DISCARDED

THE CHICANO HERITAGE

This is a volume in the Arno Press collection

THE CHICANO HERITAGE

Advisory Editor
Carlos E. Cortés

Editorial Board
Rodolfo Acuña
Juan Gómez-Quiñones
George F. Rivera, Jr.

*See last pages of this volume
for a complete list of titles.*

MEXICAN MIGRATION TO THE UNITED STATES

*With an Introduction
by Carlos E. Cortés*

ARNO PRESS
A New York Times Company
New York — 1976

Editorial Supervision: LESLIE PARR

———

Reprint Edition 1976 by Arno Press Inc.

Copyright © 1976 by Arno Press Inc.

What Price Wetbacks? was reprinted from a copy in the University of Texas at Austin Library.

THE CHICANO HERITAGE
ISBN for complete set: 0-405-09480-9
See last pages of this volume for titles.

Manufactured in the United States of America

Publisher's Note: This book has been reprinted from the best available copies of articles.

Manufactured in the United States of America

———

Library of Congress Cataloging in Publication Data
Main entry under title:

Mexican migration to the United States.

(The Chicano heritage)
Reprint of A Spanish-Mexican peasant community, by P. S. Taylor, first published in 1933, by University of California Press, Berkeley; of The wetback in the lower Rio Grande Valley of Texas, by L. Saunders and O. E. Leonard, first published in the Inter-American education occasional papers, VII, July 1951; and of What price wetbacks? by American G. I. Forum of Texas and Texas State Federation of Labor, first published in 1953, by The Forum, Austin.
  1. Agricultural laborers, Mexican--United States. 2. Mexicans in the United States. 3. United States--Emigration and immigration. 4. Mexico--Emigration and immigration. I. Taylor, Paul Schuster, 1895- A Spanish-Mexican peasant community. 1976. II. Saunders, Lyle. The wetback in the lower Rio Grande Valley of Texas. 1976. III. American G. I. Forum of Texas. What price wetbacks? 1976. IV. Series.
HD1525.M47   331.5'44'0973   76-7304
ISBN 0-405-09541-4

MEXICAN MIGRATION TO THE UNITED STATES

Introduction

The history of Mexican migration to and from the United States has been long, complex, and controversial. The three selections in this anthology provide a variety of perspectives on this process.

The first selection, *A Spanish-Mexican Peasant Community. Arandas in Jalisco, Mexico* by economist Paul Taylor, discusses the flow of Mexican laborers to and from the United States. Focusing on the small Mexican *municipio* of Arandas, Jalisco, the book describes and analyzes the history of emigration to the United States — including means of emigration, geographical distribution, and occupations held. In addition, the book relates the experiences of migrants who had returned to Arandas by the early 1930's, including the economic results of their return and the impact of U.S. culture on Arandas.

The lot of latter-day migrants — in this case, undocumented workers from Mexico — is discussed in the second selection, *The Wetback in the Lower Rio Grande Valley of Texas* by Lyle Saunders and Olen E. Leonard. The book is concerned particularly with the migrants' multiple effects on the Lower Rio Grande Valley — economic, social, health, and political — and the migrants' relations with government officials, employers, Anglo-Americans, and local Mexican Americans. The study devotes special attention to the Mexican government's dichotomous policy toward these migrants and the sometimes paradoxical relationship between undocumented migrants and Mexican Americans. Two dozen revealing maps and tables add to the book's importance.

Another perspective on the undocumented Mexican migrant in the United States is provided in the final selection, *What Price Wetbacks?* In this joint publication, the American G.I. Forum of Texas (a Mexican-American military veterans' organization) and the Texas State Federation of Labor take a strong stand against both the Bracero Program and undocumented migrants on the grounds that they take jobs from Mexican Americans. The publication also describes the negative treatment received by the undocumented worker and laments the damage to the Texas economy caused by wages being taken back to Mexico rather than spent in Texas.

The controversies and conflicts surrounding Mexican migration to and from the United States are as yet unresolved. The three studies in this anthology provide historical perspectives for the analysis of this continuing phenomenon.

CARLOS E. CORTÉS
Professor of History
Chairman, Chicano Studies
University of California, Riverside
June, 1976

CONTENTS

Taylor, Paul S.
A SPANISH-MEXICAN PEASANT COMMUNITY, Arandas in Jalisco, Mexico. Berkeley, 1933

Saunders, Lyle and Olen E. Leonard
THE WETBACK IN THE LOWER RIO GRANDE VALLEY OF TEXAS (Reprinted from *Inter-American Education Occasional Papers,* VII), July, 1951

American G. I. Forum of Texas and Texas State Federation of Labor
WHAT PRICE WETBACKS? Austin, [1953]

IBERO-AMERICANA : 4

A SPANISH-MEXICAN PEASANT COMMUNITY
ARANDAS IN JALISCO, MEXICO

PAUL S. TAYLOR

TYPICAL PEASANT RANCH-HOUSE OF LOS ALTOS, ARANDAS
The home of a returned emigrant, with evidences of American material culture

A SPANISH-MEXICAN PEASANT COMMUNITY
ARANDAS IN JALISCO, MEXICO

BY

PAUL S. TAYLOR

UNIVERSITY OF CALIFORNIA PRESS
BERKELEY, CALIFORNIA
1933

IBERO-AMERICANA: 4

94 pages, 8 plates, 4 figures in text, 1 map
Issued January 6, 1933

UNIVERSITY OF CALIFORNIA PRESS
BERKELEY, CALIFORNIA

CAMBRIDGE UNIVERSITY PRESS
LONDON, ENGLAND

CONTENTS

	PAGE
INTRODUCTION	1

I

THE BACKGROUND	3
HISTORICAL	5
POPULATION	9
AGRICULTURE	21
SOCIAL AND ECONOMIC STRUCTURE	25

II

HISTORY OF THE EMIGRATION TO THE UNITED STATES	35
OCCUPATIONAL AND GEOGRAPHICAL DISTRIBUTION OF THE EMIGRANTS FROM ARANDAS	41
MEANS OF EMIGRATION	43

III

THE INFLUENCE OF EMIGRATION ON MEXICAN ATTITUDES TOWARD THE UNITED STATES	47
THE RETURNED EMIGRANT	55
AMERICAN CULTURAL INFLUENCE IN ARANDAS	64

IV

FIELD NOTES ON FOUR EMIGRANTS	68
SUMMARY	71
APPENDIX	74

LIST OF ILLUSTRATIONS

PLATES   PAGE

1. Typical peasant ranch-house of Los Altos . . . . *Frontispiece*
2. *a.* View toward the north from the site of the ancient Indian ruins on the heights above Edificios 78
   b. Hacienda Guadalupe (Joconostle), seen from the northeast . . . 78
3. Spanish and Arandas types 80
4. Spanish and emigrant types 82
5. Spanish types; process of rope making 84
6. Process of rope making; miscellaneous types 86
7. Native homes and implements 88
8. Local Arandas scenes 90

FIGURES

1. Peasant home of "Spanish" repatriado 8
2. Hacienda San Ignacio Cerro Gordo 26
3. Leaving after early mass, Arandas 37
4. Hacienda Village, San Ignacio Cerro Gordo 74

LIST OF TABLES

TABLE	PAGE
1. Precipitation and temperature data, Arandas, Jalisco	5
2. Estimates and censuses of the population of the municipio of Arandas, Jalisco, from 1798 to 1930	9
3. Comparison of age at marriage of three groups of 100 couples each, who were married by the Roman Catholic Church at Arandas, Jalisco, during 1825-26, 1880, and 1930	10
4. Castes of children baptized at Arandas, Nueva Galicia, 1768 to 1774	15
5. Castes of children baptized at Arandas, Nueva Galicia, from 1790 to 1799, inclusive	15
6. Marriages in Arandas, Nueva Galicia, from May 17, 1802 to May 16, 1806, inclusive, by castes	16
7. Prevailing wage rates paid for town and agricultural day labor, Arandas, Jalisco, 1850-1931	24
8. Number of rural lands *(predios rústicos)* in the municipio of Arandas, and in the State of Jalisco	28
9. Money orders from the United States paid by the post office at Arandas, Jalisco, 1922-1931, inclusive	33
10. Monthly percentages of average annual money orders from the United States paid at Arandas, Jalisco, 1922-1931, inclusive	33

MAPS

following page

Mapa de la Municipalidad de Arandas (Jalisco, Mexico) by Ramón Sánchez, 1879 94

Cover map: Distribution of population, 1930, in Arandas (Jalisco, Mexico) 94

A SPANISH-MEXICAN PEASANT COMMUNITY
ARANDAS IN JALISCO, MEXICO

INTRODUCTION

IN THE HEART of the Mexican Republic is a region inhabited by people who are overwhelmingly of Spanish stock. Living in comparative isolation, these people have retained to a high degree their Spanish heritage. They have intermarried principally among themselves, absorbing the minor diverse racial elements which were originally present as separate entities, but mingling very little with the large numbers of *indígenas* (indigenous population) who inhabit adjoining regions. They even retain a few archaisms of language which have disappeared among less isolated people. They have continued to cherish their Catholic faith with the intense ardor which their ancestors brought from Spain three or more centuries ago: they constituted the bulwark of the Cristero revolution of 1926-1929.[1]

The hacienda system—agriculture conducted by large estates—which has been, and yet is characteristic of many parts of Mexico, plays a minor rôle in this region. By a process of natural agrarianism, a high proportion of the population has come into possession of agricultural land. The result is a peasant proprietorship which, with characteristic conservatism, opposes the revolutionary *agrarismo,* or forcible legal expropriation and distribution of land.

From this region many have emigrated to the United States during the past quarter of a century, and to it many have returned after longer or shorter experiences in that country. Partly, but only partly because of this migration, there has been taking place a new contact of diverse cultures, the latest of a series of cultural contacts which began with, or perhaps even before, the Spanish conquest.

For the present study, the municipio of Arandas, in the state of Jalisco, Mexico, was selected for detailed investigation, as generally representative of the larger region possessing the characteristics set forth above, of which it is a part.

---

[1] The political, and even military importance of this fervid Catholicism appears later in the description (pp. 36-40) of the effect of the Cristero revolution on emigration to the United States.

A preceding series of studies[2] concerned regions in the United States where contact of American and Mexican cultures furnished the motive for the investigations. The present regional study is also in some measure concerned with this cultural contact set in a background which is Mexican and which possesses distinctive racial and socio-economic features.

Field work in Arandas occupied portions of October, November, and December, 1931, and of June, 1932. It was supplemented by additional inquiries more profitably prosecuted in Guadalajara, among Arandas people resident in that place, and by research in libraries and archives.

The study was made possible by the John Simon Guggenheim Memorial Foundation and a supplementary grant by the Broad of Research of the University of California. Acknowledgment is due to the Governor of Jalisco, Juan de Diós Robledo, and to the Archbishop of Guadalajara, Francisco Jiménez y Orozco, for the courtesies which facilitated the execution of the study. I am particularly indebted to the following residents of Arandas: Presidente Municipal Macedonio S. Barrera, and the entire staff of government officials, Señor Ignacio Varela, *notario eclesiástico,* Señor José Hernández Orozco, and Señor Luis de M. Ramírez. Señor Pantaleón Orozco, of Guadalajara, who was born in Arandas in 1840, gave invaluable assistance by reason of knowledge of his municipio, which was as remarkable for its thoroughness as for the long span of time which it covered. The generous aid of Professor José Cornejo Franco of Tepatitlán, now residing in Guadalajara, was invaluable at a number of points. The people of Arandas, characterized generally by honesty and frankness, permitted me to go afoot into any part of the municipio with courtesy and security, and extended a reception and hospitality which I shall always recall with genuine pleasure.

---

[2] Paul S. Taylor, *Mexican Labor in the United States,* vol. 1: "Imperial Valley, California"; "Valley of the South Platte, Colorado"; "Dimmit County, Winter Garden District, South Texas"; vol. 2: Bethlehem, Pennsylvania"; "Chicago and the Calumet Region" (University of California, *Publications in Economics,* 6:1–94, 95–235, and 293–406; 7:vii + 1–24, vii + 25–284, respectively; (Berkeley, 1928–1932). Cited hereafter only by volume and page.

I

THE BACKGROUND

THE MUNICIPIO OF ARANDAS is located in the eastern part of the state of Jalisco, in the region known as Los Altos, and elevated above the great central plateau of Mexico.[3] It covers approximately 76 sitios (1300 square kilometers or 500 square miles).[4]

The surface of the municipio is in general divided into two types of country—the more or less rolling or broken upland of Los Altos which comprises the southern half of the municipio, and the northern portion which is known as El Plan because of its nearly level surface (see map). The altitude of the entire municipio rises generally from the base of Cerro Gordo in the west, toward the east; the greatest elevation, however, is at the summit of Cerro Gordo, on the western extremity, which rises to a height of approximately 2375 meters. The altitude of the town of Arandas is 1905 meters.[5] Around the rim of the municipio on all sides a series of *cerros* rise above the general level. Across the center from west to east, lies a *cordillera*. It rises in elevation toward the east, and between Cerro de Campana and the eastern limits of the municipio drops almost precipitously to El Plan, which in places is probably 100 meters or more below.

El Plan is interrupted by a series of low hills which rise in a chain across the middle in a slightly northeasterly direction. It is bounded on the northern limits of the municipio by the chain of higher cerros which rise at Caracol in the west and continue beyond the northeastern limits of the municipio. In the northeastern portion of the municipio the streams which flow eastward have cut valleys below the plain and cerros.

The uplands (Los Altos) south of the cordillera form nearly a plain from Arandas west, with gentle, undulating slope westward, except where broken by river valley and a few hills in the west. East of Arandas the surface is much more broken by hills and by the valleys of streams. In the west at the

---

[3] The town of Arandas is situated in Lat. 20° 44′ Long. 102° 20′ W (Greenwich). The term Los Altos sometimes is applied narrowly, excluding from the designation the valley known as El Plan, which comprises the northern half of the municipio. At other times the term is applied broadly to include the entire elevated table lands from Penjamo to Zapotlanejo, stretching northward over parts of Jalisco and Guanajuato. The particular use intended will be evident from the context.

[4] A *sitio de ganado mayor* (league) equals 4,428.403 acres, and contains 25 million square *varas*; a *vara* equals 33 1/3 English inches.

[5] Altitude of Arandas as reported by *Servicio Meteorológico Mexicano*. Ramón Sánchez, *Ensayo estadístico de la municipalidad de Arandas* (Guadalajara, 1889), 25, gave the altitude of Arandas as 2005 meters, and that of Cerro Gordo as 2375 meters.

foot of Cerro Gordo, it is undulating prairie elevated a little above, and separated from El Plan only by a broken chain of low hills.

The municipio is drained by numerous streams. The principal one is the Río del Tule or Sánchez, which has three sources, one in an arroyo near Edificios in El Plan, another in Arroyo de la Tinaja at the north-central boundary of the municipio, and the third northeast of Rancho Aguila. Together with numerous small tributaries which rise in Los Altos in Arandas, it drains most of the municipio. One of the tributaries, Río del Gachupín, rises just beyond the eastern boundary of the municipio at Rancho Tecolote and crosses the entire southern portion of Arandas. The Río del Tule flows past Atotonilco, and under the name of the Río Zula empties into the Río Santiago, finally reaching Lake Chapala. Along the southeastern boundary, the Ríos Aguilillas and Nacimiento unite, flow into the Río Ayo Chico, and thence into the Río Lerma and Lake Chapala.

The Río de Forlones rises in a barranca above Edificios a short distance east of the source of the Tule, joins a small tributary which rises in El Plan north of Cerro de Doña Inés, and flows eastward into the Río Turbio in Guanajuato. Just north of the intervening hills rises the Arroyo de Támara or del Pueblito, which flows to the Jalpa dam and irrigates the lands of that hacienda.

In the extreme west of the municipio rise the waters of Arroyo de Jaquetas. These flow southward into the Río de las Hormigas in Atotonilco and thence into the Río Zula. The waters of Arroyo de Tres Palos rise near Rancho Pastores, flow northward, and empty into Río Verde, which flows into Río Santiago and finally into the Pacific Ocean.

The waters of these streams are not all permanent throughout their courses. In late June, 1932, practically all of the streams within Arandas were dry. None of them are navigable at any time. The soils of the southern portion of the municipio are relatively impermeable, and the proportion of rainfall which runs off is high. The degree of erosion which results is great, and carries off much of the best surface soils. Evidence of serious erosion, which was scientifically noted as early as 1858,[6] is frequently observed in the fields.

Available data showing mean monthly precipitation and temperature are presented in table 1. The climate is mild, and rainfall is usually sufficient for crops. Details are given later (p. 22) of storage of rainfall for irrigation in some portions of the municipio.

---

[6] "Notas geográficas y estadísticas del departamento de Jalisco" *Boletín de la sociedad mexicana de geografía y estadística*, 6(1858):321.

TABLE I
Precipitation and Temperature Data, Arandas, Jalisco*

Month	Precipitation, 1921-28 (millimeters)	Temperature, 1925-28 (degrees centigrade)		
	Mean	Mean	Maximum	Minimum
January	4.0	17.2	29.5	6.0
February	12.6	19.7	31.0	6.0
March	17.2	22.0	34.5	9.5
April	.5	23.3	35.0	9.0
May	52.3	24.7	36.5	12.5
June	204.7	24.4	35.5	14.0
July	197.0	23.5	31.4	15.5
August	207.8	23.1	32.0	11.0
September	174.1	22.7	31.5	14.5
October	53.6	22.1	31.0	9.5
November	18.9	20.0	31.0	9.0
December	48.1	18.2	30.0	7.5
Annual	991.4	21.7	36.5	6.0

* Based on data of *Servicio Meteorológico Mexicano*. Equivalents for annual temperatures are:
21.7° C. = 71.1° F
36.5° C. = 97.7° F
6.0° C. = 42.8° F
Precipitation of 991.4 mm = 39 inches.

HISTORICAL

Data concerning the inhabitants at the time of the Spanish conquest of the area which is now Arandas are meager, and sometimes vague or even confused. Orozco y Berra states and shows by his map that the region of Los Altos to a distance east of Tepatitlán within the bounds of present Arandas was inhabited by the Tecuexes, and that the Chichimecs were beyond, to the eastward.[7] The term "Chichimecs," as used in this region by Spanish writers, is to be understood as a general term meaning "wild Indians," rather than a specific tribal designation. Padre Tello, writing in the 1650's of the conquest which occurred 120 years earlier, is not entirely consistent. In one place he gives the name Chichimecs to all the indigenous inhabitants of the region east of the Río Santiago, ascribing to them nomadic and idolatrous habits;[8] but in another passage[9] he refers to the Indians of

---

[7] Manuel Orozco y Berra, Geográfica de las lenguas y carta etnográfica de México .... (Mexico, 1864), 278.

[8] Fray Antonio Tello, *Libro segundo de la crónica miscelánea en que se trata de la conquista espiritual y temporal de la santa provincia de Xalisco en el nuevo reino de la Galicia y Nueva Viscaya* [written about 1650 or 1651] (Guadalajara, 1891), 11.

[9] *Ibid.*, 107.

Cerro Gordo as "Huamares of the Tzacatecas nation, who live in *rancherías*," and contrasts them with the nomadic Indians farther eastward.

Mota Padilla, writing in 1742, gives a fuller account, and, like Orozco y Berra, and Padre Tello in his second passage, distinguishes with even more sharpness the Indians of Tepatitlán, which adjoins Arandas on the west, and of Cerro Gordo, whose summit is on the boundary between the municipios of Tepatitlán and Arandas, from the Indians farther eastward. The former he describes as "political," (i.e., with organized government), and adds that "they planted maize and clothed themselves"; the latter, by contrast, had none of these characteristics, but were unorganized, planted no crops, and went about unclothed and as nomads in the manner ascribed to the Chichimecs generally in the first passage above cited from Padre Tello.[10] Thus it appears that somewhere through the present area of Arandas there passed a boundary between one type of Indian inhabitant and another.

Archaeological remains of the original inhabitants of Arandas exist on Cerro Gordo, at Caracol, along the heights and slopes of the cordillera at and above Edificios, near Mesa Meco, and on the Cerro de Farfán.[11] Three sites were visited. One site south of Edificios, on the summit above, consists of clearly defined stone walls probably forming adjoining rooms and enclosures, each in rectangular form, and so arranged as to rise practically from the northern and southern edges of the mesa upon which they are built. At the eastern end of the ruins rises a pyramid constructed of mud and stones, with a base of about 30 meters (estimated) on each side, and a height of perhaps eight meters. The distance from the eastern base of the pyramid to the westernmost wall is about 125 to 140 meters. The situation of the ruins, and their general form, indicate clearly that the structures were originally constructed for both defensive and religious purposes. The cerritos of Edificios were briefly inspected. They consist of a dozen or more mounds, one of them flat-topped, and at least two of pyramid type. Small excavations which had been made, probably by treasure-hunters, indicated the construction of these to be of thickly piled stones, the crevices filled with mud. Potsherds have been turned up by plowing in the vicinity, making it readily possible for archeologists to study the aboriginal culture. Neighbors report finding figurines, but none of these were seen. The site known as the *Plazita de los Mecos,* about a kilometer south of Mesa Meco, was also visited. It consists of a thick ring of stone ruins a few feet high, piled in circular form, with an interior diameter of about 30 meters. Surmounted with a thick growth of

---

[10] Matías de la Mota Padilla, *Historia de la conquista de la provincia de la Nueva Galicia* .... [written in 1742] (Mexico, 1870), 49. Tello, *op. cit.,* 11.

[11] There are said to be ruins also at Cerro de la Hermita, just west of the Río Tule, in the municipio of Atotonilco.

nopal (prickly pear), it furnished an admirable refuge for cavalry during the Cristero revolution.

Thus it is evident from both historical accounts and archaeological remains that the area of Arandas was occupied by Indians. Detailed knowledge of their tribes, numbers, and civilization awaits further investigation by social scientists of various disciplines.

The original entry of Spaniards into the vicinity was made in 1531 by a conquering army of 80 Spaniards and a thousand Mexican and Tlaxcaltecan Indians under Captain Pedro Almendes Chirinos. Advancing from Cuitzeo near Lake Chapala in a general but irregular northward direction, Chirinos passed Cerro Gordo and went on to Tepatitlán. It is recorded that "among the watered declivities of Cerro Gordo and in the ravines below the summits [were] many Indian ranches."[12] These Indians allowed the invaders to pass in peace rather than offer the bloody but vain resistance made by the Indians of the valley of Coynán against Nuño de Guzmán.

But subsequent Spanish colonization encountered stubborn resistance. The best available account of this conflict during the decades following the conquest was written about seventy years thereafter.[13] Like other available historical accounts, it covers the fringe of the area of present Arandas at Cerro Gordo and the adjoining area of Tepatitlán. The original description, in translation, reads as follows:

Six leagues beyond [Zapotlanejo] is the village of Tepatitlán, which at one time was composed of a people very valorous and warlike, and who are exhausted by the great wars which they had with the Chichimecs, as protection and defense of the city of Guadalajara against the passage of her enemies. Two leagues from this village there is a *cerro*, which, because of its size, is called *Cerro Gordo*, and which because of its roughness was shelter and refuge of the brave Chichimec Indians; there, from the great ravines and coves they used to go out to make their ambuscades and assaults in which they killed many Spanish and Indians, and likewise stole a great amount of property.[14]

The final pacification of the country was accomplished doubtless in part by the defeat or flight of the Indians, probably also through domestication to more peaceful pursuits. Evidence of domestication lies in the fact that by the close of the sixteenth century an *encomienda* (protectorate) had been established with 46 Indian tributaries in Tepatitlán and Acatic, while Tepatitlán had become a center for religious indoctrination of the Indians in the surrounding territory.[15] Whether the Indians who aided the Spanish to re-

---

[12] Mota Padilla, *loc. cit.*

[13] Alonso de la Mota y Escobar, *Descripción geográfica de los reynos de Galicia, Vizcaya, y León* [written between 1602 and 1605] (México, Bibliophilos Mexicanos, 1930).

[14] *Ibid.*, 111.

[15] *Ibid.*, 112, 196.

sist the Chichimecs of Cerro Gordo were of the same tribes, or were introduced from other parts is not known. Such transplantations of population to pacify a region were frequently made by the Spanish in Nueva Galicia, and the reference in the passage quoted to the wars of the Indians of Tepatitlán against the "Chichimecs" suggests that the contestants were regarded as members of different tribes. Yet specific accounts of transplantations of Indians to Los Altos for the purpose of pacifying the country do not mention Tepatitlán. The Indians in the encomienda of Tepatitlán in 1600, however, were evidently "descendants of Chichimecs" who had resisted and preyed upon the Spanish in the manner described.[16]

Peasant home of "Spanish" repatriado

The extensive colonization by Spaniards which had taken place in the western portion of Los Altos by the close of the sixteenth century was observed by the same authority (Mota y Escobar) when he wrote, "In these seven leagues between Zapotlán [Zapotlanejo] and here [Tepatitlán] there are many cattle and sheep ranches, and land planted to maize by Spaniards.[17] By the close of the century, also, some Spanish ranchers were present in the region of Arandas. Grants of land there had been made much earlier, and in the course of time some of these were followed by settlement.[18] From these grants and from documents which Sánchez cites, it appears that actual colonization was taking place in Arandas, perhaps lagging somewhat, but nevertheless proceeding during the same period in which it took place west of Cerro Gordo:

by an instrument of transfer of rights of the year 1595, we have discovered that in the said year there was already a ranch with the name of Arandas and another

---

[16] *Ibid.*, 112. The tribal designations are confused, however. Both Mota Padilla and Tello call the original Indians of Tepatitlán and the northwestern border of Arandas, Chichimecs of the Tzacatecas nation.

[17] *Loc. cit.*

[18] Copies of legal documents loaned to the writer by Don Pantaleón Orozco have proved illuminating. One recites a grant of Lagunillas and De la Hermita ranches as early as 1565. In 1568, Capuli, probably modern Capulín Verde, was granted to one Juan Rodríguez; on it was said to be "a water hole where muleteers on the road from Michoacán to Zacatecas pass the night." One document refers to an Indian renter on Carrizal ranch in 1604. Usually the grants recited that the land was unpopulated, that cattle were to be placed upon it within a stipulated period, and that the land could not be sold to a church or monastery, and, in at least one instance, that it could not be sold at all within six years of the date of the grant. Some other early grants related to Cieneguilla (1544), Carrizal (1578), and the arroyo between Cerro Gordo and the De la Hermita ranch of Juan de Villanueva (1604); from the documents it was not usually possible to ascertain whether settlement actually took place, or whether, as was often the case, the grant represented a speculation.

with that of *Agua de los Arandas*, today *Cerro Blanco;* so these territories, which we have indicated before, were populated by European colonies in times very near to those in which the conquest took place.[19]

One hundred and forty years after Mota y Escobar's early observation of Spanish colonization, Mota Padilla (1742) commented on the fact that in the *curato* (parish) of Tepatitlán "were many Spaniards dispersed in various haciendas and ranches....,"[20] and it is certain that at this date, as indeed long before as already noted, there were also many Spanish ranchers in the area of Arandas.

POPULATION

THE FIRST population figures on the municipio of Arandas are for the year 1798. These and subsequent data are presented in table 2. The distribution of population according to the census of 1930 is shown on the map opposite page 94.[21] The denser population is found in the southern portion of the municipio where the ranches are most subdivided.

Since the original settlement of the area by Spaniards, population growth has been due almost entirely to natural increase. Fecundity is great: families of ten or twelve children are common, and some have over twenty. Early marriages are the rule, although in the past century, there has been a marked progressive advance in the marriage age (see table 3). For instance: in 100 marriages of 1825–26, 49 men who contracted marriage for the first time were under twenty-one years of age, and 73 women were under nineteen years. By 1880 the numbers had dropped to 31 and 69, respectively, and in 1930 they were 16 and 51, respectively. The changes in age at time of marriage, as shown by median and mean ages, are as follows:

Age	Men			Women		
	1825-6	1880	1930	1825-6	1880	1930
Median	21.2	22.6	23.8	17.0	18.1	18.9
Mean	22.0	23.0	24.1	17.5	18.4	19.4

The mean age at time of marriage of men advanced 1 year (median 1.4) from 1825–6 to 1880; 1.1 years (median 1.2) from 1880 to 1930; or 2.1 years

---

[19] Sánchez, *op. cit.,* 36.

[20] P. 49.

[21] The census of 1930 furnished the number of inhabitants by localities within the municipio. Extensive subdivision of ranches, resulting in many new ranch names, has taken place since 1879, when the map of Ramón Sánchez was made. This necessitated reliance upon informed persons in Arandas for location of 1930 data upon the cover map. In this respect Señor Juan J. Domínguez, who was immediately in charge of the 1930 enumeration in Arandas, and Señor Luis de M. Ramírez, for many years land surveyor of Arandas, were particularly helpful. With even the best of will, this method inevitably admits of some errors, but these are believed to be few and of minor importance.

(median 2.6) during the century. The mean age of women advanced .9 years (median 1.1) from 1825-6 to 1880; 1 year (median .8) from 1880 to 1930; or 1:9 years (median 1.9) during the century. Thus postponement of the age of marriage has been more marked among the men than among the women.

One reason for these changes is undoubtedly the emigration to the United States which has been particularly important during the past ten or fifteen

TABLE 2

Estimates and Censuses of the Population of the Municipio of Arandas, Jalisco, from 1798 to 1930*

Year	Estimates	Population
1798		7,282
1820		9,185
1845		12,650
1875		27,900
1879		30,105
1885		36,617
1888		37,821
	Censuses	
1900		25,237
1910		23,689
1921		26,624
1930		27,624

* Data for the years 1798 to 1879 and for 1888 were taken from Sánchez, pp. 53, 55, who gives as sources the civil and ecclesiastical archives; data for December 31, 1885, from Mariano Barcena, *Ensayo estadístico del estado de Jalisco* .... (Mexico, 1891). The figures for 1885, 1888, and probably for other years prior to 1900, were arrived at by subtracting recorded deaths from births, and adding the remainder to a preceding figure obtained by enumeration or otherwise. This method of course fails to account for immigration or emigration. The latter has been heavy from Arandas. The result is twofold: the population figures for the years preceding 1900 are inaccurate, and probably generally overestimate the actual population; the figures prior to 1900 are *not* closely comparable with the Federal census figures which begin with that date. A much higher degree of accuracy is doubtless represented by the censuses from 1900 to date which are the only ones regarded as *oficial*.

In 1840 the population of the town of Arandas was reported as 2,241 (*Notas geográficas*, loc. cit.). In 1879 it was reported as 5,016. In 1910 the census counted 5,911; by 1921 the number had risen to 6,480, and in 1930 to 7,574. The population of San Ignacio Cerro Gordo was 980 in 1910, 1,073 in 1921, and 747 in 1930. The recency of the growth of population at Santa María del Valle is shown by its rise from 114 in 1910 to 304 in 1921, and to 480 in 1930.

years. Emigration has also contributed to a decreased birth rate through a more or less prolonged separation of husbands and wives. But it is important to observe that the advance in age of marriage was already clearly apparent between 1825-26 and 1880, and that the latter date was a quarter of a century before emigration from Arandas to the United States began. Additional reasons for the advancing age of marriage probably lie in the economic pressure of a growing population of proprietors whose land was becoming increasingly subdivided and intensively utilized, and the changing social customs involving particularly a relaxation in practice of the standards of

TABLE 3
COMPARISON OF AGE AT MARRIAGE OF THREE GROUPS OF 100 COUPLES EACH, WHO WERE MARRIED BY THE ROMAN CATHOLIC CHURCH AT ARANDAS, JALISCO, DURING 1825–26, 1880, AND 1930, RESPECTIVELY*

Age	Men					
	Number			Cumulative total		
	1825-26	1880	1930	1825-26	1880	1930
12	....	....	....	....	....	....
13	....	....	....	....	....	....
14	....	....	....	....	....	....
15	2	....	....	2	....	....
16	2	3	....	4	3	....
17	3	....	1	7	3	1
18	13	6	2	20	9	3
19	11	9	6	31	18	9
20	18	13	7	49	31	16
21	6	7	9	55	38	25
22	12	17	16	67	55	41
23	7	8	12	74	63	53
24	2	6	11	76	69	64
25	10	15	9	86	84	73
26	3	4	6	89	88	79
27	4	1	4	93	89	83
28	....	....	4	93	89	87
29	....	1	2	93	90	89
30	2	5	4	95	95	93
Above 30	5†	5‡	7¶	100	100	100
	Women					
12	1	....	....	1	....	....
13	....	1	....	1	1	....
14	4	1	1	5	2	1
15	21	15	10	26	17	11
16	24	20	7	50	37	18
17	9	12	17	59	49	35
18	14	20	16	73	69	51
19	12	4	10	85	73	61
20	5	11	5	90	84	66
21	2	2	5	92	86	71
22	5	3	14	97	89	85
23	....	1	2	97	90	87
24	....	....	2	97	90	89
25	1	4	4	98	94	93
26	....	1	3	98	95	96
27	....	2	1	98	97	97
28	....	....	....	98	97	97
29	....	1	1	98	98	98
30	1	1	2	99	99	100
Above 30	1§	1∥	....	100	100	100

* Data from *Registro de matrimonio*, Arandas. The age of persons contracting marriage was first recorded on July 6, 1825; the first 100 couples so recorded, covering the period ending May 17, 1826, constitute the first sample group above. For the second and third groups, uniform data from the months of January-April and September-November, inclusive, were taken. In every case, only data on first marriages are included.
† One person each, aged 35, 41, and 44; two persons aged 32.
‡ Ages 32, 34, 36, 38, and 43, respectively.
¶ One person each, aged 32, 33, and 34; two persons each, aged 35 and 39.
§ Aged 40.
∥ Aged 38.

sex relations, of a region whose isolation was gradually decreasing, and whose social organization was growing increasingly complex.[22]

Nevertheless, Arandas has been, and continues to be a source of great population growth. The meager statistics available confirm the contemporarily and traditionally observed high rate of natural increase. For the five years 1834-1838 births recorded in Arandas numbered 4,149 and deaths 1,979, an excess of 2,710 births over deaths, or 434 births per annum in a population of about ten or eleven thousand.[23] Sánchez, citing figures for 1877-79 showing an average annual excess of 327 births over deaths, which was below the average annual increase in total population of 551 shown by the censuses of 1875 and 1879, satisfactorily explains the discrepancy by pointing out that the Arandas ecclesiastical registration area at that time was materially smaller than the census area.

Not only has Arandas supplied its own population increase, but it has been an important source of emigration as well. In large part, this emigration has been stimulated by civil disorders. From the outbreak of the War of Independence in 1810, the municipio of Arandas has been the scene of military occupation and intermittent combat. When the movement for independence broke out, the royalist government concentrated the people of the municipio in Arandas town, as was again done during the Cristero revolution of 1927-29. One result was that many went to Guadalajara and settled, principally in the *barrio* of San Juan de Díos, where their descendants still live. The most serious of the various internecine wars which swept over the country occurred in 1854 with the revolt against the dictator Santa Anna. The disorder subsided somewhat in 1867, with the death of the Emperor Maximilian and the triumph of Benito Juárez, and finally ceased upon the accession to power of Porfirio Díaz in 1876.

Between 1854 and 1867 alone the municipio of Arandas was visited at least seventeen times by armed bands, usually military forces but sometimes bandits, who exacted in forced loans, ransoms, or simply by robbery and sack, aggregate sums estimated at 325,000 pesos. Many other occupations by government and revolutionary forces took place, whose petty exactions raised the estimated losses to 500,000 pesos.[24] In addition to financial loss, there were the usual accompaniments of guerrilla warfare and banditry, combats, shootings, sack, and rape. Because of these, many people emigrated from Arandas, seeking greater security in León, La Piedad, and elsewhere,

---

[22] For additional discussion of customs affecting population growth, see p. 66.

[23] Longinos Banda, *Estadística de Jalisco*.....(Guadalajara, 1873), p. 61.

[24] Sánchez, *op. cit.*, pp. 38-47, details the most notable events of revolution and banditry which took place in Arandas between 1810 and 1876. He notes five occasions between 1867 and 1876.

especially after an invasion in 1863 by 150 bandits from the Río Verde. The number of those who left the municipio during these twenty-odd years is reliably said to have been thousands, probably the major part of the population. Not again until the Cristero revolution of 1927–29 did the exodus reach comparable proportions. For more than a century, however, emigration from Arandas has been more or less continuous, with excess of population relative to economic opportunities the basic cause. The emigration to the vicinity of La Piedad and elsewhere in 1836 was stimulated by the new economic opportunities offered through the general sale of lands belonging to Hacienda Santa Ana Pacueco.[25] At practically the same time, Spaniards built the textile factory of Atemajac near Zapopan, and numbers left Arandas to take advantage of the opportunity for employment offered women and children at attractive wages, while the men found work in the surrounding agriculture. Furthermore, it has long been customary for one or more of the family to leave Arandas in search of greater opportunities elsewhere. When, upon the death of the parents, the lands of the family are divided, those remaining in Arandas have generally bought the shares of those who have left.

There are at the present time large clusters of Arandas emigrants or their descendants in Guadalajara, León, Piedra Gorda, La Piedad, and Penjamo, Guanajuato, Atotonilco, Venta del Astillero, Hacienda del Plan, and Zapopan. The neighboring town of Degollado was practically founded as an Arandas colony. As long ago as 1879 all these localities were known as places where important groups of Arandas people had colonized.[26] Most of the larger of these places as well as many other parts of the Mexican Republic from Mexico City north, have continued to receive Arandas emigrants in numbers to the present time. Thus as a result of population pressure on lands which have been increasingly subdivided,[27] of political disorder, and of religious war, large numbers of people have left Arandas permanently.

It is noteworthy that not only laborers have emigrated to find work elsewhere, but persons of all occupations have gone, finding employment not only in labor and commerce, but attaining to a notable degree, places of importance in the cultural, professional, and political life of the Republic.

In the perspective of extensive emigration in the past, the movement during the past quarter-century to the United States appears as but a modern and expanded phase of a fairly continuous historical exodus from this populous district. Its details will be presented later.

---

[25] See p. 27.
[26] Sánchez, pp. 45, 55.
[27] See pp. 27 ff.

Race—

The people of Arandas are generally regarded, and they so regard themselves, as of Spanish stock. The great majority are white in color, often with blue eyes, and in general Spanish rather than Indian in their physical characteristics. Documentary evidence of their origin in Spain was not obtained, but inquiry of persons who know the region and who know Spanish types, indicated that their ancestors were from northern Spain. Many are tall and well built. There are some Indian and mestizo (white-Indian mixture) types, with strong Indian characteristics, but these are a minority. Sometimes one sees a combination of Indian pigmentation or other Indian characteristics, and blue eyes. Occasionally, but less often, one sees Negro characteristics.

The early Spanish ranchers were served not only by Indians, but by Negro slaves who were introduced into the region. Little documentary material on slavery in Arandas was obtained, but reliable tradition states that it was frequently customary before general emancipation in 1810 for the master to emancipate slaves, usually by the terms of his will; in harmony with this tradition, church archives frequently recorded mulattoes as either slave or free. Sometimes Indians sold themselves, or their children, into virtual slavery, but these cases were very few. Some of the descendants of the Negro slaves of Arandas are today proprietors of ranches.

The earliest statistical data on races in the population of Arandas were found in the church archives. In table 4 are presented the castes of children baptized during the six years immediately following the establishment of the *congregación* of Arandas. Approximately two-thirds of the children baptized were classed as Spanish, one-seventh mestizo, and one-tenth as mulatto. Examination of the records for a ten-year period at the close of the eighteenth century yielded data which are very similar to those just presented; table 5 shows somewhat higher proportions of Spanish and of Indians (doubtless including most mestizos of dominantly Indian type), and a slightly lower percentage of mulattoes. These tables reveal with substantial accuracy the racial composition of the Arandas population during the first forty years after the foundation of the congregación. It should be noted that to arrive at the full proportion of Spanish blood in the population, some addition to the percentage of "Spanish" must be made in order to allow for the Spanish blood present in mestizos, mulattoes, and other mixed castes.

Since the Spanish colonization of Los Altos, the process of intermixture of races has been going on. Clear documentary evidence of this is found not only in the two tables preceding, but in the record of legal intermarriage of persons of different races. These data, covering a sample four-year period from 1802 to 1806, are shown in table 6. The great majority of the marriages

TABLE 4

CASTES OF CHILDREN BAPTIZED AT ARANDAS, NUEVA GALICIA, 1768 TO 1774*

Caste	Number	Per cent
Spanish	668	69.4
Mestizo†	139	14.4
Mulatto‡	104	10.9
Indian	26	2.7
Coyote‖	13	1.3
Slave§	7	.7
Zambo¶	2	.2
Morisco††	2	.2
Negro	1	.1
Lobo‡‡	1	1
Total	963	100.0

* Data from *Registro de bautismo de la capilla de Arandas, Nueva Galicia*, from February 22, 1768 to February 21, 1774, inclusive. Since the ecclesiastical régime was well established in Los Altos at this period, it is very improbable that non-Spanish children were less likely to be baptized than Spanish children. The race of both parents was recorded when the child was Spanish; otherwise only the caste of the child was noted.
  † Spanish-Indian mixture.
  ‡ Spanish-Negro mixture. Probably many of these were slaves, although many were listed as *mulato libre*.
  ‖ Spelled "collote" in the *registro* at Arandas. The classifications of the more mixed castes were not uniformly made. See, for example, Gregorio Torres Quintero: *Mexico hacia el fin del virreinato español. Antecedentes sociologicos del pueblo mexicano* (Mexico, 1921). According to one system, *collote* meant the offspring of Indian and *mestizo*. According to another system, it meant a person whose ancestry was divided by a complicated series of intermarriages as follows: 463/1024 Spanish, 449/1024 Negro, and 112/1024 Indian. The former usage seems more likely to have prevailed in Arandas.
  § Almost certainly all these were Negroes or mulattoes. All were recorded as *natural*, i.e., illegitimate; the name of the father was not recorded, although the ranch to which they belonged was usually given.
  ¶ Indian-Negro mixture. See also ‡‡.
  †† Spanish-mulatto mixture.
  ‡‡ According to the classification probably in use in Arandas, *lobo* meant a person who was half-Indian, 15/32 Spanish, and 1/32 Negro; according to another system it meant the offspring of Indian and Negro, for which *zambo* is the more usual term; according to a third system it meant a person who was quarter-Indian, 15/32 Spanish, and 9/32 Negro.

TABLE 5

CASTES OF CHILDREN BAPTIZED AT ARANDAS, NUEVA GALICIA, FROM 1790 TO 1799, INCLUSIVE*

Caste	Number	Per cent
Spanish	2,372	71.0
Indian†	667	20.0
Mulatto‡	304	9.0
Total	3,343	100.0

* Data from same archives as those of table 4.
  † Undoubtedly includes mestizos during this period. Sixteen years earlier (see table 4), only 2.7 per cent of the children baptized were recorded as "Indians," and 14.4 per cent were recorded as mestizos, making a total of 17.1 per cent. This combined total is not far from the 20 per cent listed as "Indian" in the present table, and verifies the definition of "Indian" suggested here.
  ‡ Spanish-Negro mixture. The 9 per cent of mulattoes shown in this table checks closely with the 10.9 per cent of mulattoes shown in table 4, verifying this definition of mulatto.

which took place during this period were between persons both of whom were of Spanish stock, but it is interesting to observe that while Indians participated in 25 *mixed* marriages, only 22 marriages between Indians were recorded; and, even more interesting, that while mulattoes participated in 15 mixed marriages, only 4 marriages between mulattoes were recorded. The population of all castes was so thoroughly Catholic at this time, that the records may be regarded as approximately complete. Absorption of mestizos and mulattoes by the dominant whites was evidently proceeding at a rapid rate, even by legalized intermarriage alone.

TABLE 6

MARRIAGES IN ARANDAS, NUEVA GALICIA, FROM MAY 17, 1802, TO MAY 16, 1806, INCLUSIVE, BY CASTES*

Marriages between persons of:	Number	Per cent
The same caste:		
Spanish	268	75.9
Indian	22	6.2
Mestizo	10	2.8
Mulatto†	4	1.1
Total	304	86.0
Different castes:		
Spanish-Mestizo	18	5.1
Spanish-Indian	5	1.4
Spanish-Mulatto	3	.9
Indian-Mestizo	11	3.1
Indian-Mulatto	9	2.6
Mestizo-Mulatto	3	.9
Total	49	14.0
Grand Total	353	100.0

* Data from the *Registro de matrimonio*, Arandas.
† The mulattoes whose marriages were recorded were sometimes slave, sometimes free.

It is significant that some legal marriages of every possible major race crossing were found in the records, even during so short a period as four years. It is also worth noting that the women of Spanish blood were apparently only a little less ready to intermarry with men having less Spanish blood than themselves, than were men of Spanish blood to undertake such intermarriages. Thus, of the 18 Spanish-mestizo marriages, at least 8 involved Spanish women; of the 5 Spanish-Indian marriages, 2 involved Spanish women; and of the 3 Spanish-mulatto marriages, one involved a Spanish woman. Of the 11 marriages of Indians with mestizos, 3 involved mestizo women. The 9 Indian-mulatto intermarriages involved 5 mulatto and 4 Indian women. The mestizo-mulatto intermarriages were participated in by one mestizo and two mulatto women.

Perhaps even more important numerically than the intermarriages undertaken with church sanction were the irregular liasons which took place. These unions were principally between Spanish men and women of other castes, probably for example, between master and slave, such as occurred in the southern part of the United States before emancipation; or between employer and Indian or mulatto women-folk, directly or indirectly in his employ. The existence of these irregular unions under the social and economic conditions which prevailed is not only plausible, but is practically evident from the entries which appear in the baptismal register, of children born of non-Spanish mothers and unnamed but doubtless very often Spanish fathers, and it is confirmed by the most reliable tradition.

It is probable, though not susceptible of conclusive proof, that the racial strains in the present population of Arandas are mingled in proportions not greatly different from those which existed in the last third of the eighteenth century, the period sampled by the data in tables 4 and 5. Differences which may have existed during the past century and a third between the respective rates of immigration and emigration from the municipio, and respective rates of natural increase of the racial groups, are not known. It is extremely unlikely, however, that Negro or mulatto blood has been added through immigration; to a small degree Spanish, Indian, or mestizo elements have so entered. All the racial elements have felt the effect of emigration. But although there has been some variation, therefore, in rates of increase and decrease of these various elements it seems likely after diligent inquiry and observation, that the proportions of the racial strains have not greatly altered to the present time, except for a probable relative diminution of the Negro element. What has occurred is that, through intermixture, the numerically subordinate racial elements have tended to disappear as separate elements in the population, while the dominance of the Spanish strain has become apparent in an increasing proportion of individuals of the population. The consciousness of a black strain has practically disappeared from the community, although its presence is conceded upon presentation of historical data and upon questioning; its existence is scarcely noticeable in Los Altos, though it is more prevalent on the ranches of El Plan. Slaves were introduced more extensively into El Plan because there the haciendas and ranchos were larger than in Los Altos. The more well-to-do owners of the former region sought Negroes for use as field laborers, vaqueros and pastores, and house servants. The Indian element in the population, usually much diluted, is generally recognized, and is plainly evident in all parts of the municipio, more especially in the town of Arandas, and on the larger ranches. Among the small ranches of Los Altos, the Spanish strain predominates greatly.

In 1889 a local writer stated:

.... the greater part of these inhabitants are of Spanish race, and the rest of indigenous race; among the former, the men are of very good constitution and of white color, the women of the same color and of beautiful features, holding a reputation for beauty in the neighboring territory, inasmuch as some are of a truly Grecian type.

It may very well be asserted that two-thirds of the population is of European origin, and the other third, indigenous.[28]

In 1932 the same statement may be accepted with the exception already stated concerning the presence of a black strain; and the observation that the proportion of Spanish blood is probably even higher than the two-thirds claimed by Sánchez in 1889.[29]

Racial attitudes—

In view of the racial composition of the population of Arandas, the racial attitudes of the people are of particular interest. These were found to be by no means uniform. At one extreme were a strong pride in Spanish ancestry, a feeling of superiority, and opposition to mixture with mestizos or indígenas. A prominent business man said:

The señoritas here do not want to marry mestizos or indígenas. They do not want to mix. It is something like the negroes in your country, but that is a much bigger problem.

The speaker just quoted had never been outside of Mexico. A young woman of whitest Spanish type, recently returned from the United States, cited an illustration:

Parents don't want their daughters to marry Indians; they want them to marry white blood. Of course they're proud, proud of clean blood and old customs! A girl here wanted to marry a dark complexioned young man. You know people here look up your ancestry; they looked up his, and found Indian blood. The parents of the girl wouldn't give their consent, and when the couple were married anyway, they said, "She is not our daughter."

Similarly, a Spanish-type young man, just returned from steel work in Ambridge, Pennsylvania, replied to a remark that the people of Arandas are *buena gente* (good people):

Yes, that's because they're white people; you know, not dark like the Indians. When I get a girl to marry, I want to get a girl like I am; that's the way the boys here feel.

---

[28] Sánchez, *op. cit.*, 65.

[29] It is interesting to note that the Mexican census of 1921 classified the population of the municipio of Arandas as follows: indigenous race, .7 per cent; mixed race, 97.1 per cent; white race, 2.2 per cent. While technically a high proportion of the population may be the result of mixture of races, in so many of them the degree of intermixture is so small that the census figures give an utterly erroneous idea of the racial composition of the population of Arandas.

Characteristically, a Spanish-type land-owner explained the social and economic qualities of the population in terms of race:

This is a white race, with a tendency to improve and economize. The people are better dressed than in many other parts of the country. I attribute these things to the white blood in these people.

These attitudes probably were but slightly, if at all, influenced by dominant race attitudes in the United States; rather they are of local, or of European origin. Sometimes, however, there are direct indications of United States influence. The terminology employed may be one of these. One returned emigrant of predominantly Spanish type, for example, used the familiar distinguishing term "white" as applied to white Americans in most parts of the United States where there are many Mexican laborers.

How is the hotel; is it clean? It's not so good for a white fellow like you; there are better hotels in the United States.

He also said of his baby which had been born, and had died in the United States:

He was good—white.

Another returned emigrant, of practically pure Spanish type, combined curiously a defensive assertion that there *are* white people in Mexico, and an unconscious acceptance of the color terminology:

In Mason City, Iowa, they said to me, "Your people are all black." I said, to come to the center of my country [i.e., doubtless to Los Altos] and you will see white people..... The Mexicans married to white women in the United States may stay there..... In Mason City I got more friends among white people than among my own.

But the appreciation of whiteness as a desirable personal attribute is frequently encountered in Mexico, and in this instance could not have been more than reinforced by experience in the United States. Two women with amounts of pigmentation of the skin varying from extremely little to a great deal expressed clearly their disparagement of dark skin color, and their appreciation of whiteness; in the language of one, the metaphor appropriate to the comparison was a "fly in milk." Neither of the women had been in the United States. A Spanish-type merchant who had never emigrated joined class and color in a protest against the general American conceptions of Mexicans:

They think we are all *prieto* (dark) and wear poor clothes.

While these statements reveal the existence among some people of a strong race consciousness and feeling of superiority or occasionally of inferiority, there was never the slightest indication of any public distinctions such as are common in some parts of the United States. Furthermore, there were many, naturally including persons who obviously had some Indian ancestry but also some who did not, or at least in whom it was not evident, who denied the existence of race feeling. In one or two cases, superiority was claimed even for Indian ancestry. For example, an extreme attitude, strikingly in contrast to those which placed more or less of a premium upon Spanish blood and whiteness of color, was vigorously expressed by a young mestizo boy with good European dress and manners, who was probably less than one-quarter Indian; he voiced the assertive pride in Indian ancestry which recently has been stressed by revolutionary elements in Mexico:

La sangre gachupina es una desgracia. (Spanish blood is a misfortune.) We are mixed Spanish and Indian. The pure Indian blood is best.

This view, however, is not at all characteristic in Arandas.

A moderate attitude, minimizing the importance of race, is more general, and is well illustrated by the following statements of a professional man and a ranchero; they are not correct, however, in attributing the same attitude to the whole community of Spanish stock:

There is almost no mixing with Indians here; we are of the *raza española*. But there is not race prejudice. Although of the white race, the people do not regard with prejudice those who are indígenas. There is a more universal spirit here—more a spirit of social distinction and class than of race. There is no prejudice here. We are all Mexicans—but individuals.

The Spaniards came here with their families. They married with the indígenas but very little, because few indígenas were here; not because of race prejudice.

The dominant racial attitude of the community is thus one of tolerance. The racial minorities have been largely absorbed without stress or friction. Those who are most purely Spanish, and have somewhat higher social position than most of their fellows, show sometimes a strong feeling of pride in Spanish ancestry, and of clannishness, but these are effective only in private social relations, particularly with respect to marriage, and are not manifested in the slightest public ostracism. It is an interesting commentary on the importance of point of view, that when, upon inquiry, I admitted ancestors from three north European countries, one of the auditors exclaimed "¡Qué tanta mezcla! [What a mixture!]".

Schools, parochial and private.—The earliest schools in Arandas were parochial and private schools. The date of establishment of the first state school is uncertain, but probably it was about the middle of the nineteenth century. In the late 80's, according to Sánchez,[30] there were two state schools in the town of Arandas, with an enrollment of from 220 to 250 boys and from 40 to 58 girls. A parish school enrolled between 90 and 120, and there

---

[30] P. 68.

were a few private schools on haciendas and ranches. Probably not over 500 pupils were enrolled in all the schools. In 1932 there were 12 state schools with an enrollment of 1,294 pupils, and four federal rural schools with an enrollment of 293 children and 89 adults. The total enrollment of 1,676 in all schools was divided practically equally between the sexes. Parish schools were not permitted to exist legally. Their attempts to function were necessarily *sub rosa,* and these schools were unimportant as a factor in public education.

Sánchez reported that in 1879 there were 1,262 males and 617 females who could read and write, and 243 males and 81 females who could read but not write. Thus, 2,203 of an estimated total population of 30,105 could either read, or read and write. The latest available figures on literacy, those of the 1921 census, are not closely comparable with the data of Sánchez. Of persons 21 years of age or over, 2,026, or 35.6 per cent, could read and write. The comparable percentage for the State of Jalisco was 42.6 per cent; but a fairer comparison is with the State of Jalisco omitting Guadalajara; the percentage of literacy among adults in the rural portion of the State thus defined was 37.7, only slightly above that which prevailed in Arandas. Schools are few and communication by road is yet meager in Arandas, so many children living in smaller ranches never go to school. In recent years, however, educational facilities have been increasing.

AGRICULTURE

IN GENERAL, the soil of the rocky uplands of the southern half of the municipio is of the type known as *tierra colorada,* a red soil with high content of oxide of iron and low content of humus. In parts, especially near the Cerro de Ayo in the south, there are patches of *tierra parda,* or brown soil, which contains more clay. The soils of El Plan are not of uniform character, but vary even in the same vicinity. There is much tierra parda in El Plan, usually of a somewhat better quality than the tierra parda in the uplands. There are small patches of *tierras blancas,* gravely soils which contain more lime and which are hard to cultivate. These are scattered over El Plan, especially in the region of Piedras Blancas and Sauz de Cagigal. Also relatively small, are patches of *tierra negra,* or black land, which contain more humus than any of the other soils. A few soils, of cinnamon color, and of poor quality for agriculture, are known as *tierra canela.* On the crests are gravelly soils which support only *monte,* or brush, and pasturage.

The red soils are relatively poor except when fertilized with manure or wood ashes, which are frequently used. Maize, *frijoles* or *habas* (beans), barley, *calabazas* (squash), *linaza* (linseed), and some wheat are practically the only crops grown on these soils. The brown soils produce the same crops as the red. The black soils are best for *garbanzos* (peas), but they produce all the other crops found generally in the municipio.

As noted earlier, the Indian inhabitants of the area of present Arandas practiced agriculture at the time of the Spanish conquest, at least to the extent of raising maize, and probably beans and garbanzos. The Spanish colonists added barley. Wheat was first planted in Arandas in 1868. After about ten years' experience without irrigation, it was planted on irrigated lands. At present it is grown under irrigation in El Plan, for it is not well suited to *temporal*[31] agriculture. When grown with reliance only on rainfall, the lands are seeded in the latter part of May in order to take advantage of the rains which come soon thereafter. In 1930 and 1931, for the first time, potatoes were planted with success in the vicinity of the town of Arandas. In about half a dozen mills tequila is manufactured from mezcal plants.

Linaza (flax) is one of the most important crops produced. It was first introduced into Arandas about 1850 by an Arandas rancher who was familiar with the crop in Zamora, Michoacán. At the present time it is raised both in El Plan and in Los Altos, but it grows best in Los Altos. Linseed oil is extracted from the seeds. The fiber is generally fed to cattle, although in previous years some has been sold for manufacturing cloth. The factory which utilized the fiber has been closed for several years because of lack of sufficiently continuous and ample water supplies to make satisfactory and economical operation possible.

Irrigation is practiced in El Plan by means of low earth and stone dams, or *bordos*, erected along small streams, particularly the Río del Tule, and in low spots where water collects during the rainy season. There are probably from sixty to eighty such little artificial lakes in the municipio; one hacienda alone has forty bordos, and from the site of the Indian pyramid above Edificios, fifteen small lakes were visible. The largest of the old reservoirs is at Hacienda Guadalupe (Joconostle); it dates from the early 1870's and was the second or third to be erected in the municipio. Its capacity is approximately five million cubic meters; curiously it impounds water by means of two dams, the outlet from one of which is in the drainage basin of Arroyo de Tres Palos, the other in the basin of Río del Tule. The largest dam in the municipio is Presa Nueva of Hacienda Jalpa, constructed in the closing days of the Díaz Régime, which has a capacity of between 25 and 30 million cubic meters.

In the temporal agriculture characteristic of the uplands, the schedule of operations of a typical small ranchero is about as follows:

---

[31] i.e., dependent on the seasonal rains.

Agriculture

Beginning about April first, lands are plowed and cross-plowed, by means of the usual Egyptian style wooden plow and oxen. This occupies about a month. Then the rains are awaited, which usually come in late May or early June. In 1932 they did not arrive until the end of June.

After the first rains, planting begins. The plow is followed by a boy who plants alternately a kernel of corn and a bean. The field is immediately plowed again to cover up the seeds. Planting requires about nine or ten days' work.

Immediately after corn-planting, the linaza fields are plowed so as to open up rows, the seed is broadcast by hand, and the field is plowed again to cover up the seed. This occupies from three to six days.

After the corn has well sprouted, it is cultivated, each row being plowed twice in order to throw the earth to the stalks both ways. The same wooden plow is used, but with a different cross-stick (*telera*), which is more effective in throwing the earth. This requires about eighteen or nineteen days. After more rains, the corn is plowed once again, requiring about eight or nine days.

In the latter part of July the fields of linaza are weeded with the sickle, an operation performed in about five or six half-days of work.

About the latter part of October, the harvest starts, the crop which ripens first being harvested first. Usually this is the linaza. The linaza, which is a small grain, is cut by sickle, collected with pitchfork and cart, and hauled to a large pile on the grass. There the oxen walk round and round until all the seed is loosened from the plant.[32] The straw is then lifted with a pitchfork to let the wind blow away the chaff, and the seed falls to the ground.

Corn is cut by hand with a sickle, shocked, and allowed to dry from fifteen to twenty days. Then the ears are husked in the field, the stalks carried to the corrals in bundles, and the ears carted or carried in baskets (*canastas*) on the back of a man to the ranch house. There the corn is shelled by scraping with cobs, and the kernels put in a *petate* (container made of a tule mat) for storage.

The beans are pulled up by the roots, piled like linaza, and beaten from the pods with a stick used as a flail. Harvest is usually ended between the first and the middle of January. Wheat, which is raised principally on the larger ranches and haciendas of El Plan, is planted usually in October and harvested in May.

At intervals during the season, small ranchers occasionally work by the day for another rancher. Frequently they exchange labor with their neighbors. Throughout the year they are occupied with cutting wood, building stone fences, or carrying and filtering water, etc.

In the vicinity of the Tule ranch, ropes are made of maguey fiber and sold. At San Ignacio Cerro Gordo, the wood of the cerro is used to make plows, carts, etc., for the entire region.

On one hacienda in El Plan eighty iron plows are used, with oxen for traction. Iron plows are used also on some of the larger ranches both in El Plan and Los Altos. One tractor—and perhaps a few more—is used in El Plan. At least one rancher in the same region uses a truck for hauling on his ranch, and for transporting his produce.

---

[32] Sometimes horses are used, and sometimes cylindrical stones, drawn by animals, are used to expedite the threshing.

During the past fifty or sixty years the utilization of the land has been progressively more intensive. Sánchez estimated fifty-odd years ago that the lands were used for diverse purposes in approximately the following proportions: agricultural land, 16 per cent; pasture land, 59 per cent; brush (monte), 25 per cent.[33] An estimate of the uses at the present time by a man thoroughly familiar with the changes which have occurred, places the proportion of land devoted to agriculture at 50 per cent; of pasture land at 25 per cent, and of monte, at 25 per cent.

TABLE 7

PREVAILING WAGE RATES PAID FOR TOWN AND AGRICULTURAL DAY LABOR ARANDAS, JALISCO, 1850-1932*

Year	Town labor	Agricultural labor
1850		12½ centavos and maize†
1879		12½ centavos and maize†
1896	25 centavos	12½ centavos and maize†
1900	31¼ centavos	18¾ centavos and maize†
1904	31¼–37½ centavos	25 centavos and maize
1906	43¾ centavos	25 centavos and maize
1914	50 centavos	25 centavos and maize
1915	75 centavos	25–31¼ and maize
1920	75 centavos–1 peso	50–75 centavos without maize‡
1921	75 centavos	50 centavos without maize
1928	1 peso	75–1.00 without maize‡
1930	75 centavos–1 peso	60–75 centavos without maize‡
1931	40–75 centavos	40–50 centavos without maize, or 25 centavos with maize

* Data for 1879 taken from Sánchez, *op. cit.*, 81. Prior and subsequent data based on the memory of reliable citizens, and upon contemporary observation.
† The amount of maize customarily given since about 1896 has been 5 liters (3½ kilograms); prior to that time the amount of maize was an *almud*, or a little less than 4 liters. In some parts of the municipio the lesser amount continued until much later; see text.
‡ In some outlying portions of the municipio, maize was probably always included as part of the wage, with a somewhat lower money wage than is here indicated for the years in which purely money wages predominated.

Wages.—From the 1850's, and how much earlier is not known, the wages of farm laborers in Arandas were 12½ centavos and an almud of maize a day. At the close of the 1870's the daily wage of *peones de labranza* (farm laborers) was 12½ centavos and 1/24 of a *fanega*[34] of maize, practically the same as for decades preceding. In harvesting grain crops, the wage was 25 centavos with no allotment of maize. Vaqueros and pastores received from 4 to 6 pesos monthly, with the same ration of maize. For yet another twenty years wages of farm laborers continued about the same; then they began to

---

[33] P. 79.
[34] A fanega is equal to 1.526 bushels. The wage data for the 1870's are from Sánchez, *op. cit.*, 81.

advance. Table 7 has been prepared to show the generally prevailing wage rates, with the approximate dates when changes took place. In the vicinity of the town of Arandas higher wages and earlier advances in wage rates than those in outlying portions of the municipio have been characteristic. As late as 1910 wages in the vicinity of San Ignacio Cerro Gordo were still 12½ centavos and 4 liters of maize, when they were generally 43¾ centavos and maize, usually 5 liters, in the vicinity of the town of Arandas. It will be noted that by the depression years of 1930 and 1931 wages had dropped back to their level of fifteen years earlier. Hours of labor in both field and town, in 1931 as before, were from sun to sun. In the fields it is customary to give only enough time off to eat lunch; in town this is more liberally estimated at half an hour.

With these wage rates may be compared the $1.25 (pesos 2.50) per day of 10 hours received by the man who left Arandas in 1905 to work on the track in Kansas, or the 35 and 40 cents per hour paid on the track in 1929, or the coal-mining, steel, or automobile wages which mounted in some cases to the heights of $6, $7, or even the $9 per day (12, 14, and 18 pesos) which one barefooted ranchero claimed he had earned two years before in the Buick plant at Flint, Michigan. The tremendous disequilibrium created by these enormous wage differentials would alone suffice to cause the heavy emigration that is described later.

SOCIAL AND ECONOMIC STRUCTURE

AFTER THE CONQUEST the land area of the present municipio of Arandas was originally granted to individuals by the *Real Audiencia* at Guadalajara, in parcels of one or two *sitios*[35] for purposes of pasturing stock. One such grant of two sitios was made as early as 1565 to Andrés de Villanueva, alderman of the city of Guadalajara; these were located at Lagunillas and de la Hermita in the western portion of present Arandas, and perhaps spread over into the adjacent municipio of Atotonilco.[36] Many of the grants were never occupied by the original grantees. In the course of many decades, however, some of the more enterprising grantees obtained ownership of a number of sitios, exercised possession over others, and then perfected titles in a series of *com-*

---

[35] A league, equal to 4,428 acres.

[36] Concerning the activities of Villanueva, whether at these particular ranches or not is not stated, it was written in 1858: ".... on one hacienda alone, D. Andres de Villanueva, one of the foremost *conquistadores* [conquerors] of the kingdom in the year 1570, brought together thirty thousand head of cattle. Actually this estate amounts to much less today, because one of its owners disposed of many portions of it; but what he lost others gained, which is the way the fortunes of this kingdom diminish; since the land is becoming every day more thickly settled, naturally the property has to be divided more."—Joaquin F. Escovedo, "Apuntes históricos sobre la conquista de la provincia de Nayarit," *Boletín de la Sociedad Mexicana de geografía y estadística*, 7(1859):14.

posiciones and *confirmaciones;* these procedures were conducted by royal officials sent by the King of Spain to confirm or reject the validity of titles, and for clearing titles to secure appropriate fees for the service of His Majesty in such matters as the maintenance of the fleet or the army. All, or practically all, of the area of Arandas was thus ultimately absorbed into three large haciendas:[37] Milpillas, Santa Ana Pacueco, and Jalpa. All three still exist today as agricultural units, though much shrunken in area. A portion of one of them, Jalpa, yet remains within Arandas at its extreme northeastern limits. Hacienda San Ignacio Cerro Gordo, which by the middle of the seventeenth century had come to belong to the owner of Milpillas, has comparatively recently become separated from Milpillas. It is operated in two or three units, and its owners are now numerous.

Hacienda San Ignacio Cerro Gordo

The three haciendas met at Caracol, in the northwestern portion of the municipio. Jalpa, covering approximately 16 sitios in the municipio, lay north of the line formed by Caracol, Saucito, Presa, and Fresnos. Milpillas, occupying 20 sitios in Arandas, lay west of the line formed by Caracol, Tule, Sauces, and Hermita. The remaining major portion of the municipio, approximately 40 sitios in extent, was part of Santa Ana Pacueco.

The original use of the land was for pasturage of stock, principally sheep, cattle, and horses. Exploitation of the range was partly by the owners themselves, with Spanish colonists serving as *mayordomos* or *capataces,* while Spanish, Indians and mestizos, Negroes and mulattoes served as laborers, the latter often being slaves. In part, the range was rented to Spaniards and a very few Indians at an extremely low figure, which tradition places at one peso per year. It may well have been set low by those interested in possessing it, in order to promote Spanish colonization and effective occupation of a region of comparatively poor lands.

By some date probably not long before 1760, three sitios had been sold to Spanish families from the lands of Santa Ana Pacueco. These sitios covered the site of the present town of Arandas and stretched from San Francisco,

---

[37] Milpillas and Cerro Gordo were organized as haciendas before the middle of the seventeenth century. A *Composicion de las haciendas de Milpillas y Cerro Gordo celebrado entre Sebastian de Andia y la Audiencia real de Guadalajara* is dated January 21, 1645.

Nopal, and Santa María ranches to Carrizal.[38] These sitios were used by their owners, and by Spanish families who rented from them. About 1760 the population felt itself sufficient in numbers to establish a chapel and *congregación*. According to reliable tradition, two chapels were started, one east and one west of Arandas, but by superior order these were discontinued in order to unite upon a single chapel to be built midway between. This middle site, now the site of the present town, chanced to be on the ranch rented by a family named Aranda, and from this family name the town name Arandas was derived.[39]

As early as 1804 thirty *caballerías*[40] of land in El Plan belonging to Milpillas were bought by one of the Spanish residents for 200 pesos per caballería. The general sale of the hacienda lands in Arandas, however, took place after the War of Independence, which broke out in 1810.

The heirs of the Marquis of Altamira, original owner of Hacienda Santa Ana Pacueco, which covered more than half of the present municipio, returned to Europe during the wars, leaving their numerous stock to fall a prey to the contending groups of the time. Guanajuato was an important center of activity of the *Insurgentes*. The position of the hacienda was thus particularly exposed, and as a result it was practically deserted. Jalpa was less disorganized than Santa Ana Pacueco, and Milpillas, less exposed, survived in better fashion.

In 1836 when Spain finally abandoned its claims over Mexico, an *administrador* was sent to take possession of the lands of the Hacienda Santa Ana Pacueco and to rent them. This he did until some time in the 1850's. But by that time the majority of the heirs, who numbered some 72, were ready to sell and did sell their fractional shares. The purchasers in Arandas were principally renters occupying the land at the time; a few came from Atotonilco and Ayo to buy. The 28 owners who were unwilling at first to sell their interests, finally sold them in 1860 to a Mexican, grandfather of the present owner. The purchaser at once sold off still more land to renters at a capitalization of their annual rental. Thus was completed the sale of all the hacienda lands in Arandas, and from this time began the general division by sale of the lands of Arandas. About the same time Hacienda Jalpa also sold off land in Arandas and only Rancho Ordeña yet remains in the possession of Jalpa. In approximately 1850, six sitios were sold, which today form Hacienda San Sebastian. In 1854, as already noted, Hacienda San Ignacio Cerro Gordo was separated from Milpillas.

---

[38] The price was 200 pesos per sitio, paid at the rate of about 5 per cent annually.

[39] Sánchez, *op. cit.*, 36. Don Pantaleón Orozco states that he has seen the remains of the chapel started on Rancho Santa María.

[40] A caballería equals 107.948 acres.

The process of subdivision was rapid. By 1879 the real property of the municipio was already so much divided that it was said:

> The property of few *municipalidades* of the State, and perhaps of the Republic, is so divided as this, which brings a great benefit to society, because it gives no opportunity for monopoly of grain, and serves well the stimulation of commerce and the common prosperity.[41]

The process of increasing subdivision of the land in Arandas has continued to the present, as is shown by the data assembled in table 8. The increase in number of properties (*predios*) and of proprietors, however, is not identical; of the increase in the latter only estimates can be made. Sánchez estimated that in 1879 there were 3,000 proprietors of both rural and urban properties.

TABLE 8

NUMBER OF RURAL LANDS (*predios rústicos*) IN THE MUNICIPIO OF ARANDAS AND IN THE STATE OF JALISCO*

Fiscal year	Number of rural lands	
	Arandas	Jalisco
1879	1,316	
1895–1896	2,610	68,930
1900–1901	2,497	110,945
1905–1906	4,205	139,804
1910–1911	5,932	162,851
1922–1923	6,838	181,167
1927–1928	7,588	198,348

* Data from the Cuenta general del tesoro público. Estado de Jalisco, Mexico; data for 1879 from Sánchez, *op. cit.*, 71.

Assuming the existence of the same relation between number of rural proprietors and of rural properties as between total number of proprietors and properties, there were about 2,250 rural proprietors in 1879. Relying upon estimates from a source comparable to that used by Sánchez, there were 5,000 rural proprietors in 1927–28. According to these estimates there were relatively fewer owners of land in common in 1927–28 than in 1879, and more persons with one or more predios. But the increase in proprietors, while much less than the increase in number of predios, has nevertheless resulted in a greater percentage of the rural population which owns land. In 1879 the proportion of estimated number of rural proprietors to rural population was approximately 9 per cent; in 1927–28 it was approximately 25 per cent. These figures are subject to all the limitations of estimates and

[41] Sánchez, *op. cit.*, 71.

the inaccuracies of population data, but they are the best data available, and they do show a trend which the general observation of old residents clearly confirms.

It will be noted from the table that, from 1879 to 1927–28, the number of *predios rústicos* in Arandas increased 191 per cent, while the number in the entire state of Jalisco increased 187 per cent, practically the same rate. Land division has taken place at a rapid rate in many parts of the state, particularly in the important region of Los Altos but also in other portions, even before the agrarian decree of Carranza in 1915. These figures obscure the fact that many large haciendas still exist in the state: proportionately, land ownership is more widely distributed in Arandas and other portions of Los Altos, than in the state as a whole.

While the distribution of rural land ownership has been increasing in Arandas, some individual proprietors have lost their lands, and have become laborers. Thus, frequently when properties have been small and heirs numerous, some heirs have sold out to others and have become laborers; some have simply spent what they inherited and have lost their lands in a way reminiscent of the American saying, "from shirtsleeves to shirtsleeves in three generations." Furthermore, while most properties have been dividing, at least one hacienda was built up by an Arandas renter, originally landless. The grandson is yet living. But at his death it will be divided among nine heirs according to legal arrangements already made. Another hacienda was similarly built up by purchases of small tracts, and a fourth was separated as a small tract from a larger hacienda. But even these haciendas have been undergoing division under the influence of normal inheritance or desire to forestall *agrarismo* by partition of some of the lands of the living hacendado among prospective heirs.

The custom of equal division of inheritances and the fact of large families have been largely responsible for the increasing subdivision of the land. In general, the people esteem ownership of land highly, and save to purchase it. As I was repeatedly told:

When a man gets 40 or 50 pesos, he seeks to buy a *pedazo de tierra*.

Some people rise to ownership by buying a pig, feeding it scraps at their house in town or in the country, selling it, buying another, and so on, until they accumulate enough to purchase. Others save from their wages in Arandas, and rise from laborer to metayer to proprietor, or directly from laborer to proprietor. Yet others, during the past twenty years, have purchased land with the earnings of their labor in the United States. Many in the rural parts of the municipio own only one, two, or three *solares*, or twenty or thirty, and there are many who begin by purchasing only a few square meters for their houses.[42] Because of this insistent demand, the price of land in Los Altos has long been relatively well above the price of more productive lands elsewhere.

A further important factor in the development of a community of peasant proprietors is the composition of the population. In this predominantly Spanish community, its members were accustomed to the European traditions of husbandry, agriculture, and property ownership. Thus they possessed a cultural background fitting them to make more rapid economic advance than the Indians. Also, by reason both of their European background and their membership in the conquering race, they were doubtless imbued with ambition to advance themselves economically in the New World.

In addition to the large number of proprietors, there are many who cultivate land on shares. Poorer lands are usually rented on thirds, and the better lands on halves. The terms of the leases are essentially the same as those which obtain in Texas for leases on halves, i.e., the landowner furnishes everything except the labor.

The larger proprietors have generally been willing to sell pieces of their land, using the money for stock for their own ranches, for commercial activities, etc. More recently, apprehension of agrarianism has been an additional impelling factor. The subdivision of the land is most marked in the southern half of the municipio. In El Plan, where the surface is more nearly level, irrigation is used on fields, some of which formerly were regarded as less desirable, and the agricultural unit is larger partly for this reason. All the haciendas of the municipio are in El Plan, except San Ignacio Cerro Gordo at the western extremity, which has remained large from the beginning—though now with divided ownership—with a diversity of resources, timber, soil suitable for making pottery, broad pastures for cattle, and nearly level fields for crops.

Agrarianism—

The extensive distribution of land ownership leads to the emphatic declaration, upon inquiry, that

There is no agrarian problem here—none!

Or that

There is a *natural* agrarianism here!

The latter statement accurately sums up the historical process already described. The former is a mixture of fact and usually of fervent thanks or hope as well.

---

[42] A *solar* (50 *varas* square) equals .4428 acres.

In general, it is true that agrarian sentiment is absent from Arandas. As early as the Madero campaign more than twenty years ago, a leading agrarian went to Los Altos to win support, but he states that he was unable to make any impression. And in the recent Cristero revolution, when *agraristas* fought with the government against Cristeros, Arandas was practically unanimously Cristero.

Agrarismo was generally attacked as unethical. For example, a ranchero said:

The laborers here do not want to take the lands; they are honest men. If they want land, they want to buy it. They do not want to despoil anyone.

Similarly, a young metayer, son of a proprietor, said:

The agraristas come to the big haciendas and take everything. I don't like that.

A poor laborer, also a metayer on a small scale, confirmed the view:

No, we are not agraristas here; we do not believe in taking what belongs to another.

The alignment of church against government and agraristas which broke into war was clearly revealed by a young rancher of Cristero sympathies:

The war is over. But it would start again if the agraristas and government became active as they are in Vera Cruz. The agraristas want to take the bishops' lands and kill them, and take the lands of us Catholics and shoot us. I don't believe in robbing people of money or taking their land, but only in buying it. The *hacendados* should pay more wages and give more work, but the agraristas should not rob them of their land.

The interesting conflict of moral and religious sanctions for agrarismo was further illuminated by the observations of a clergyman:

The agraristas say that God gave all to all, but those who believe in God do not want to take what does not belong to them.

On one hacienda in the municipio, a town had grown up on land which belonged to the hacendados. Prior to 1919 the inhabitants of the town desired to purchase their house-sites, but the owners preferred not to sell. Under pressure from political leaders who used the threat of expropriation of agricultural lands by means of the agrarian law, and with the priest siding with the householders, the owners made donation to the inhabitants of their house-sites and to the town collectively, of additional land surrounding it for expansion.[43] In 1931 another incipient agitation for agricultural lands failed to mature. A townsman gave one reason for the failures:

We are artisans here, and we didn't want farm lands. We already owned the houses, but not the land on which we built them.

---

[43] See Appendix.

Other reasons were given by a clergyman and a landowner:

> Politicians from outside stirred up the people here. But the people didn't want *tierras,* only their houses. They didn't want what didn't belong to them.....
>
> Agrarismo is a part of communism, but it doesn't profess all the doctrines of communism. The communists are against ecclesiastical authority.
>
> There *was* agrarismo, but they changed the padre. Now there is none.

Thus, agrarianism had appeared in a truncated form even in Arandas, where landowners, large and small, were practically unanimously against it, the small owners as ardently opposed, or more, than the large; and where the influence of the church, which dominates the minds and holds the affections of the population to an extraordinary degree, is generally hostile. The local priest, who had been sympathetic to the desires of the people for land, was transferred to another parish. Some local government officials in the past have shown sympathy toward local agrarismo, but no agrarian activity from that quarter was manifest in 1932, nor did it appear likely. The rise of a large landless class of potential agraristas in Arandas, and the economic hardships of increasing population have been checked or mitigated by emigration to other parts of Mexico or to the United States. On the whole, the wide distribution of land ownership among a very high proportion of the population even though the amount owned individually was usually very small, together with the dominance of the church, make Arandas a powerful bulwark against agrarismo.

Ever since emigration to the United States has assumed large proportions, the earnings of Arandas emigrants have been an important addition to the purchasing power of the poorer elements of the community. The number of postal money orders and amounts remitted annually during the past ten years appear in table 9. The fluctuations parallel fairly closely those exhibited by the total money order remittances by emigrants from all parts of Mexico during the same period.[44] The average monthly fluctuations of remittances over the ten-year period are shown in table 10. In the six months, June to November inclusive, 62.2 per cent of the money orders and 63.6 per cent of the amount of money were remitted. This coincides with the period of fullest employment in the United States.

In addition to postal money orders, there were remittances by registered mail of bank drafts or United States paper currency. Registered letters (first class) from the United States received at Arandas numbered 1,076 in 1929, 895 in 1930, and 332 in 1931, exceeding in each year the number of postal money orders received. It was estimated that 90 per cent of the registered letters contained either bank drafts or currency. The average amounts sent

---

[44] Manuel Gamio, *Mexican Immigration to the United States: a Study of Human Adjustment* (Chicago, 1930):5.

TABLE 9

Money Orders from the United States Paid by the Post Office at Arandas, Jalisco, 1922-1931, Inclusive*

Year	Number of money orders	Total amount remitted (pesos)
1922	436	$35,093.73
1923	1,110	94,471.88
1924	659	53,176.72
1925	555	41,351.25
1926	1,033	83,507.30
1927	1,153	91,479.37
1928	1,213	75.575.42
1929	661	50,157.94
1930	490	31,189.83
1931	360	24,715.57
Total	7,670	580,719.01
Annual Average	767	58,071.90

* Data by courtesy of the *Dirección General de Correos Mexicanos*. They include the post offices in the towns of Arandas and Santa María del Valle; the post office at San Ignacio Cerro Gordo is under the jurisdiction of Atotonilco.

TABLE 10

Monthly Percentages of Average Annual Money Orders from the United States Paid at Arandas, Jalisco, 1922-1931, Inclusive*

Month	Percentage of number of money orders	Percentage of amounts remitted
January	5.2	5.1
February	6.8	6.9
March	5.9	5.5
April	5.7	4.9
May	6.6	6.0
June	9.1	9.6
July	10.7	10.3
August	11.5	11.6
September	10.7	11.0
October	10.7	11.5
November	9.5	9.6
December	7.6	8.0
Year	100.0	100.0

* See footnote to table 9.

per draft were probably greater than the average amounts per money order, as minimum remittance charges for drafts are usually greater. The average currency remittances, which were in violation of Mexican law, were probably smaller, and much less numerous. Therefore, while it is impossible to know the amounts sent to Arandas by registered letter, they probably were even greater than the amounts sent by postal money order.

These remittances were an important factor in temporarily raising the standards of consumption of many Arandas families, and in supporting the market for American as well as Mexican goods sold in Arandas. Their sharp decline in 1930 and 1931 was an important local factor in the economic depression in Arandas in those years.[45]

---

[45] It is significant that a considerable number of laborers of Hacienda Jalpa, overlapping into Arandas, bought small pieces of land from the hacienda, principally with their earnings in the United States, but, although the owners favor these sales, they have practically stopped with the cessation during the past two or three years of liberal remittances from the emigrants.

II

HISTORY OF THE EMIGRATION TO THE UNITED STATES

THE FIRST EMIGRANTS to the United States from the municipio of Arandas left in the early years of the twentieth century. About two decades before, in 1884, the rail connection from Mexico City to El Paso, which passes through the eastern corner of Jalisco, had been completed, and an increasing stream of Mexican laborers had begun to move northward from the country adjacent to the railroad to take advantage of the employment made available by the new means of transportation.[46] Before many years the news reached Arandas, and laborers from that isolated region began to join the tide of emigration.

The earliest emigrant from Arandas with whom I talked left the town in 1905; he asserted, plausibly, that he was the first to go from that region. Having heard from prisoners sent north to Sonora to fight the Yaqui Indians, that "the United States was a good place to work," he and his brother decided to take some of their savings, go to San Francisco del Rincón on the railroad, and entrain for El Paso. Upon arrival at El Paso they were sent by an employment agency to work on the track near Independence, Kansas, at $1.25 per day of 10 hours. After about six months, they returned to Arandas. In 1907 my informant went again to El Paso, accompanied by two friends; this time he was sent by employment agents to Fresno, California, for track work. At least by 1909, and probably earlier, men from the Arandas ranches, distant from roads and towns, were also beginning to go north for seasonal employment as track laborers in the United States.

The news of attractive work spread rapidly. Doubtless the ranchers and small merchants who for many years previous had gone on horseback as far as Aguascalientes, Querétaro, Guadalajara, Guanajuato, and Michoacán to market their produce of butter, *tequila* (strong alcoholic drink made from mezcal plant), linseed oil, animals, etc., were among the first to carry to the ranches the news of the employment offered by the railroads, and with the return of the first few emigrants to Arandas there was a wave of enthusiasm to take advantage of the wages in the United States. Naturally; for wages in Arandas were from 31 centavos to 36 centavos Mexican, which was one-half the value of the same figure American, and in the country wages were 25 centavos and 3½ kilograms of maize for a day from sun to sun, as against

---

[46] See Victor S. Clark, "Mexican Labor in the United States," U. S. Bur. of Labor, Bulletin 78 (September, 1908): 466–522.

United States wages of $1.25 for 10 hours.[47] Besides the wage and hour differential in favor of the United States, there was some direct stimulation of emigration by interests not content to rely on chance methods of disseminating information to potential emigrants. Two Arandas Mexicans reported the early activity there of Mexican employment agents, and one of my informants asserted that he received free passage to the border from an agent securing railroad labor. In these various ways the stream was started.

No statistics are available whereby to chart historically the course of the emigration. It is therefore necessary to rely upon the memory of residents who have observed the emigration since its inception. According to their recollections the numbers of emigrants steadily augmented from 1905 to 1914 as word spread of the attractiveness of labor in the United States, and as it was made concrete to all with the seasonal return of those who had gone. About 1914 the number of emigrants rose somewhat more rapidly, partly as a result of increasing opportunities in the United States and increasing knowledge of them, and partly as a result of disturbed conditions in Mexico. In May, 1914, the first of the revolutionary armies—troops under Estrada—passed through Los Altos; later came the armies of Carranza and Villa. The effects of the economic stresses of the revolution—the inflation of the currency through use of paper money, greater insecurity of persons attendant upon less effective maintenance of order, etc., all these were felt in Arandas. But, in a military sense, there was no serious revolutionary disturbance of the people in this region.

The demand of the United States between 1917 and 1920 for laborers, because of war and immediately post-war conditions, was strongly felt in Arandas, and it gave great impetus to emigration from that region, as well as from other parts of Mexico. In 1921, because of post-war depression in the United States, the return movement was heavy. A few emigrants, however, set out for the north even in that year. With returning prosperity in the United States, the tide of emigrants from Arandas rose higher than ever in the years 1923 and after, though the revolutions which continued to sweep over Mexico had comparatively little direct effect in Los Altos. Even the Huerta revolt in 1923 and 1924, during which occurred the battle at near-by Ocotlán, was without any marked effect on Arandas. The rising emigration was influenced chiefly by conditions in the United States.

Cristero Revolution—

Between 1926 and 1929, however, local revolutionary disturbances in Los Altos sent fresh recruits to swell the tide of emigration. In August, 1926, the

---

[47] See table 7, p. 24.

national conflict between church and state in Mexico reached an open breach, and in January, 1927, armed insurrection broke out in Los Altos.

With the general political phases of the conflict, the more or less formal alliances of government and agraristas, of church and conservative landowners, this study is not primarly concerned. In order to reveal the temper and power of religion in Los Altos, however, as well as to show the effect of civil war on emigration, the details of the conflict in that region are presented here briefly.

In Arandas all the principal elements of the national conflict were present, but the people regarded the revolution as entirely religious in character—as a great popular uprising to demand that priests be allowed to say the mass. With agrarian agitation almost absent from their midst,[48] and with strong, even fanatical religious convictions, the people of this region were practically unanimously Cristeros, either actively or sympathetically. A ranchero described the situation from the local point of view:

Leaving after early mass, Arandas.

> It was a religious war purely, for liberty of belief and tolerance like in the United States. The people were all in sympathy with the Cristeros; they gave them moral and financial aid, if they did not bear arms.

On January 9, 1927, armed Cristeros took possession of Arandas and burned some of the municipal archives; simultaneously other bands entered Atotonilco near-by, and a number of other towns. Guerrilla warfare dominated the region for two years and a half, until a nation-wide agreement was reached in June, 1929. Strong bodies of federal troops occupied the town of Arandas practically throughout the revolution. But the demonstration of force was not sufficient to suppress the revolt. When the soldiers went out into the countryside for provisions or other purposes they were subjected to heavy and effective fire whenever the Cristeros, most of whom were ranchers, could attack them to advantage. But when the advantage lay with the troops, the Cristeros simply avoided combat, thus giving the soldiers no opportunity to inflict a decisive defeat upon them. Small combats in the fields were almost daily occurrences and usually took place under conditions which favored the revolutionaries. Upon at least one occasion a battle took place within the town of Arandas itself, as also in numerous other towns of

---
[48] See pp. 30 ff.

Jalisco and adjacent portions of Guanajuato and Michoacán. Indeed, on April 19, 1927, a Cristero force, shouting "Viva Cristo Rey," assaulted a train en route from Guadalajara to Mexico City between Ocotlán and La Barca, killed the guard of some 52 soldiers and about 56 passengers who were caught in the line of fire, burned the train, and made off with a rich prize of silver.

In their struggle, the people of Arandas were sustained, according to a local account, by such teachings as:

> Our religion is twenty centuries old, and cannot be killed. If you lose today, tomorrow you will win. The soul is over all, and the religious leaders are always right.

A small rancher assured me:

> God was with us. We started the revolution armed with clubs and implements of labor, but soon we had rifles which we took from the soldiers.

The local conflict proceeded so favorably for the Cristeros, despite hardships, that the belief was general among the common people of Arandas that they were winning. Even in 1931 I was told by a laborer, for example,

> The Cristeros were satisfied with the peace, because then they could have masses again. That is what they fought for. The people here are *muy católicos*. If it had lasted a year more, the Cristeros would have won.

And a resident reported what, judging from the temper of the people of Arandas, was entirely plausible:

> If the government starts to persecute the church, the war will start again in two weeks.[40]

Because of the difficulty of dealing with a rural population in rebellion, concentration of all the people into the towns was ordered. It was enforced upon three separate occasions—approximately from October to December, 1927, January to May, 1928, and January to May, 1929. While the countryside was vacated, the ranchers were despoiled of stock, clothing, and anything of value. Some buildings, too, were burned or destroyed. Part of the

---

[40] For the Fifth of May, 1932, army officials instituted an "Olympiad at Arandas," including athletic games, musical contests, and the usual festival attractions, which was attended by people from far and near. Included in the ceremonies was a military demonstration by crack regiments, the purpose of which was doubtless to impress the people with the futility of military resistance to the government anti-clerical program. There is considerable evidence that this program, together with war-weariness from the preceding experience, has had a pacifying effect. On the other hand, I was told in June, 1932, that the demonstration was not effective, that in view of the regional successes in the previous Cristero revolution the people of Arandas "no longer feared the government troops," and even that "many people here want another [religious] revolution." Within a month after the preceding was written, reports came of a clash near Atotonilco between soldiers and an armed band led by an ex-Cristero chief, in which the former were badly worsted (see *El Informador* and *Las Noticias* of Guadalajara, July 27, 28, 1932); this was followed shortly by a public statement of a high church official in Mexico City to the effect that the clergy were not authorized to advocate resistance by force of arms.

spoliation was charged to the government troops, part to the Cristeros; naturally, in a region so unitedly in favor of the latter, the spoliation of the former was bitterly condemned, and similar acts of the latter were condoned as necessary to appease hunger and need or to prevent supplies from falling into the hands of the government. Some of the losses of stock, of course, resulted simply from lack of care. Captured persons accused of active aid to the Cristeros were frequently shot or hung in Arandas—on the edge of town, in the atrium of the church, behind the temple which is under construction, or in the cemetery. The most famous of the Cristeros to be shot in this manner was General Aristeo Pedraza, a valiant priest from Ayo, who was wounded and captured in battle near Arandas.

Life during this period was very difficult for the inhabitants of the region. Strict martial law prevailed, and the movements of civilians were sharply restricted. Concentrated in the towns, they were often without sufficient means of support, while their ranches were being stripped. The men often brought their families to town, then slipped out at night to join the Cristeros. Some families were maintained by remittances of relatives working in the United States (see table 9). Suspected persons were liable at any time to detention and even death at the hands of the military. On the other hand, those who performed functions for the local civil government or at the behest of the military incurred the hostility of their neighbors of Cristero sympathies; as one civil employee described the bitter denunciation,

They say we are Bolsheviks; that we do not believe in God.

Neutrality was almost impossible. One citizen who interceded with generals to spare the lives of accused Cristeros, and frequently succeeded—sometimes with the aid of money—described his difficult position:

The Cristeros said, "Why are you so friendly with the generals? The military inquired, "Why are you asking us to let the Cristeros escape?"

A town laborer voiced the general sentiment when he said:

We all were in fear.

Thus, a religious motive became an important incentive to emigration from Arandas, as well as from other disturbed portions in the central part of Mexico. Many went to live in Mexican cities or other places not torn by war, for the sake of the physical security or the employment which they could not obtain in Arandas under revolutionary conditions. For the same reasons many emigrated to the United States, raising the volume of emigration above its previous totals. No accurate data are available, but rough local estimates placed the departures from the municipio for the United States at 400 in 1926, 600 in 1927, and 200 in 1928. Relatives already in the United States were advised not to return to Arandas, both in the interest of personal security and because of the greater need for the wages which the emigrants remitted, and thus the usual temporary return movement to Arandas was retarded. In 1929, the year during which the war ended and employment in the United States began to slacken, the estimated emigration from Arandas dropped to 100. The revolution caused a loss of population to Arandas estimated locally at several thousand persons who either settled in other portions of Mexico or went to the United States. Since the peace many have returned, but many have not.

In 1930 and 1931 practically no one emigrated to the United States from Arandas except a few who returned to previous employments after short vacations in Mexico. In those years the tide of migration, responding to depressed employment in the United States, was moving back to Arandas.

When interrogated concerning the causes of emigration, the replies of the emigrants usually stressed economic factors—the scarcity of employment in Arandas, the desire to gain a better livelihood, the great differential in favor of wages in the United States. An illiterate metayer, who regretted his inability to emigrate, pictured the glamour with which work in the United States had been surrounded:

> The worst work in the United States is better than the best here. The *repatriados* say that treatment is good and wages are good, and there is much machinery. Here we work like burros, from sun to sun. And they say there is good order in the United States.

One emigrant, more articulate than the others, summed up the factors of poverty, revolution, and the common complaint against heavy taxation:

> People are too poor here; all the time they want to fight, and they take all you have in taxes.

Only the more educated citizens of Arandas explained the emigration in terms of population pressure.

A minor but appreciable element in the emigration was represented by the young boy who ran away from home, not from economic necessity, but to *aventurar* in the United States.

But important as the internal economic, religious, and political conditions in Arandas have been, the chief stimulating, and limiting factor as well, in the emigration to the United States has been the fluctuating demand for common laborers in the United States.

OCCUPATIONAL AND GEOGRAPHICAL DISTRIBUTION OF THE EMIGRANTS FROM ARANDAS

ALMOST ALL OCCUPATIONS and classes in the community have been represented among those who have gone from Arandas to labor in the United States. Only the wealthier merchants with stores, the professional men, the larger *rancheros,* and the hacendados, have refrained entirely from joining the ranks of the emigrants, and even some of these have contributed sons. Small street vendors, small rancheros, both proprietors and metayers, day laborers with or without property, handicraftsmen such as shoemakers, carpenters, stone masons, *sombrereros,* and many young sons of persons of practically all classes, have been among those to go. While the majority of the emigrants have been drawn from the rural portions of the municipio where the bulk of the population resides, the town itself has also contributed heavily.

In the United States the geographical and occupational distribution of the Arandas emigrants has been wide. Although frequently they lived and worked in small clusters in various parts of the United States, there was no tendency to form large and distinct Arandas colonies.

A complete list of the places and jobs at which they had worked was not obtained, but the summary of a representative sample is illuminating. These Arandas Mexicans had been employed in 24 states, in 20 of these, on the track: California, Arizona, New Mexico, Texas, Oklahoma, Kansas, Missouri, Oregon, Nevada, Utah, Wyoming, Colorado, Nebraska, North and South Dakota, Iowa, Illinois, Ohio, Michigan, Pennsylvania. In steel mills, foundries, etc., they had worked in Indiana, Illinois, Colorado, Pennsylvania, and West Virginia; in the automobile industry some had been employed at the Buick factory in Flint, Michigan. In agriculture some had worked in the varied agriculture of California, in onions, vegetables, and cotton in Texas, in sugar beets in Idaho, California, and Minnesota, in vegetables in Kansas, in vegetables and fruit in Oregon. Other occupations, reported by one or two emigrants each, were employment in pipe-line, oil, dry-dock, hotel kitchen, and soft-drink stand in Texas; by a public utility in Wisconsin, at a cement plant in Iowa; at meat-packing plants in Illinois and Iowa, in the lumber industry and in aqueduct construction in California, in highway construction in Oklahoma and Iowa, and in coal mining in Utah and New Mexico.

Employment by railroads on maintenance of way, work in round-houses, etc., was by far the most common experience of the emigrants. Persons who had worked in the steel industry and in coal mines were frequently encountered, and many who had worked in agriculture. The proportion that had worked in sugar beets was comparatively low, since relatively few families had emigrated and the beet sugar industry prefers, and is preferred by, those who labor in family groups.

A good conception of the characteristic movement from place to place in the United States can be had from the following illustrations:

An emigrant, owner of two auto trucks which he drove to Arandas from the United States, went first to the United States in 1913, returned to Mexico twice temporarily, and finally in 1929. His principal places of employment in the United States, arranged chronologically, were as follows: railroad labor in Houston, Texas; Kansas; Oklahoma; Missouri, and Aurora, Illinois; Centerville, Iowa; near Lincoln, Nebraska; Frost, North Dakota; town labor in Butte, Montana; coal mining near Helper, Utah; sugar beet labor near Twin Falls, Idaho; picking pears in Oregon; railroad labor at Elko, Nevada; coal mining at Gallup, New Mexico.

The itinerary of one railroad laborer was as follows: Entered the United States at El Paso, in April 1926; track labor for the Santa Fé at Plymouth, Emporia, and Lyon, Kansas; at Tulsa and Oklahoma City, Oklahoma; at Joliet, Illinois; for the Milwaukee railroad at Kadoka, South Dakota; at Savanna, Illinois; for the Milwaukee railroad at Davenport and Maxwell, Iowa; for the Santa Fé at Oklahoma City; for the Southern Pacific at Ogden, Utah, and Reno and Sparks, Nevada; for the Oregon Short Line at Burns and Lawrence, Oregon. Twice in 1931 he returned from the United States to Arandas.

A ranchero first went to the United States in 1910, worked for the Southern Pacific in New Mexico, and returned to Arandas in 1911; went to the United States in 1913, worked for the Santa Fé in Kansas, and returned to Arandas in 1914; went to the United States in 1916, worked on a pipe line being laid from Kansas City to Chicago, and returned to Arandas the same year; went to the United States in 1918, worked on the track and in cotton picking, and returned to Arandas in 1920; went to the United States in 1922, worked in the Santa Fé yard in Kansas City, and returned to Arandas in 1924; went to the United States in 1925, worked for the Southern Pacific at Phoenix, Arizona, and returned to Arandas in 1926; went to the United States in 1928, worked for the Rock Island at Denver, and returned to Arandas in 1929. This emigrant had a family, but each time he went to the United States alone.

A ranch laborer, owner of about one acre of land, first went to the United States in 1922, worked on the track in Colorado and Kansas, and returned to Arandas the same year; went to the United States in 1924, worked at a foundry in Chicago, and returned to Arandas the same year; went to the United States in 1926, worked in an oil refinery at Port Arthur, Texas, and returned to Arandas in 1927.

The Mexicans, chiefly young fellows in their twenties, who had worked in the steel plants of Chicago, Indiana Harbor, and Pennsylvania, usually had remained fairly steadily at the same plant.

The experience in the United States of the emigrants from Arandas was probably as representative of emigrant Mexicans generally as it would be possible to find in any small locality in Mexico. This was true not only occupationally and geographically, but also with respect to the time of emigration and return. Among those with whom I talked in Arandas in 1931 were emigrants ranging from the man who had gone to the United States first in 1905 to a recent emigrant who returned on the same train and stage which took me to Arandas in October, 1931; some had been back fifteen years or more, some but a day, or a month or two; some had lived eight or ten years or more in the United States, some but a few months. In 1931 some Mexicans from Arandas were living in the United States and were expected to live there permanently; others were yet in the United States, but their ultimate return to Arandas was looked for. Only in the percentage of families to emigrate, which was even lower than for Mexico generally, and perhaps in a somewhat higher proportion of rancheros and of Spanish blood, was there apparent deviation from the average character of the national migration.

The failure to take the women folk to the United States sometimes wrought hardships upon the latter. Usually the wives and children remaining in Arandas were supported by remittances from the emigrants. A few, however, were abandoned. As one person in San Ignacio Cerro Gordo said bitterly,

There in the United States they are riding about in automobiles; here their families are without food to eat, and must eat nopal (prickly pear cactus). Many —perhaps one-third—don't write; one man with many children hasn't written for eight months. Two men from San Ignacio have families there, and here, too.

Such instances of abandonment of families, however, were comparatively few. Somewhat more numerous were prolonged separations of husbands and families, sometimes commencing almost immediately after marriage and lasting for years, and entailing emotional distress and other inevitable hardships.

Most of the emigrants from Arandas have entered the United States at El Paso, but in recent years, particularly since 1923 when demand for Mexican labor in the north and east strengthened, they have entered at Laredo. After the Southern Pacific completed its connection with Guadalajara in 1926, and the American consular service in 1928 began to exert pressure on emigrants to secure the necessary papers at the nearest consulate, some began to move northward along the west coast to Nogales.

MEANS OF EMIGRATION

IN ORDER TO MAKE the journey from Arandas across the northern frontier it was necessary to raise money to pay transportation, immigration fees, and expenses en route. The amount needed varied with individual requirements and changes in American immigration fees. In the early years of emigration, emigrants from Jalisco provided themselves with from 30 to 50 pesos for the trip.[50] In recent years, emigrants from Arandas have usually started with from 80 to 100 pesos.

This money has been obtained in a variety of ways. Some have been able to draw upon personal savings—usually money hidden away in their houses. After their first trip to the United States, a much larger proportion saved enough from earnings in the North to pay for the next trip. Some obtained money from the savings of friends or relatives, without interest charge. Others sold animals in order to raise funds for the journey—a horse, cow, or pigs. Some even sold houses, at prices from, say 80 to 200 pesos. Upon return some of the houses were repurchased, usually at a good advance in price. The majority, however, went to the United States on money obtained at a price, usually a high price.

Since there are no banks in Arandas, money was borrowed from individuals. These were frequently merchants, who often were also owners of ranches. These, and rancheros, both proprietors and metayers, or indeed, anyone with money to lend, engaged in the business of assisting persons to emigrate. Apparently there was not the slightest fear of depleting unduly the local labor supply. The paucity of large employers of labor, the ample supplies of laborers produced locally by a prolific people, the remunerative rates of interest, with the knowledge that if one person did not lend, another would eliminated any possible reluctance to assist emigration.[51] Furthermore, since the rise of agrarianism, especially since the Carranza decree of 1915, there has been a desire on the part of the small hacendados and large rancheros of Arandas, at least, to provide an outlet for landless laborers, who are potential agraristas. An informed ranchero said:

> The hacendados prefer to let the workers get away so they won't concentrate in *pueblos* [towns] and ask for land. They would [be willing to] loan money to emigrants. The laborers go from the haciendas here the same as from elsewhere.

Sometimes loans were made in the form of purchases of linseed oil, with six months to pay. No interest was due unless repayment was not made within six months after which interest of from 10 to 15 per cent per six months was charged. It was reported, however, that the price at which oil was purchased usually was well above market price, sometimes almost double, and that, in the anxiety to depart quickly, it was usually sold below the price which could have been obtained in the market with a little more time and patience. Sometimes similar transactions were made with corn or beans, instead of linseed oil.

---

[50] Clark, *op. cit.*: 473.

[51] Clark, *op. cit.*: 472, doubted in 1908 that employers of Mexican laborers, who were generally hostile to emigration would lend even at very high rates of interest. But the class of hacendados of whom this was probably true, practically did not exist in Arandas.

More often, however, the loans were in cash. The lowest rate of interest reported to me was 6 per cent in six months. To this was added a penalty of an additional 5 per cent per six months if repayment was not made within the first six months. From 1 to 2 per cent per month was said by a lender to be a common and comparatively low rate. Emigrants who had borrowed money practically always reported higher rates than these. One man, for example, borrowed 130 pesos, and returned 160 pesos in eight months, equivalent to an interest rate of 34.6 per cent per annum. Fifty per cent interest in six months was reported by those who had paid it, to be a frequent charge. A man who had gone to the United States five times between 1919 and 1927 said that he had paid this rate of interest each time. Another stated that he had paid 6 pesos for 5 in six months, i.e., 20 per cent in six months. Some emigrants were reliably reported to have been charged $100 for 100 pesos in six months, i.e., 100 per cent in six months. In some of the latter cases, restitution was brought about by local religious authorities.

Usually security for the loan was insisted upon—a house or other property and two signatures. As a matter of practice, repayment was made within the allotted time in almost every case. If the emigrant experienced difficulty in meeting his payments, he usually was aided by his fellows in the United States. Sometimes it was difficult for a propertyless laborer to obtain a loan. But more often someone was ready to loan to even this class of emigrant. It was reported that one man, who twenty years ago owned only two or three *hectareas* of land, now owns a ranch of about 100 *hectareas,* purchased with the gain from loans without security made to laborers at the rate of a peso for a dollar in six months, or 200 per cent per annum.

Only one emigrant reported that he had been assisted to the frontier by employment agents. This man, who had lived many years in the United States and spoke fairly good English, declared of his first trip north:

In 1913, an agent [Mexican] from the Santa Fé railroad came to Arandas and took three or four of us by auto to the railroad, and north. I did not pay anything to go to the frontier; they paid all.[52]

A number of the Mexicans from Arandas had entered the United States illegally in past years. Some had paid from four to eight pesos to cross the Río Grande at unguarded points, others had made their own way over the boundary. In 1931–32, however, there was general knowledge of the economic depression in the United States, of the reluctance of the consular service to grant immigration papers, and of the activities of the American

---

[52] Clark, *op. cit.*:471, stated in 1908 that "there is doubtless recruiting, direct or indirect, by the representatives of American employment agencies." A reliable ranchero at Atotonilco, on the edge of Los Altos, states that American *contratistas,* representing railroads and mines, had been all through the region twenty-odd years ago.

immigration service in apprehending and deporting aliens illegally in the United States, knowledge which spread through personal experience of Arandas emigrants, Mexican official propaganda,[53] and newspaper publicity. Under these conditions, no spirit of again adventuring surreptitiously across the international boundary was evident at that time.

---

[53] In 1931–32 the writer observed in the second-class compartments of the cars operating to Atotonilco, the nearest line to Arandas, the following notice:

"The Department of Interior brings to the knowledge of all emigrant workmen of Mexican nationality [the fact] that those who go without suitable papers and the necessary money will not be admitted by the American authorities. Any individual who attempts to enter American territory illegally will be severely punished by the government of that country, and the so-called 'Coyotes' who deceive our workers within the republic will be dealt with by the proper authorities. The people of Mexico must cooperate with the government to keep those who cannot be admitted to the United States from leaving the republic, denouncing the 'enganchadores' and 'coyotes' to the authorities and spreading active propaganda among the workers *who do not know how to read* so that they will realize that it is in reality a dangerous adventure for Mexican laborers to try to reach the United States without meeting the requirements which that nation imposes on emigrants, because, as warned above, they will expose themselves to destitution, followed by incarceration and deportation. Mexico, D. F., May, 1930." In earlier years when emigration was at high tide, and enforcement of the United States immigration laws on the Mexican border was lax, similar and even stronger efforts of the Mexican government to check emigration were unavailing.

III

THE INFLUENCE OF EMIGRATION ON MEXICAN ATTITUDES TOWARD THE UNITED STATES

THE ATTITUDE toward the United States of those people in Arandas who have not emigrated to work in that country must be considered simultaneously with the attitude of those who have emigrated. At one extreme is the underlying hatred of the more powerful and richer nation to the north, its very power and riches obviously aggravating the dislike. The antagonism is collective rather than individual, and may be—indeed, was—accompanied by the utmost and genuine friendliness and courtesy to the individual American. For example a merchant-ranchero who had not been to the United States said:

> Down in their hearts the Mexicans do not like the Americans, collectively. Individually, they often like them; those who have seen the Americans in the United States like them better. But the United States took more than half of this country [Texas, California, etc.]. But [with intense emotion] I tell you, it will be Mexico again, not now, but in hundreds, or a thousand years.

This declaration was followed by an account of the rise and fall of nations, and the intimation that the United States also was destined to fall. Others, too, usually persons who had not been to the United States but including one who had worked there, mentioned the loss of Mexican territory to the United States as a grievance, and intimated, hopefully, that the United States might not recover its economic prosperity, and that it might be torn by revolution or even worsted in war by a ring of hostile nations against her.[54] By the merchant-ranchero quoted above, the United States was condemned as largely responsible for the continued internal disturbances which weakened Mexico and for a tariff policy which throttled Mexican industry. Under stress of economic depression and the campaign to buy Mexican-made goods, he added:

> Ten years ago it was a good advertisement to say, "It's American." Now, it is practically the opposite; it is a mistake to say, "It's American." Now we say "Made in Mexico"; and if we don't have it in Mexico we buy it from Europe.

He added that though he hated the United States for its asserted strangulation and division of Mexico into factions,

> "We would do the same to you. I do not blame you."

---

[54] See, for example, pp. 54, 55.

Another grievance arose from the relations of Mexicans and Americans in the United States. Practically the first person with whom I talked in Arandas, a young man who had *not* been to the United States, volunteered:

> *Se ve mal a los Mexicanos en los Estados Unidos* [they regard the Mexicans badly in the United States]. They regard them as an inferior race. They fill the jails with them. Do you know that the Mexican students were killed by the sheriff [Guess] in Oklahoma?[55]

Characteristically, another Mexican, though he, too, had not been in the United States, made a defense of Americans:

> The treatment depends on the man. Some of the Mexicans who go to the United States are vicious. Some of the Mexicans who come back have told me that they can say nothing bad of their treatment in the United States.

Only one of the many returned emigrants of Arandas with whom I talked in Arandas *volunteered* grievances; he was a mestizo of light complexion:

> Here they treat the strangers very well—with respect. But the *gente blanca* [white people] don't always treat the Mexicans well. The Los Angeles police treat the Mexicans badly. The officer at the Plaza tells the Mexicans to get out of town when they have no work. He kicks the Mexicans. The mayordomos—some are bad and some good. They drive the Mexicans too hard, and say, "If you don't like it, go."

The sullen manner of this man stood out in sharp contrast to the reception accorded one by the other Mexicans of Arandas upon the same and other occasions. My guide informed me immediately upon the man's departure, apologizing for the attitude and deprecating the complaint, that the man was a *borracho* (drinker) and didn't observe filial obligations by sending money to his father from the United States. A neighbor added that, though he had financially aided the complainant to emigrate to the United States, shortly afterwards the latter had stolen $15 more from him and departed. These explanations were offered in the spirit of statements made repeatedly in very similar language:

> If a man works well, they treat him well. But if he drinks and shoots, they treat him badly.
>
> Some say the treatment is bad because if they got into trouble, they don't like it. If they don't want to work, then the mayordomos call them names, etc.

Another explanation was offered by a Mexican who had lived eight years in the States:

> Some Mexicans come back and say they have been robbed, after they have drunk and gambled away their money. Sometimes the Mexicans rob each other, and then say the Americans did it.

There were, however, some genuine, and probably well grounded complaints, voiced, after questioning on my part, by returned immigrants of the

---

[55] Cf. II, 149 ff.

best type. One of them independently corroborated the evil reputation of Los Angeles police:

> In Los Angeles they say the police are pretty bad. They say that at the Plaza an officer called "Red" kicks the Mexicans.

Another Mexican of the best type told an experience with the police of Pittsburgh, Pennsylvania, which is only too tragically plausible:

> Some Mexican fellows who were drunk with whiskey made noise in the street and were shooting into the air. Somebody telephoned the police. I was not with them, but was asleep in bed in my room. The police came to the boarding house to get the whole bunch. They came to my door. I got up in my underwear and opened it. The cops tried to find if I had a gun; I did not. They said "Get up and dress." I said, "What you going to do to me?" They said "Arrest you." "Why?" "You're going to find out in jail." At the jail, an officer said, "What you rob?" I told him I didn't rob, and showed him my number at the steel company. He asked me again what I rob, and because I said I didn't do anything he hit me across the ear with a black jack, and across the head and face [splitting the ear and breaking the cartilage]. Then he threw me into the cell with the others [without giving any attention to the bleeding wound].
>
> In the morning in court the police told the judge I was shooting. The judge asked me what kind of a gun I had. I told him I was asleep in bed and had no gun. The policeman told me to shut up. The judge asked me what was my nationality. "Mexican." Then he said "$10 or 30 days." I said, "Here's $10." I was working and had money and paid. Then I went to the doctor, who sewed my ear. I couldn't work for ten days, because I worked in a hot place, putting billets in the furnace.
>
> I feel sorry when I was in jail when I do no trouble. My father lived 52 years here and never was arrested. I am born here, and never was arrested until I went to the United States, and I feel sorry.

Two Mexicans each admitted that upon one occasion they were at least technically at fault when arrested and fined, but made no complaint of their treatment upon these occasions.

Two other returned emigrants, the first of them now a Mexican federal rural schoolteacher near Guadalajara, described high-handed treatment by farmers in Nueces County, Texas, giving accounts which are entirely plausible and in harmony with complaints made when I talked with Mexicans in that county in 1929:

> We were supposed to be paid $1.50 a hundred pounds for picking cotton, but we received only $4 or $5 a week in cash. We were paid partly in money and partly in credit at the ranch store, and the prices at the store were high. Some of my friends left, and caused much disgust to the farmer. So they gathered the rest of us in the garage and posted the mayordomo at the door with a rifle. Then the owner came with a pistol and threatened to kill any man who left.
>
> Soon afterwards the mayordomo kicked a boy—the son of an attorney in Guadalajara—who was lying down because of the effects of heat, sun, and bad water. I protested. Then I left on a train for San Antonio and arrived with ten cents in my pockets. A Mexican there gave me a meal.

A farmer near Petronilla employed me at $6 a week, with board, clothing, and washing, and six acres of cotton on halves. He asked me if I wanted my money each week, and I told him no. So he just gave me board and washing, and once he bought me a pair of shoes. One day I was playing with the son. His mother came out with a pistol and said, "You were fighting with Louis." I said "No," and so did Louis. So I went to the house and said, "Give me my money; I'm going." The farmer said, "I don't owe you anything; I paid your money to the mayordomo. I haven't any money; I might pay you after cotton picking." The Texas-Mexican mayordomo told me to "get out of here; I'll kill you if you bother me."

I was green. He ran me off when there were six acres of cotton—pretty good, too—about that high.

There was occasional complaint against foremen and also commendation for them; for example:

Some treat pretty good; some treat bad—call bad names and bawl out the Mexicans.

Interestingly, one Mexican made particular complaint against the Texas-Mexican track foremen:

The *Mexico-Texanos* are *malos;* the *Mexico-Texano mayordomos* [assistant foremen] treat the Mexicans badly and drive them very hard.

Similarly, but without distinguishing between Old Mexicans and United States born Mexicans, another Mexican said,

The worst foremen are the Mexicans.

The familiar distinction in favor of Americans as against recent European immigrants[56] was expressed by a Mexican who had worked in Flint, Michigan; for the Poles especially, there was hostility:

The man who is good is the true American, not the immigrants. The Poles are the most Catholic people in the world. They take out citizens papers. But *tienen pretensiones;* they think the Mexican people are not smart. The immigrant foremen give their people the jobs, and if they are told to lay off men, they lay off other nationalities. My American foreman was a good man; he treated all nationalities good.

The question of race distinction was never raised voluntarily by the returned emigrants. When asked about it, the answers were of various types; sometimes the individual's answer combined the elements of more than one type. The first and most common answer was a denial that discrimination had been personally experienced.

They never refused me to go into any place—restaurants, movies, etc.

Even stronger was the statement of a girl of pure Spanish *criollo* type:

There wasn't a bit of difficulty between us and the Americans. They even forgot I was a Mexican.

---

[56] See II: 15, 113, 239 ff.

Others, too, in whom European physical characteristics predominated, naturally remarked that the Americans did not regard them as typically "Mexican," or even mistook their nationality.

A second form of answer was to observe that the race distinctions had affected Mexicans poorer, darker, or less clean than the speaker:

> The poorer people complain more.

> When I went into a theater I was clean, with good clothes. But some went like I am now—nasty; they ought to refuse me this way.

In the matter of uncleanliness, it will be observed, the usual justification for *distinción* was offered. Another answer was to recognize the existence of race discrimination in the South, particularly in Texas, and to point out that it is absent [at least relatively] from the North:

> Distinción? Yes, in Texas; the Mexicans look too much like niggers. In Flint, Michigan, no.

> You know; the Mexicans have darker face. In Pittsburg [Pennsylvania] I go every place. But in Texas—that's why I was living good and liked it in Pittsburg.

The treatment of Mexicans in the relations of employer and employee, as in social relations, was also said to be better in the North—an observation made frequently by Mexicans in all parts of the United States:[57]

> The treatment is very good in Pennsylvania; bad in Texas. On the frontier are people who exploit labor, who are less educated than those in the rest of the United States. A good percentage in the southern states exploit. I have good impressions of the other states because of the better education of the people of the central and northern states.

The complaints made against treatment of Mexicans in the United States thus stressed essentially the same points as those expressed by Mexicans interviewed in the United States. It is significant, however, that in Arandas complaint was made much more vigorously, although in less detail, by persons who had never emigrated than by those who had; the single exception to this has already been noted. In the minds of the returned emigrants, the agreeable aspects of their experience in the United States far overshadowed the disagreeable. Even the young man who sustained brutal treatment at the hands of Pittsburgh police told of his experience only after prolonged conversations, and then with humiliation and regret rather than bitterness; he would like to return to live in Pennsylvania all his life. The man who was "run off" the Texas farm without pay was pathetically eager to return to the United States. Discouraged by the American restrictive immigration policy he said wistfully:

> I don't think I can ever get there anymore—maybe—maybe—maybe.

---

[57] See II, 16.

Frequently comments were made on the good treatment and conditions experienced in the United States:

The Americans are *muy buenos hombres* for us. If a man is a good worker, they can't treat him badly. A man who is *trabajador* [industrious] likes the Americans.

Señor Zárate [a former labor agent in El Paso] is *muy correcto, muy buen hombre*.

The people where I worked treated me good.

A number of times it was said that in times of good employment the United States are fine, but that in bad times it is better for a Mexican to be in Mexico:

If one has no work, it's better here. One can always have something to eat, even if little—*siempre* [always]. In the United States one walks around the streets and begs money at American houses, and eats a cup of coffee and some bread. One suffers without work in the United States. This is my country and *paisanos* aid. In the United States when there is good work it is fine—much wages.

I liked it when I was in the United States, and came back when no got a job. I like United States—wear good clothes, parks, etc. I've got my people here, when no work there, I like it here better.

A Mexican who had worked as a coal miner in Utah was unwilling that his countrymen should seek American charity.

I wish all the Mexicans would come back to Mexico. I don't like to see them have to beg for charity in the United States.

A large proportion of the Mexican emigrants preferred, naturally, to live in Mexico. The easier pace of life, the mild climate, the greater assurance of a minimum of subsistence, and the inclusive fact that Mexico is their native country, were all mentioned by them:

I like it better in Arandas. The climate is better than the heat and cold of Chicago. This is *mi patria*.

I would go back if there was work. I was contented there with work at good wages and the treatment was good. But I am *más contento* here; *es mi patria*.

I am *más contento* here. When I work in the United States, I make money only to eat. Here with only a few pesos I make a good living. Corn and beans never fail. In the United States, you work every day, and if no work, no eat. Here I work three months in a year and live. I like it best here.[58]

But with a large proportion of the returned emigrants, the happier life in Mexico was more than counterbalanced by the higher material standard of living in the United States. Many asserted that they were happier in Arandas, and almost in the next breath, that they would go back to the United States if work was plentiful, and would gladly live there the remainder of their lives, apparently seeing no contradiction in their statements. In ex-

---
[58] See also Field Notes, pp. 69, 70.

planation they repeatedly said that it was hard to make a living in Arandas, because there was little work, and low wages; that, on the contrary, work and wages were good in the United States, and one could have good clothes and autos, and there were pretty parks, too.

The overwhelming majority of emigrants wished to return at least temporarily, and both they and others who had never been to the United States very often inquired hopefully of the employment situation in the United States,

"Are conditions in the United States improving yet?"

A few returned emigrants frankly preferred to live indefinitely in the United States; if work was harder, nevertheless it paid better. The son of a large ranch proprietor who had worked in Pennsylvania steel mills said:

> I was living nice there. Sure I'd live there all my life. I live good here, only work's too slow here, and one needs work to live..... It's no good living if you don't work and make a lot of money. With money you can do anything, and live better, and I'd rather work harder [and have money].

The *tequila* maker on an hacienda was impressed by the domestic tranquility of the United States and the extensive public activities in such matters as water supplies, health, and sanitation:

> This is my country; I am Mexican; I love my country. But we are disunited here; we are like cats and dogs. If I had a recommendation to a *dueño* who would know that I am a good worker, and he would treat me accordingly, I would gladly go to live in the United States. I like your ideals there, and everything [public works, etc.] is methodically arranged.

It was a rare person among the ranchers who had no interest in emigration. A young fellow herding burros said,

> No, I don't wish to go; it is too far. This is *mi tierra*.

And to my remark that many others go, he gave an answer similar to one frequently made by Southerners in the United States to the northward migration of Negroes or Mexicans:

> Yes, and they return.

But in each instance the reply overstresses a partial truth.

In general, the emigrants held a better opinion of Americans after working in the United States than before they went, despite the genuine grievances which some voiced. Said a young ranchero who had lived eight years in the United States:

> Before I went, I thought that Americans treated people about the same as Mexicans. Now I think Americans are better than we are. There if a poor man tries to make a business, the Americans help him, whether he is American or Mexican. .... I wish I were there now. [Do I] want to go back? Sure I do. I like that

country; I do like it, and I would like to live there. I am going to the United States as soon as it gets good..... I like it there better than I do like here. This is my country, but after the day you were at my ranch, I dreamed that I was back in the United States.

Naturally, the better feelings toward Americans were closely related to material advantages in the United States. As a returned emigrant said:

> Sure they like the American people better than before they went. Before, they never made $4 or $5 a day; so they don't know.

A professional man confirmed the representative character of the specific cases cited and observed above:

> Those who stay in Mexico say the Americans have prejudice against the Mexicans. Those who go [to the United States] say that it is not as the *gente vulgar* say. Those who go say they receive good treatment, and in the North, better treatment. They say, "Our people don't give us work, and let us starve; we have more *cariño* for the Americans. Our government hasn't compassion for its own sons.

To a leading merchant, as to many Mexicans elsewhere, this increased friendliness of Mexicans toward Americans was anathema.

> Every Mexican who goes, likes the United States better than Mexico. He gets a better life there than here. After 100 years, it will be good-bye to Mexico. I am afraid they will like America better than Mexico. We are making "war" [nationalistic propaganda] so they won't become Americanized.[59] They will not like the Mexican flag; they have not love of country, and that is a great danger to Mexico.

An interesting corroboration of the "Americanophile" tendencies of some emigrants, as well as an illustration of the utterly fantastic and confused rumors which find credence, was the statement of an emigrant:

> A friend told me a few days ago that there are lots of American soldiers on the border, and there's going to be a revolution [i.e., war] in the United States. Fifteen days from now, Mexico is going to be part of the United States. He said it was true; he had seen it in the papers. I don't care; I'd rather work for Americans than for the government here. I'd rather be under American laws than under the Mexican government; I had more guaranties over there than in my own country. We are ignorant here; you know that.

At the opposite extreme from those who hated the United States, a prominent citizen of Arandas, like a small percentage of Mexicans elsewhere, hoped for what he called the "peaceful conquest" by Americans, as a means of ameliorating the disordered political and economic conditions in his own country.

Midway between the two extremes of attitude toward the United States was an interesting union in the same person of a scarcely concealed desire to see the United States sink as a world power, and a genuine liking for life in

---

[59] See for example, II, 216-218.

the United States; the man who exhibited this contrast had formerly mined coal in Utah:

The United States is now in worse condition than we are. They cannot sell. Many banks have failed. The farmers have a hard time. I don't think it will recover as it was. They produce too much and cannot sell it. Japan and Austria may attack the United States. They may have a revolution inside, too, breaking out in various parts of the United States, because now they give work to the Americans first and not to the foreigners.

It makes my life easy to live in the United States. There I had my own car. Here it is hard to make a living. When you going to take some more back there; sure, I would like to go there again.

Thus, the customary viewpoints of the emigrants contained all the varied elements of the attitudes toward Americans and the United States which are found in the Arandas community generally. But it was abundantly clear that with very few exceptions, the attitude of the returned emigrants was distinctly more friendly because of their experience in the United States.

THE RETURNED EMIGRANT

IN ARANDAS one is impressed more by the relatively small degree of change in the attitudes and ways of living of the returned emigrants than by the material change which experience in the United States has sometimes produced in the economic condition of individuals.

A conspicuous index of the lack of effective contact with American culture is the high proportion of returned emigrants who could speak practically no English. Usually ability to understand English was slightly in advance of ability to speak it. A notable instance of failure to learn any English was a ranchero who had been seven times to the United States between 1910 and 1929, working principally on the track, but at times in cotton picking and on an oil pipe line; he could not understand the simplest questions in English, and after a number of efforts on my part to open a conversation in English, he said only with difficulty, "No spik Inglis." I was told of another Mexican who had been twelve times to the United States, yet could speak no English. Similar instances of persons who had been to the United States from one to four times were common. The correct explanation was given by a Mexican who, in three trips between 1925 and 1929, had worked on the track in California, Nevada, Kansas, and Arizona:

I didn't learn English, because I worked with *puros Mexicanos*.

It was the experience of the majority of Mexican track workers in the United States that the foremen as well as the laborers spoke Spanish.

This failure to establish one of the most important media of cultural contact, which was particularly conspicuous among the railroad workers, was to a lesser degree true also of persons who had worked in agricultural employments. Those laborers who spoke English best were almost invariably persons who had worked in the industries of the North and East, or in coal mines in Utah. Often they had lived longer in some one place, the foremen usually had spoken no Spanish, the proportion of Mexicans in the total population had been smaller, and their consequent social isolation was less. Furthermore, a few in industrial centers had taken advantage of night schools in order to improve their English. Three young Mexicans, two boys and a girl, who had left Mexico when very young, had been educated a number of years in public schools of the United States; these spoke nearly perfect English.

In matters of dress, the daily costume of the returned emigrants was usually about the same as worn by others of the same occupational status. In town, trousers or overalls, shirt, a felt hat or cap, and shoes, were common. But similar garb was also worn by many young men who had not been to the United States. A few returned emigrants in town wore *guaraches* [the customary sandal of the majority]; one of these, for example, had formerly worked at Wisconsin Steel Works in South Chicago.

In the rural parts of the municipio, the usual costume of the returned emigrants was even more nearly identical with the costume of those who had never emigrated. The palm *sombrero*, cotton *camisa* and *calzones* (cotton shirt and trousers, or "pyjamas"), and guaraches were often worn.[60] One returned emigrant wearing the typical sheepskin apron, and another at work in the fields barefooted were also seen. A few wore shoes, shirts, and trousers or overalls. The customary blanket was also used for warmth in morning and evening. For Sunday dress the returned emigrants, both in town and from the ranches, sometimes had tailored or ready-made suits, and the hats and shoes which they had brought back from the United States. But the great majority had no suits.

Before commencing my field work I had been told that the returned emigrants, at least, would not resume the wearing of guaraches. Whatever the situation elsewhere, it is clear that in Arandas they did so readily, and in the rural area the camisa and calzones as well. Both in town and in country it was impossible to determine with certainty, merely from dress, whether or not a man had been an emigrant.[61]

It would be incorrect, however, to say that migration had no direct effect on the dress of the emigrants. That it had, was frequently evident. Many wore somewhat better clothes than they would have otherwise, although because of the economic depression and the disappearance of savings many

---

[60] See plates 3*f*; 6*d*.   [61] See plates 3*b, c, f*; 4; 8*e*.

were selling the excess supplies they had brought from the United States in order to realize small amounts of cash, even though for the same reasons, they found it impossible to replenish their stock. Both on a ranch and in town, suits "like yours" were taken out of trunks and exhibited with pride. In each of two instances, three suits were shown. One of the rancheros showed also two hats and a pair of oxfords, and pictures of himself taken in Pennsylvania in American garb, remarking,

> I like good suits, even in this country, but here nobody use it.

Repeatedly he apologized for wearing guaraches instead of shoes, explaining that this was necessitated by an infected foot. Another ranchero had returned with five suits, but said that under economic pressure he had sold various hats, boots, suits, etc. In addition to the evidence of acquisition of better clothing by the emigrants, it was obvious that their standards of dress had been a factor in setting the standard for non-emigrants who could afford it.

The effect of life in the United States on the customary dress of women was evident in the declaration of a girl educated in a Utah high school:

> Here the girls all dress alike, in black. But I'll never dress in black in all my life. Here it seems that when a girl is married, it's all over; then they don't care about clothes any more.[62]

Comparatively very few Arandas women had gone to the United States, so that there was very little penetration of American ideas concerning the social rôle of women. However, a professional man expressed the characteristic effect of contact with American customs:

> The women learn American customs. The women want more liberty, but the husbands don't want it.

One emigrant, however, who knew the greater ease of women's life in the United States, wished that kind of liberty for his wife:

> I like liberty for women. If I had money, I wouldn't have my wife work so hard.

The enthusiasm of an emigrant in the first flush of his return, for alteration of local standards was revealed by one who had arrived in Arandas but five days before:

> I wish all the people would go to the United States. They would learn to eat better, and have a better place to sleep, and clothes that are pretty good, and to be clean. But [by way of explanation] they are poor here, and if you're hungry and have only 20 centavos, you don't get a haircut.

Some persons who had not emigrated commented on changes in the personal habits and standards of emigrants, but often the comment ended with

---

[62] Her impressions of Arandas were generally favorable, nevertheless.

a discouraged observation of the ephemeral nature of the change. Said a merchant:

> When the Mexicans come from the United States they are converted. They have better manners, dress, and more money. They learn to wash their faces, to have clean hands and clothes. Many live in a *jacal*, and upon return, make a new house..... But after he has been here for a time, he loses his learning and his wishes [i.e., his ambitions] and makes his living as before.

A physician observed,

> The nutrition is poor here, and the people lack strength. Yes, in the United States they eat better, but upon return they eat as before.

A ranch proprietor, himself a returned emigrant, explained that there were obstacles to maintenance of the new standards:

> Cleaner? Yes, two, three, or four months, and then they are the same as before. The water is sometimes cold here.

It was a common observation in the United States that the active adherence of the Mexican immigrants to their Catholic faith was weakened by the migration; this was true apart from, and in addition to, the proselytizing efforts of some Protestant denominations. Similarly, a priest in Arandas observed:

> Emigration lowers the moral level; while they are in the United States they forget their religion. The most important reason is that they are isolated; also they see a different mode of life, go to dances, movies, etc., and have other diversions. The propaganda of the *evangelistas* is not so important."[63]

But the returned emigrants of Arandas, in religion as in most other respects, generally slipped back readily into the old ways. The situation was described by a local clergyman:

> There is hardly any alteration in the religious attitude of the returned emigrants. Two or three have changed their faith, and some are less Catholic than before, but most are the same as before they went.

The economic status of the great majority of repatriates was practically the same as before they emigrated to the United States. During the years when they could enter the United States freely, many spent their money in ways which made no permanent change in their status. The practice of many, after return from the States, was

> to come to Arandas, stay without working until their money was gone—drinking, dancing, etc.,—then to return to the United States; but they are ragged now.

Of course many spent their money for better clothes, food, etc., for themselves and their families. But in their expenditures, the same lack of foresight or exercise of what others regarded as wise choice in purchases, which was

---

[63] Cf. Manuel Gamio, *The Mexican Immigrant: His Life Story* (Chicago, 1931).

observed in the United States,[64] was commented upon by an Arandas merchant.

When the money was sent to the families, it was like throwing it out the windows. They bought *anything*.

Such thought as they gave to the future was to rely upon making another trip to the land of high wages when previous earnings were gone. In 1930 and 1931 it was not easy to cross the frontier, as it had been before. However, the attitude of those who had neither saved their money nor used it to better their status by purchase of land, animals, etc., was generally without noticeable regret for the course followed. For example:

I spent my money on an auto [which was left in the United States], and for the family; I'm not sore.

I spent my money in the United States or after return, mostly in drinking and investing in the "stocking bank" [i.e., women]; it never breaks [referring humorously to the common lack of confidence in banks].

My money? I'm young; I spent it.

The last speaker, however, had bought some cattle with earnings which he had sent from the United States.

A contrary attitude was expressed by a young metayer who had lived eight years in the United States and was eager to return:

I wish I could have saved all the money I made there; I could buy a big ranch of my own.

The very wide variety of experience of the Arandas emigrants in American agriculture, mining, and industry suggests that much should have been learned by them. Doubtless something was learned, but the outstanding fact is that generally the knowledge obtained is not put to use in Arandas.

Some returned emigrants were ready to give assurance that valuable knowledge had been gained. One of the most positive, for example, said first that he had learned to speak English. This was true, for he spoke well. But he also said a moment later that he did not speak it with the other returned emigrants, because "one should not speak English in Mexico." Next he said that in the United States he had learned to dress better; but he admitted at once that had he never left Arandas, he would probably have dressed about the same. Finally, he said that in the United States he had been a mechanic's helper, that this would help him to get a job if he went to Guadalajara, and that his English would help him if he ever returned to the United States. But now he was in Arandas, and was operating a pool hall.

The situation of the many rancheros who had worked on the track in the United States was summed up by one who had emigrated five times:

Our business is *agricultor*, before and after.

---

[64] See I, Index, under "Improvidence of Mexicans."

In Arandas there is no railroad track on which to work. Similarly, a Mexican who had worked for fifteen years on the fertile islands of the Stockton delta in California, said:

> I learned much, but here we have no water for irrigation.

Two rancheros observed:

> Whatever I learn there, there's nothing like that over here. There [in Texas] they use mules, or plant with machines. Here we haven't got the materials, plows, etc. Our land is different; it has too many stones; we use a wooden plow with an iron point.

> There I was just working [in a steel plant]. I don't learn nothing that helps me.

Another young ranchero who had worked in steel plants of Pennsylvania spoke of similar difficulties:

> I would like to know the metallurgical industry better, but there are no plants here.

A returned emigrant generalized:

> For many, the experience in the United States *vale nada* [is worth nothing].

The tenacity of old ideas was well illustrated by the affirmation of belief in the danger of bathing by an intelligent young ranchero who had lived nine years in the United States, was eager to return, and had adopted a contrary practice with avidity while there:

> I used to like to take a bath after work every day in Texas, but you can't do it in this climate. If you even wash your hands after work while you're hot, it will make you stiff. That's why you notice so many rancheros whose hands are dirty.

The fact that the emigrants so readily readapt themselves to the ways of their home community can be ascribed only in small degree to the hostility of those who have not emigrated. True, there were some jibes at their expense, principally at their poverty. For example:

> Look at that guy; he has good clothes, but not a centavo in his pockets.

But a professional man pointed out the significant fact:

> They used to joke about them, and criticize their better clothing, but not now. Now they imitate them.

Naturally those who had not gone to the United States were unwilling to admit inferiority to those who had gone. The mingled envy of the emigrant and denial of his superiority appear from the statement of an illiterate metayer who, with his companion, inquired eagerly whether employment conditions were not improving in the United States:

> The *norteños* [those who have gone north to the United States] gain from their experience because they learn English. They can get good jobs in hotels in Mexico City, and other cities. Here, no. They come back with *pretensiones* that they have much money, but they do not. They come back with clothes which last a year or two; then they dress the same as the rest of us.

They think they are better than we, but they are not. Some go there, but not really to work, and would be better off if they had stayed here and worked..... The *norteños valen* less than we, as workers, because they don't want to work for so little.

Another ranchero did not even reveal envy:

What do they learn? *Nada!* A few words of English; they only learn to work on the track. Their *pretensiones* are that they have money, and have earned much, but they come back without money. They are *iguales* with us who have not gone; they say they worked for $4 or $5 a day, and do not like to work for 50 centavos.

A laborer who had not been to the United States described the frequent practice of idling at ease, which doubtless only added to the envy of the others:

Many come back and spend in a month all they made, and when their money is gone, they return to the United States. The others envy them, and want to go also.

But in 1931 the possibility of return was shut off.

The charge advanced by those who had not emigrated, that the returned emigrants worked less readily in Mexico, is similar to the frequent accusations of farmers of the southwestern United States that the immigrant Mexican soon becomes spoiled for work. The opposite observation, however, is usually made by American industrial employers. In Arandas, two proprietors of larger ranches confirmed the opinion that the laborers returned from the United States worked less; the second proprietor, however, distinguished between work for others and work for themselves:

They got more there, and so they work a little less here.

The returned emigrants work better for themselves. But we [employing rancheros] prefer our own [men who have not gone]; we pay too little for repatriados. They are used to $3, $4, or $5 a day and don't like to work for so little; so they are lazy.

This preference for the employment of Mexicans who had never emigrated was common in Mexico, but was of relatively little importance in Arandas because of the paucity of large employers, and the relatively large amount of independent work.

Despite the general tendency to spend for ephemeral things, the higher wages gained in the United States about as fast as they were earned, there were many instances, doubtless numbering hundreds, of purchase of land, animals, tools, trucks, etc., which improved the economic status of their owners. For example, a man who operated two Ford trucks, which he had driven from the United States, for hauling live stock, produce, etc., to market, said:

Now I own a house and two trucks; it makes me a living. I was a laborer here, and never could have bought trucks [with my wages] here.

There was even complaint that too many had brought back trucks, resulting in competition ruinous to all. Some emigrants who had returned with automobiles, had operated them until they broke down; unable to repair or replace them, they left them to rust uselessly. Some had taken the motors out for use in local linseed oil factories or other small enterprises using power.

One emigrant had returned with a bottling machine purchased in the United States, from which he made an income of about 4 pesos a day, and "no worque hard." Yet another had brought machinery for making shoes, and some carpenters and other craftsmen had purchased tools with which to carry on their trade. Some emigrants had set themselves up in business with capital gained in the United States. To cite a notable example, two brothers operated an oil station and sold automobile parts, and also aided a younger brother to open a pool hall. The father had been a laborer, but

The sons do not let the father work; they give him money, because they are good sons.

A ranchero, son of a *propietario,* had made himself a small capitalist. Saving carefully the wages which he had earned principally by working in the dry salt department of a Mason City, Iowa, meat-packing house, he had returned to Mexico with 6,000 pesos. Of these, he loaned 2,000 pesos at interest of one and one-half per cent per month, yielding him approximately a peso a day, or double the prevailing laborer's wage. A large part of the balance of the amount saved was apparently secreted in a hole in the ground, or some other place of safekeeping.

Many Arandas Mexicans had bought cows, pigs, oxen, etc., usually so as to improve their income from their ranches; occasionally the smaller animals were kept in town.

The most permanent improvement in individual status undoubtedly resulted from purchase of land. A good many had bought houses in town. Numbers of others had purchased small ranches, or added to the holdings they already had. A metayer, for example, who had worked on the track in Texas, Colorado, Illinois, and Wyoming, and had laid concrete highways near Onawa and Missouri Valley, Iowa, returned to Arandas with 1,000 pesos. With 300 pesos he purchased 55 solares of land—about twenty acres. But he was clad in the usual cotton camisa and calzones and guaraches of the region, and his agricultural methods, like his dress, had undergone no change.

Another young Mexican, obviously mestizo, who had been in the United States from 1923 to 1925 and from 1926 to 1931, had worked on railroads in

Oklahoma and Pennsylvania, and for the Bethlehem Steel and American Bridge companies in Pennsylvania. With his earnings, 53 solares of land had been purchased for 1,200 pesos, and added to his father's original 40 solares; later, an additional 100 solares (about forty acres) had been purchased for the emigrant himself for 2,000 pesos. He also bought a yoke of oxen and a horse, and he was provided with the usual wooden plow. With appreciation of what his experience in the United States had meant to him, he wrote on November 19, 1931 (translation):

.... the U.S.A., to which I am grateful for my fortune, and when you return to the U.S.A., tell the great functionaries that a son of Mexico says that he is very grateful and that he sends the most repeated thanks.

For the most part, then, the cultural effects on the returned emigrants of Arandas have generally not been great. The majority did not even learn to speak English. Their dress, which in the United States they had changed most easily to accord with American standards, was generally indistinguishable from the dress of others. This was true partly because many readily resumed the native costume, and partly because American garb—overalls and ready-made suits, especially the former, was used in Arandas by many who had never gone to the United States.

The majority of the emigrants had spent their money as fast as it was earned, in the United States, in Mexico, or in both countries, for food and clothing for themselves and families or for pleasures of various kinds. For the most part, the material gains were ephemeral. Lest it be thought that the ablest, most economically progressive young men were always those who had been to the United States, the striking instance to the contrary should be cited of my young illiterate, car-owning chauffeur who had never emigrated, but who employed at day wages as a *mozo* (servant) a literate young repatriate. A minority only had invested in livestock, land, tools, etc., with a consequent relatively permanent betterment of their position. Even this betterment was largely individual, and affected very slightly if at all the attitudes and ways of living and working in the community. Probably the emigrant most fired with enthusiasm for an altered mode of life was the young Pennsylvania steel worker who had purchased land, oxen, and horses. His words showed both the hopes and the difficulty of realization:

I have many desires to do things in the style of the United States. For example, I would like to have a pump for irrigation so I could have better crops *every* year. Here we need money for machinery for our farms; we have oxen and no machinery and can't do much without money. Money is a good help.

I would like to have a house in American style..... But .... here we build thick so no bullet can come through, and no windows, so when the door is shut, no one can come.

AMERICAN CULTURAL INFLUENCE IN ARANDAS

The returned emigrants are not the only source of American cultural influence in Arandas; probably not even the chief source. It is of course impossible to separate completely the influence of emigrants from that of American goods and ideas brought by salesmen, newspapers, books, movies, etc. Furthermore, it is not always possible to separae American from European influences, for often they are intermingled.

The culture which superseded the Indian was predominantly Spanish, brought there by the colonists who populated Los Altos after the conquest. Principally during the past century the center of its economic life has shifted from cattle and sheep raising to agriculture. It remains a simple peasant society, using primitive methods of production. For example, an early resident ascribes to his father in the year 1810 the introduction of the simple iron crow bar yet in common use, as a new device to remove from the fields and place in fences or houses the large stones so common in the region. Since the beginning of agriculture the Egyptian-style wooden plow has been in use; sometimes the point is tipped with iron, sometimes it is not. In 1931 the only iron plow seen in the vicinity of the town was on display by a merchant; the only ones in use were on a few haciendas and large ranches. Sickles are commonly used for harvesting corn, linaza, and wheat. Most of these are made by Arandas smiths, but a few of American manufacture are sold.

Probably the first important American mechanical device to come to Arandas was the sewing machine, which entered probably in the third quarter of the nineteenth century. At first its use was limited to the few well-to-do families, but by about 1900 it was spreading rapidly; in 1931 practically everyone, even the poorest, possessed a machine. The telegraph was brought to Arandas probably during the same third quarter of the nineteenth century. In 1931 the only telephone was a local line from the house of the *cura* to the church. There were perhaps half a dozen radio sets in town. Stations at Los Angeles, San Antonio and Dallas, Texas, and Villa Acuña, Coahuila, were heard as readily as those in Mexico City.

A mill to grind corn was erected toward the close of the nineteenth century; it was followed by steam boilers, motors, etc., for use in tequila and linseed oil factories,[65] and for a few other purposes. In 1905 electric lighting was introduced in the town; in 1931 it was used in practically all town houses. Kerosene open wick lamps and candles are used on the ranches. A

---

[65] Sánchez (p. 83) noted the existence of eight linseed oil mills in the municipio when he wrote.

few houses in town are supplied with water from pipes, but distribution to the majority is yet by *aguadores,* who carry or cart it from door to door.

Recently a machine to extract ixtle fiber from the maguey plant was installed at one of the haciendas. The reaction of the ropemakers along the Río del Tule, who extract the fiber by hand, was one of apprehension; nor was the apprehension allayed by such knowledge of American experience with machines as they possessed. A group of ropemakers, led by a returned emigrant who had worked in steel mills of Pennsylvania, said:

> That machine is stealing work from everybody. So the men who use the machine spoiled it—broke it. The people don't like the machine because it will do *mal* to them. I see in the newspaper that Henry Ford made a machine so that where he had 100 men, he only needs 10, and 90 have no work. That is why so many are unemployed now in the United States.

The first automobile was brought to Arandas in 1908 by a well-to-do rancher and merchant; by 1916 the auto was coming into "general" use as a stage and for hauling. On December 31, 1929, there were twenty-six motor vehicles in the municipio, nine of them used for commercial purposes; there were also fifteen bicycles. The first movie appeared in 1912; in 1931 there was one motion picture theater in town.

The watches long possessed by only a few of the wealthier persons were first of European make. The spread of the use of watches has come largely through the returned emigrants, who bring them back from the United States. Often these are costly, and of the best American manufacture. A young man, for example, exhibited a $75 railroad watch which he had purchased when for a short time he had been an assistant track foreman.

The furniture in the houses of the wealthier members of the community used to be brought from Spain; but more recently, American furniture has entered. The merchandise in the stores is often American—toilet articles, clothing, electric equipment, etc. Undoubtedly, the entry of these goods was stimulated because of the desires of the emigrants, and made possible by their remittances of money from the United States.[66]

In the matter of dress, the most conspicuous innovation due to American influence is the overall. This was brought back by the first emigrants, and others have brought them ever since, though there are now overall factories in Mexico. Overalls cost about 3 pesos as compared with 80 centavos for the material to make the customary white cotton calzones and camisas. The latter are still worn almost universally in the rural parts of the municipio, and widely in town also; but most people, especially in town, possess also an overall suit.

---

[66] See pp. 32-34.

The dress and customs of young women in the towns show marked changes. This is to be attributed less to emigration than to movies, book and newspaper advertising, merchants, visits to Guadalajara, etc., through which styles and customs elsewhere become known. The long black shawl habitually worn by women is giving way, among the young women, to a short black shawl worn only to church as the necessary head covering. Young women dress in color; black is reserved by them principally for mourning. The young women wear short skirts and low shoes, like American girls. Bobbing of the hair has become general among younger women practically contemporaneously with the spread of the custom in the United States.

The custom of arrangement of marriages by parents, which held sway a half-century ago, has given way to choice by the participants, usually with, but occasionally against the consent of the parents. The custom of the *serenata*, or walk about the plaza, the sexes marching in opposite directions, is still observed. In part it is an opportunity for courting, and it is supplemented by the recognized method of sly courting at the barred window. The women, however, remain in their houses practically all the time, going out little more than to church services daily, and to the evening serenata.

Divorce is practically non-existent in Arandas, I was informed with pride; but one young man, insisting that he was a sincere Catholic, observed,

Now everybody knows he can break the marriage; but very few do it.

It was clearly evident that in general no form of birth control was practiced. As a prominent citizen assured me,

There is much morality here. People never commit an offense against nature; they are *muy moral,* and never use drugs, etc.

But a younger citizen, also Catholic, was not so sure; he thought that even here an entering wedge of change had appeared:

Contraception? *Perhaps* a few learn about drugs, etc., in Guadalajara or in the United States—probably some of the better class families, and some who have been to the United States.

Further evidence concerning population limitation was the citation of cases of "taking medicine" to produce abortion, and recent instances of abandonment of newly born babies, one of which was found dead; the motives appeared to be evasion of the social consequences of irregular sex relations, however, rather than direct limitation of numbers. But the general attitude toward the birth of children was expressed by the words of a town laborer who said simply: "God sends them."

The life of Arandas is characterized by a non-resident Mexican as "monastic" in comparison with life in such a town as near-by Ocotlán, the railroad junction and port of Lake Chapala, where the disintegration of the old culture is clearly evident. This characterization faithfully mirrors the domination of religion and old customs over the life of isolated Arandas.[67] But even here, the old order is slowly beginning to change under the impact of forces, some of which are American.

---

[67] A good insight into the mental life of youth in Arandas may be obtained from the poems *Alma solariega* (Mexico, 1923), of Manuel Martínez Valadez, who was born and raised in Arandas.

IV

FIELD NOTES ON FOUR EMIGRANTS

THESE INTERVIEWS are presented in order to portray more vividly without dissection, and in detail, a few emigrant types, some of their experiences in the United States, and their readjustment to life in Arandas upon their return.

The young son of the proprietor of a large ranch:

In 1923 I went to San Antonio, where I worked for the Southern Pacific. Soon a friend working at Inland Steel Company in Indiana Harbor sent me $100 and told me to come there. I reached Chicago, but could find no one who knew where Indiana Harbor was [the post office address of Indiana Harbor is East Chicago]. I knew no English, and for six days I was in Chicago, trying to find Indiana Harbor. I got on street cars, and asked the conductors, but they said, "This car doesn't go to Indiana Harbor." I would ride a long time, hoping to see Indiana Harbor, and then get off and take another car. I couldn't order in restaurants so I couldn't get anything to eat except in stores with some fruit which I could see and point to. At night I slept in box cars, or any place; I couldn't go to a hotel, because I didn't know how to ask for a room. I'm scared of policemen, and I didn't think I would stay so long in Chicago, so I didn't ask them. I saw people with dark faces [Negroes?] and asked them, but they couldn't understand Spanish. In all that time I saw no Mexican. Finally, in a railroad station I found a man who spoke Spanish; he was a Cuban. He took me to the place to get my train to Indiana Harbor.

After working at Inland Steel Company for a time, I went to a steel company in Pittsburg, where another friend was working. Except for a short time when I worked at a steel plant in Wheeling, West Virginia, I continued to work in Pittsburg until I came back to Arandas last year.

If work's going to be all right, I think I'll go again to the United States. I had an auto, and sold it to a friend in Homestead when I left. Would I live permanently in the United States? Sure! Many come back from the United States and say the Americans treat the Mexicans badly, and don't want to talk with the Mexicans, and don't want to be friendly with them. But when I was there, many talked to me, and they didn't treat me bad. They treated me the same like everybody; I didn't do no trouble. The American girls don't like to speak to the Mexicans; they speak to all others except Mexicans. But the girls treat me nice and say hello when I was alone [the speaker was less dark than many Mexicans are]. The Americans who knew me talked to me. [The unfortunate experiences with the Pittsburg police quoted on p. 63 were recited by this speaker.]

A small proprietor and laborer, who was engaged in making rope when interviewed:

A friend loaned money without interest to pay transportation to the frontier. Went to improve living; it was hard here. Went to Colorado and Kansas to work on the track in 1922; returned to Arandas the same year. In 1924 went to United

States again for the same reason, and returned the same year. Through an *enganchista* at Kansas City went to Chicago to work in a foundry on the north side. Liked Chicago, it was *bonito* [pretty]—much traffic and big buildings. In 1926 made a third trip for the same reason, returning in 1927. Went to Port Arthur, Texas, where a friend was working, and worked at oil refineries. Each time returned from United States with about 40 pesos, and once sent 15 pesos home by money order. Owned house and three solares (about 1¼ acres) of land before going to the United States, and made a living principally by making rope and working for others. Owns no more land than before emigrating and makes living as before. Says attitude toward Americans is the same as before he went. Speaks very little English.

A returned emigrant who bottles and sells soda waters:

In 1917 because of the Carranza and Villa revolution, and paper money, poor business here, and robberies and fights, and also to see the country, I went to the United States. I entered at Laredo, and went to Fort Worth, where I had a friend, and worked in a roundhouse for six years. In 1923 I returned to Arandas for two years, and married. In 1925 I went to California, and worked for a year on the track at Corcoran where our first baby was born. Then I went to Redlands, where I worked in citrus fruits for two years. In July, 1928, I went to Chicago to work at Illinois Steel Company, where my brother-in-law was working. I stayed there until July, 1931, when I returned to Arandas because there was no work. The baby died. He was good—white.

We drove down from Chicago in our auto. At San Luis Potosí it broke down, and the mechanic wanted 450 pesos to fix it. So I sold it, and came the rest of the way by train and stage.

I had a bottling machine before I went to the United States, but when I came back I bought another machine from Baltimore and shipped it to Arandas. It is good for me, no much "worque" and I can sit and read the papers. I make often 4 or 5 pesos a day.

United States gave me good treatment. It is more better than this country for me. All American people are good; I like them; I like the United States for me. Bad treatment of some Mexicans? If I treat you bad, you treat me bad; if I treat you good, you treat me good. All the foremen were good to me.

In the United States all the time I am stranger—just work; and if there is no work, it is hard. But I like it in the United States; there is more money than in Arandas. Here no worque hard—two, three hours' work—it's all right. In the United States I am up at six o'clock, worque hard, they pay me good money—all right. I like it better there to make money, but I am more happy here. I know the language, I know everybody here.

His wife: I like it better in Arandas. The climate is better than the heat and cold of Chicago. I like California better than Chicago. This is *mi patria*.

The husband: I like it too much; it's good, your country Maybe in 1933 it will be better, and I will see you in Chicago.

In the United States every man work all the time, morning and night. You stay at the hotel [in Arandas]? Is it clean? Not so good for a white fellow like you. There are better hotels in the United States.

The son of a small ranchero:

In 1923 I went to the United States. When I reached San Antonio, I had no money. A friend took me to eat with him, and asked me if I wanted to go some place which pays too much [i.e., very much] money. So I signed a contract to go to Bethlehem Steel in Coatesville, Pennsylvania. In 1925 I returned to Arandas. With the money which I earned my father bought 53 solares [about 19 acres] of land for 1200 pesos.

In 1926 I went to the United States again and worked two weeks on the railroad. But it is a too much heavy job, and little money, so I went to an enganchista who sent me to work for the Pennsylvania railroad. I worked there for two weeks, and then went to the American Bridge Company at Ambridge, Pennsylvania. There I liked it too much; I sent back money by the post office to my mother who bought 100 solares [40 acres] of land for me for 2,000 pesos. When I came back I bought a yoke of oxen and a horse. In April, 1931, I returned to Arandas; I was working only 5 hours a day, 5 days a week in Pennsylvania.

In Ambridge I went to night school to learn English. I got books in English too; I like it. Some say the Americans are bad; some say they are good. But I can't talk like that [i.e., can't say they are bad]. In the United States there are many nationalities and scarce work. Maybe they make a revolution in America. But I don't want it, because we are brother countries. If they make fight there, it will come over here; and if they make fight here, it may go over there. [Can revolution aid there?] No, on the contrary.

Very many went to the United States during the [Cristero] revolution. We lost about 2,000 pesos because of the revolution. We buried these trunks to save them. The war is over, but it would start again if the agraristas and government become active as in Vera Cruz [referring to drastic laws against the church passed in that state shortly before]. The agraristas want to take the bishops' lands, and kill them, and take the lands of us Catholics, and shoot us. I don't believe in robbing people of money or taking their land, but only in buying it. The haciendas should pay more wages, and give more work, but the agraristas should not rob them of their land. The lands are already divided here. Are you a Catholic? Well, if you are or are not, you are my friend. My father was a Cristero.

Here we need money for machinery for farms. Here we have oxen, and no machinery, and can't do much. Money is a good help.

I have many desires to do things in the style of the United States. I would like to have a pump for irrigation, so that I would have better crops *every* year. I would like to have a house in American style. I like lumber houses, but they cost much and bullets can go through like paper. Here we build thick so no bullets can come through, and no windows, so when the door is shut no one can come in.

I am more content here than in the United States. When I work in the United States I make money only to eat. Here with a few dollars, I make a good living. Corn and beans never fail. I only work two or three days a week. [The rest of the time?] I rest. If there is good work in the United States, I like to go again.

[See also p. 63 for excerpt from letter of appreciation of the United States written by this emigrant.]

SUMMARY

The municipio of Arandas, situated in Los Altos of Jalisco, is inhabited by a population which is overwhelmingly of Spanish stock. In the process of conquest and settlement which began in the middle sixteenth century, the original invading army was not met in open battle. The Indians, variously called by historians and writers the "tecuexes," "huamares of the Zacatecas nation," or "chichimecs," relied rather on forays against the Spanish settlers who followed the military invaders and against the Indians friendly to these settlers—tactics similar to those employed by many Indians in the United States. Resistance ended in domestication of some Indians and perhaps the flight of others.

The minor elements of both Indian and Negro stocks, the latter introduced as slave labor, have been almost completely absorbed by intermixture. The dominant Spanish constituted approximately from 80 to 85 per cent of the blood strain of the population as a whole in the latter part of the eighteenth century, and the proportion is probably not greatly different today. In a large number of individuals, non-white physical characteristics are entirely absent; one often sees the idealized tall, lean, well-built figure, dark-haired and blue-eyed, of the United States pioneer in the white-skinned, black-bearded Spaniard. Race prejudice is weak, and, when exhibited, appears as a distinction privately applied by the whites in such matters as social intercourse and intermarriage; it is not manifested in the cruder public discriminations practiced in many localities in the United States.

The lands of present Arandas, which through the seventeenth century had come step by step under the control of three large haciendas, were originally utilized for pasturage of cattle, sheep, and horses. Commencing very slowly in the second half of the eighteenth century and first years of the nineteenth century, pieces of land were sold from the haciendas, principally to renters of Spanish race, who were occupying them. In the second quarter of the nineteenth century, after the close of the War of Independence, most of the hacienda lands in Arandas were sold to small proprietors. Four smaller haciendas yet exist in the municipio, one of them built up from successive small purchases by a renter during the first part of the nineteenth century, the others separated at a stroke from the original haciendas, two by sale and one by inheritance. But by inheritance and sale, the major part of the land of the municipio has become very greatly subdivided among many owners. By such a "natural agrarianism" a peasant proprietorship has been built up.

The faith of the Arandas community in the vigorous Roman Catholicism brought from Spain centuries before by its ancestors has remained extremely ardent. Isolated, deeply religious, economically conservative, the community was at the center of the Cristero revolution of 1927-29, and stood united practically to a man against the armed forces of government and agraristas.

The rate of natural increase of population has been, and is, very high in Arandas. Since at least 1810 this region has been a source of emigration which was stimulated by intermittent civil disorders from 1810 to 1876, and from 1927 to 1929, but which had as a constantly underlying factor the pressure of numbers of people on economic resources. Population within the municipio has greatly increased, and with it has come more and more intensive cultivation of the land. At the same time many people have left for residence elsewhere in Mexico where they or their descendants yet live. From about 1905 to 1930 the Arandas emigrants went increasingly to the United States, but they have continued to go also to other places in Mexico.

Those who have emigrated from Arandas to the United States have been generally young single men. Although there was some activity of labor agents in Arandas during the early years of the emigration, most of the direct stimulation of movement came from the example of those who went and received money wages five times as great as could be obtained for farm labor in Arandas. When the demands of expanding agriculture and industry in the United States made employment at comparatively high wages available to them, many emigrated. When, as in 1921 and again in 1930-31, demand for labor slackened and wages fell, few went, and many returned to Arandas despite their poverty at home.

The emigrants made their way to the border, usually with the aid of money borrowed at exorbitant rates of interest ranging from 12 per cent to frequently 100 per cent and even 200 per cent per annum. There they were usually met by labor agents, who distributed them to various parts of the United States. Emigrants from Arandas worked in at least 24 states of the United States, from California to Pennsylvania and from Texas to Michigan. They engaged in a wide variety of occupations, particularly labor on the track and labor in agriculture, steel mills, and coal mines.

In general, the treatment received in the United States was reported to be satisfactory; there were some complaints of maltreatment, but usually even the victims, like the majority of repatriates, were ready and even eager to return to the United States if economic conditions and immigration regulations shall permit. The existence in the United States of race discrimination against Mexicans was known to all, but few had personally experienced it, doubtless chiefly because of their Spanish, rather than Indian physical characteristics. Almost without exception their attitudes toward the United States were more favorable than the attitudes of those who had not emigrated.

Sums of money which, in some years, must have reached a total of 200,000 pesos, were remitted home by the emigrants. Some individuals made purchases of land, houses, stock, auto trucks, etc., with their earnings in the United States, and thus effected notable improvement in their economic condition. But in general there was comparatively little advance in their permanent economic status. The economic advantage derived from their experience was in the main limited to a higher material standard of living for themselves and their families while they were in the United States and for a short time thereafter so long as their savings lasted. Similarly, American cultural influence was but slightly transmitted to Arandas by the returned emigrants. Indeed, such American cultural influence as was evident, appeared to have been transmitted principally by other means, such as the sale of American products, the showing of American motion pictures, and the indirect entrance of American ideas or practices by way of printed media.

The failure of the returned emigrants permanently to raise their economic status more than they did was due either to insufficient earnings in the United States or to preference for purchasing temporary satisfactions as compared with saving for the acquisition of land or other relatively permanent goods. The failure of the returned emigrants more markedly to affect the culture of Arandas was not so much because of hostile pressure from the community, except possibly in religion, as because of their usual inability to make effective contact with American culture when in the United States, their insufficient economic power to put into effect such ideas as they brought back, and the great difference in physical and economic conditions, which made it extremely difficult to apply in Arandas methods learned in the United States.

APPENDIX

Documents Relating to the Transfer of Land by the Hacendados to the Inhabitants of the Hacienda Village of San Ignacio Cerro Gordo

(*Translation. Letters have been substituted for names of persons.*)

To the Governor of the State.
Guadalajara, Jalisco.

We, the undersigned, inhabitants of the *Comisaría Política* of San Ignacio Cerro Gordo, *municipalidad* of Arandas, for ourselves and representing the other inhabitants of the locality, respectfully submit the following to you, the Governor:

Hacienda Village, San Ignacio Cerro Gordo.

Under date of February 5 of the past year, we brought a petition before the Executive of the State, requesting a decree expropriating the land occupied by our houses in this *Comisaría*. Governor A., disregarding the just and forceful arguments brought forth, rendered a negative judgment, based solely on the principle that this locality should not be a *comisaría* but a *casco de hacienda* (hacienda village) by virtue of a decree of the First Chief of the Constitutional Army in pre-constitution days in which he declared invalid all the acts of legislature of the time of Huerta.

The arguments of real weight with which we defended ourselves on that occasion were the following:

"1. The *Comisaría* of San Ignacio Cerro Gordo has a population of 1157 inhabitants.

"2. Of the number of inhabitants given above, not one works for those known as *hacendados* (large landowners), and by that token this place cannot be considered an *hacienda*.

"3. The buildings are ours, but we cannot improve them without the previous consent of the landowners who claim the control of the lots and even attempt to regulate our houses.

"4. For a CENTURY the inhabitants of this place have been paying rent for the land.

"5. AT PRESENT THE LANDOWNERS PAY THE STATE FOR THIS COMMUNITY AS THOUGH IT WERE RURAL LAND, AND WHEN ONCE THE EXPROPRIATION IS DECREED THE STATE WILL PERCEIVE HOW WELL IT RETURNS THE FAVOR, SINCE SEVERAL HUNDRED HOUSES ARE INVOLVED.

"6. A company attempted to establish a small electric light and power plant in the locality, but it did not do so because the *latifundistas* (large landowners) prevented it.

"7. In this locality we possess inexhaustible sources of water which are actually shut off, solely through the egoism of the proprietors, who are only determined that the people do without necessities and therefore remain subject to their legendary control.

"8. The three or four landlords of the locality possess more than 500 *caballerías* of land."

These were the principal arguments advanced. For the rest, we ask but one just and lawful thing, since we are prepared to pay what is due under the terms of the law itself. When once the expropriation is decreed, the Executive of the State shall arrange what is to be paid.

It is to be noted that the only legal motive claimed by Ex-governor A. was that this *Comisaría* was only a *casco de hacienda* by virtue of the decree already made, but this argument has ceased to have any foundation by reason of the fact that this community has been newly raised to the status of *Comisaría Municipal*, BY DECREE OF THE EXECUTIVE OF THE STATE, ISSUED UNDER DATE OF AUGUST 11 OF THE CURRENT YEAR.

Because of what has been explained, and considering the revolutionary and liberal spirit that has animated all your acts, and because of this completely anachronistic colonial vassalage to which we have been subjected for more than a century; and looking toward the progress of this *Comisaría* which desires to attain its proper importance.

Of you, the Governor, being strictly just, we request the following:

1. That there be a reconsideration of the decision of Ex-governor A. which denied the expropriation of the land of this *Comisaría*, since its legal basis has disappeared; and

2. That the expropriation of the said lots of the *Comisaría* be decreed, taking into consideration the map attached to the relevant file of documents.

We affirm to you our respectful and sincere regard.

San Ignacio Cerro Gordo, (Arandas,) November 2, 1920.

In the city of Guadalajara, on the twenty-fourth of June, 1921, the following persons, present in the Office of the Governor of the State, Attorney B. as counsel for señor C. F., señor D. F., and señorita E. F., owners of one part of San Ignacio Cerro Gordo, *Municipalidad* of Arandas; señor G. also representing the F.s, in order to submit data and give the information necessary, señor H. as representative of the inhabitants of the hacienda of San Ignacio Cerro Gordo,— declared: That a number of the inhabitants of San Ignacio Cerro Gordo petitioned some time ago for a *dotación de ejido* (donation of expropriated land according to the terms of the agrarian law), notwithstanding that being *casco de hacienda* instead of *pueblo* (village) there was no right to obtain a donation: That subsequent to that petition the Local Agrarian Commission sent one of its engineers to survey the land to be made into the *ejido* and then the people told the engineer that they did not seek *ejidos*, which would be of no use to them because most of the inhabitants were not engaged in agriculture but in arts and business, and that it was a mistake to have applied for an *ejido*, since they had wanted only to request land for the town, and were urging that the *casco* of San Ignacio Cerro Gordo be made into a town with political autonomy: That the engineer returned without having made the survey, and then señor H. and also señor I., both representing the inhabitants of San Ignacio Cerro Cordo, went to the F.s, telling them that they were disposed to withdraw the petition for grant of an *ejido,* and that they offered to buy from the F.s the land of the *casco,* with some additions to form and enlarge the town: That the F.s were well disposed to aid the inhabitants to form an autonomous town, and made an offer to señor I. and señor H. to give freely to the inhabitants, instead of to sell to them, the lots or ground-plots on which are built the houses of the said inhabitants, as well as contiguous property, which will be described below, and to give them the use of other land, also described below, for three years, for the making of adobe and for extracting earth to be used as clay in making pottery, all on the express condition, to be duly guaranteed, that they will not insist on a *dotación de ejido*: That as a result of this they made a resolution or agreement which is stated in the following clauses:

1. Señor D.F., señor C.F., and señorita E.F., personally or through their agent, will issue in this city deeds for lots for houses already constructed, or lots on which to build them, and land intended for expansion, in that part of San Ignacio Cerro Gordo which belongs to them, in accordance with the following terms:

A. Each resident of San Ignacio Cerro Gordo who has his own house built on the property will be given the lot occupied by his house.

B. The inhabitants of San Ignacio Cerro Gordo who have no house for themselves and their families will be given a lot large enough for building a house, on one of the following plots of land: I—Orchard of señorita E. F. which adjoins the property of señorita J. on the east, the town on the west and north, and the Atotonilco Road on the south; II—The portion of the land of señor C. F. bounded by the inner gate on the north and the pasture of señor K. The orchard will be turned over after the harvest of the present crop.

C. This agreement does not include the lots, plots or sites where the F.s have houses, dwellings or buildings on their property, such as the manager's house at present occupied by señor L., granaries, carriage houses, shed used for a slaughter house, stables, the place for watering horses in the orchard, as well as the orchard known by the name of MANGA or Jesús Vázquez, etc.

D. Only the inhabitants of San Ignacio Cerro Gordo have the righ to the donations mentioned in the foregoing paragraphs.

E. The division of the property destined for expansion will be effected by a Commission elected by the said inhabitants. The lots for each dwelling shall be of the dimensions necessary for the construction of houses and not unduly large.

2. The said F.s will issue to the *ayuntamiento* (governing commission) of Arandas, in which *municipalidad* San Ignacio Cerro Gordo is located, a deed of gift of the streets and *plazuela.*

3. The donations to which the foregoing clauses refer will be made on the recissory condition that the village or town of San Ignacio Cerro Gordo shall not be granted an *ejido* (expropriated agricultural land). Señor I. and señor H.

agree to withdraw the petition already filed for a grant, and no other shall be made. The inhabitants of San Ignacio who signed the petition must ratify the withdrawal, and all shall ratify the agreement not to request or accept a grant.

4. The donations to the inhabitants of San Ignacio Cerro Gordo will be made with the proviso that those who acquire lots shall be under obligation to sell the manure from their houses to señor D. F. and señor C. F. at a price of $2.25 [pesos] per cart-load. Those who use the manure to fertilize their own fields or orchards shall not be under this obligation.

5. The F.s agree to concede, and henceforth *for three years* concede to the inhabitants of the *casco* [the right] to take earth to make adobe for the construction and repair of their houses and for clay for making pottery, from the portion of land three *hectáreas* in size situated in the lower part of "El Refugio" pasture. These three *hectáreas* will be measured and landmarks erected. Within this same area the inhabitants may open wells or water-hoists which they shall fence in to prevent danger of fall of animals, and *in no case may they take or use the water of the Sangrado dam*.

6. The F.s will issue the deeds as soon as the representatives of the inhabitants of the *casco* withdraw [the petition] and give them the necessary data regarding the inhabitants to be allowed donations and regarding the lots which are to be given to each one, with a statement of the measurements and boundaries.

7. All the costs of transfer will be borne by the inhabitants.

Señor G. stated that señor K. and señorita J. indicated to him that they would adhere to this agreement, drawing up a similar one with regard to certain portions of land for expansion of that which is incorporated in the town. These portions of land are two which belong to señor K. or his sisters: one is approximately 120 meters wide and lies north of the *casco,* and the other, about 100 meters long, lies on the west. The portion belonging to señorita J. is about 28 meters wide and adjoins the *casco* and señorita F.'s orchard. Señor I and señor H. will deal directly with señor K. or his sisters and with señorita J. to make whatever arrangements they agree upon; for the F.s commit themselves only to what is contained in the present agreement.

The Governor ordered that what is herein contracted be recorded in duplicate and triplicate to be signed by the parties and made known to the F.s and señor I., who did not personally attend.

By virtue whereof this contract is drawn up in triplicate.

(Signed)   G.   B.   H.

We, the undersigned, advised of the foregoing contract, are in agreement with it and sign it.

(Signed)   I.   C. F.   D. F.
                   E. F.   M. (an owner)

EXPLANATION OF PLATES

PLATE 1

(See frontispiece)

PLATE 2

a. View toward the north from the site of the ancient Indian ruins on the heights above Edificios (see p. 6). Note the semicircular configuration of the eroded edges of the heights, and the fact that the plain, El Plan, lies below. These were inaccurately represented on the original map of Ramón Sánchez in 1879, and have been corrected on the cover map. (Both maps accompany this study.) Fifteen artificial reservoirs of water stored for irrigation behind low dams, or *bordos,* were seen from this point, although not all are clearly visible in the plate.

b. Hacienda Guadalupe (Joconostle), seen from the northeast. The structures in the foreground are laborers' houses; at the extreme right and left are the walls of stock corrals. In the background, right center, stands the chapel; in the left center rises the smoke-stack of the *tequila* factory, where the strong alcoholic drink of that name is manufactured from *mezcal* plants. See plate 8*f.*

PLATE 3

a. Spanish-type ranch woman, in typical workaday costume, with apron and shawl (*reboso*). Her home is shown on p. 8. Compare with the young townswomen shown on this plate, *e*, and plate 6*e*.

b. A young *proprietario*, returned emigrant, whose wife is shown in *a*; he is dressed in his best native costume, including pistol, dagger, and fine leather equipment. The same man is shown at work harvesting maize, in the article by the present author, "Vignettes from Old Mexico" *(University of California Chronicle*, vol. 34, plate 3, opp. p. 126).

c. Spanish-type ranchero. After seven trips to the United States where he labored on the track, an oil pipe-line, and in the cotton harvest, he was still practically unable to speak a word of English.

d. Spanish-type professional man of Arandas; a land surveyor.

e. Young women of Arandas town. Note the American style of dress. The two women at the left are of Spanish type; the one at the right shows evidences of Indian admixture.

f. Young ranchero, a returned emigrant, in typical peasant costume of *camisa*, *calzones*, and *guaraches*.

PLATE 4

a. An *hacendado* (wearing white jacket). A Spanish physical type. None of the persons shown in *a* or *b* had ever emigrated to the United States.

b. A *cargador*, or porter, of Spanish physical type.

c. The two men are returned emigrants.

d. A returned emigrant, *proprietario*, in characteristic peasant costume with leather apron, prying rocks from a field with which to build a fence. Physical type predominantly Spanish, with some Indian admixture.

e. An emigrant, returned but two weeks from the sugar beet fields of Colorado.

f. A returned emigrant who had worked in the steel mills of the Calumet region, engaged as a stone mason in construction of the new temple, Arandas. A pure Spanish type.

PLATE 5

a. Spanish-type peasant, because of long delayed rains, carrying water in *cántaros* to cattle, and to irrigate a small patch of corn.

b. Typical group of Spanish-type peasants, illiterate, engaged in moving a stone fence.

c. (This picture, and *d*, *e*, and *f*, and *a*, *b*, *c*, of plate 6, depict steps in the process of rope-making.) Stripping spines from the leaves of maguey plant, in preparation for extraction of ixtle fiber, and manufacture of rope.

d. Stripping outer skin from the maguey leaf. The leaf is then pounded with a wooden mallet, a large rock serving as an anvil, to reduce the meat of the leaf to a pulp.

e. The long fibers are separated from the pulp by scraping the pulp off with the downward push of a rude scraper resembling a draw-shave.

f. The ixtle fiber, thoroughly dried, is spun into the strand of a rope. The spinner is a ranch laborer, resident in house shown in plate 7*b*, and a returned emigrant who had worked in a Chicago foundry (see pp. 68, 69).

PLATE 6

a. Four (sometimes as many as five) strands are woven into a rope. A returned emigrant of predominantly Spanish type, but with Indian admixture, turns a wheel which separately twists each strand. This man lives with his parents, who are small proprietors, in the house shown in plate 1 (frontispiece). Like many others in Los Altos, this house is constructed of stones, plastered on the inside with mud, unfloored, and roofed with tiles supported by log rafters and by tule. In the yard are fruit trees, and prickly pear cactus (*nopal*) raised for its fruit (*tuna*). A shallow well supplies water not only for domestic purposes but for the fruit trees and a few rows of cabbages which were carefully tended. The son had worked in steel mills of Pennsylvania.

b. At the other end of the rope-making process the four strands are twisted tightly together immediately after they pass through grooves of a wooden *piña* (a truncated cone with four grooves lengthwise) which is advanced slowly as the completed rope is formed.

c. Reeling the finished *riata* or *soga* onto a revolving drum.

d. A returned emigrant, in native costume, even to *guaraches* and *faja* (sash), plowing up potatoes with wooden plow drawn by a yoke of oxen.

e. A Spanish-type señorita of Arandas town.

f. Hacienda Sauz de Cagigal.

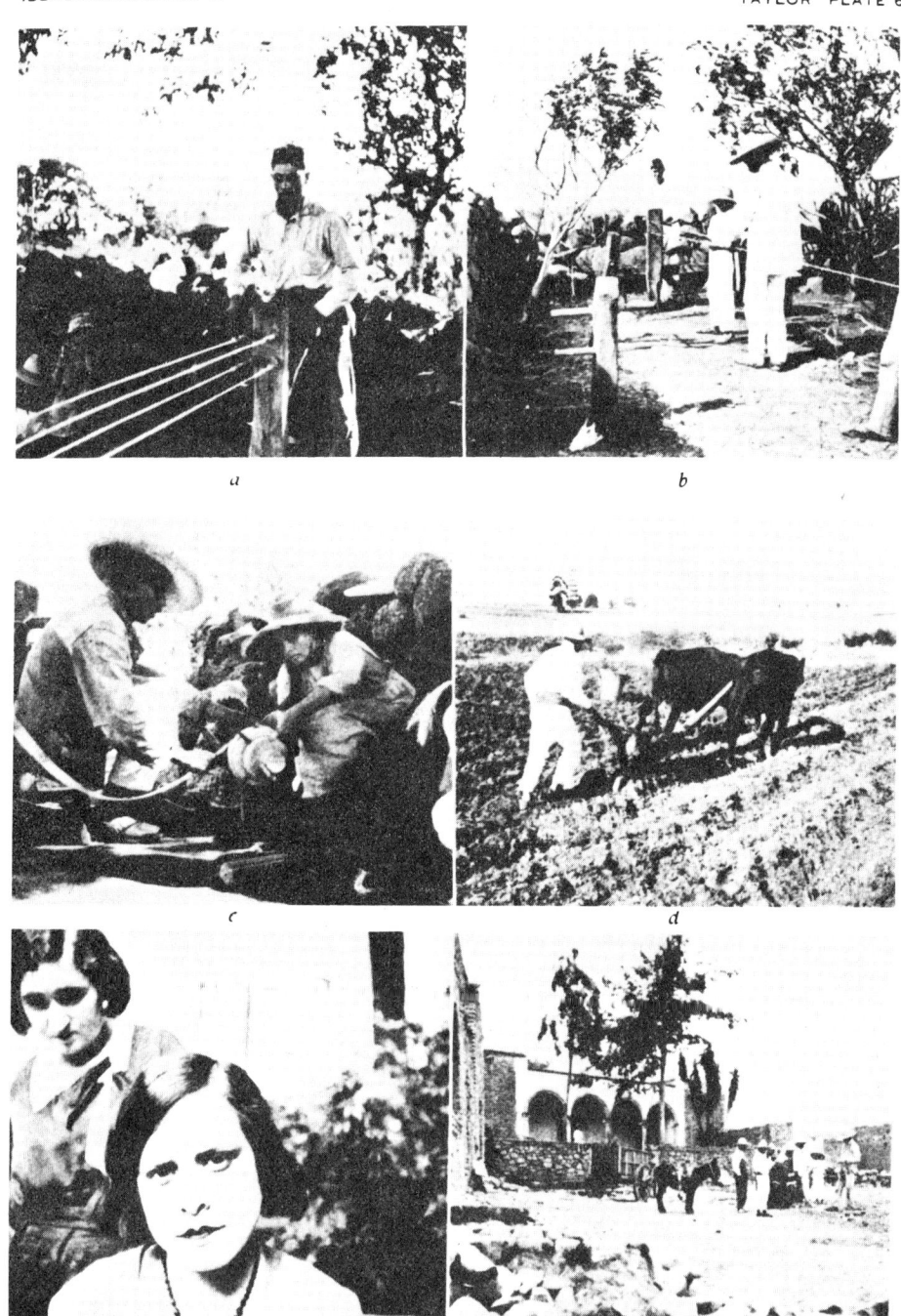

PLATE 7

a. Ranch house of a prosperous proprietor, constructed of adobe. The proprietor's sons had worked in steel mills of the Calumet region.

b. Adobe house of a rural laborer who owns only a small plot of ground, making his livelihood chiefly by rope-making and by field labor for others. See plates 5*f* and 6*c*.

c. Typical solid-wheeled wagon, San Ignacio Cerro Gordo.

d. Bringing in the corn harvest for winter storage by ox-cart, Hacienda Guadalupe, Arandas. See also "Vignettes," *op. cit.*, plate 5 opp. p. 126.

e. Wooden plow used generally in Arandas. Sometimes the point of the share is tipped with iron. A curved cross-stick (*telera;* not shown) is inserted in the hole to throw earth as desired.

f. Laundering on the stones bordering a lake-reservoir. Unlike the French peasant women, Mexican women do not use wooden paddles, but instead slap the wet clothes against the stones.

PLATE 8

a. Sunday afternoon scene in the plaza of Arandas, showing vendors in the *portales*, and the church. Note the burros, automobile, and telegraph and light wires.

b. Plaza of Arandas, showing *portales* and *kiosk* (see also "Vignettes" *op. cit.*, plate opp. p. 130). Here the social life of the town is centered, *serenatas* are held to the music of the municipal orchestra, and citizens of all ranks come to promenade with their families and friends (see description in "Vignettes," *op. cit.*, 127-8).

c. Looking eastward from the roof of the Arandas church.

d. Sunday morning scene in the street in rear of the church, used as part of the town market place.

e. Group of young men and boys in the plaza of Arandas. It is not possible to determine by costume alone which members of the group have been to the United States and which have not.

f. Transporting *mezcal* plants to *tequila* factory for maceration and distillation. Hacienda Guadalupe.

a

b

c

d

e

f

The Wetback in the Lower Rio Grande Valley Of Texas

By

LYLE SAUNDERS
University of New Mexico

OLEN E. LEONARD
Vanderbilt University

Editor's Foreword

Two years ago, Lyle Saunders and I said the following in a preliminary report (mimeo.) on wetbacks:

One of the most serious problems facing the people of Texas is the presence in the state of a very large, but as yet undetermined, number of wetbacks—illegal aliens who cross the border from Mexico mainly in search of agricultural employment but who are to be found in many cities of the state and in many non-agricultural jobs. The Spanish-speaking Texans are not the only ones affected. Every citizen of the state, Spanish- and English-speaking alike, shares, to a greater or lesser extent, in the evil effects and devastating repercussions that derive from the presence in the state of from a hundred thousand to half a million homeless wanderers—men, women, and children without legal status, without skills, without knowledge of our ways and customs, without protection, and without opportunity for improving their condition. No citizen of the state, or of the other states into which many of the wetbacks eventually drift, can escape the consequences that grow out of the importation of this contraband labor—consequences which appear in the form of poverty, disease, slums, ignorance, dependency, low wages, and social and personal disorganization not only for the wetbacks themselves but for the Spanish-speaking citizens whom they displace and the English-speaking Texans in whose communities they and the thousands of displaced persons come to live . . .

A large part of the economy of central, western, and south Texas is being founded upon most dangerous ground: the shifting quicksand that is the wetback—contraband labor. The cotton and citrus industries, vegetable farming, and similar enterprises there, by the shortsighted dependence on wetback labor, are sowing the wind—and, as a result, the state and nation will long reap a whirlwind of social misery and unrest, of expensive remedial action, of international embarrassment. Those enterprises, by their very dependence on wetbacks and on modified peonage, are exposing themselves to economic disaster. The flow of contraband labor, like that of contraband goods, is subject to legal sanctions and to control; and a sudden turn of events could bring a sudden removal of this mainstay of a warped economy.

All in all, the ill-gotten profits from the exploitation of this illegal labor seems poor compensation for the myriad real evils and potential dangers attendant on the use and encouragement of wetbacks. It is the conviction of the authors that measures for the solution of the wetback problem should be given highest priority by state and national officials, as well as by the leaders of private enterprise in Texas. This is a major problem, of far-reaching consequences, and its solution calls for the best that the co-ordinated intelligence of our top-flight leadership can offer in the way of social and economic inventiveness and of truly enlightened social consciousness.

Since the time that the above statement was made, the wetback issue has received a great deal of national attention, and various studies and reports have dealt with the subject. Among the most notable of these is the recent report of the President's Commission on Migratory Labor, *Migratory Labor in American Agriculture*. All of these studies and reports have corroborated the conclusions which Saunders and I reached in 1949. However, we have felt that none of the studies was detailed and thorough enough to satisfy our desire for a complete picture of the wetback in the Lower Rio Grande Valley of Texas. Because of this, the Study of Spanish-Speaking People undertook the investigation reported in this bulletin. Saunders and Leonard, and their assistants, have done an excellent job, and we are happy to release their report through *Occasional Papers*.

George I. Sánchez
Sutton Hall 212
The University of Texas

Preface

On June 3, 1950, President Harry S. Truman issued an executive order creating a President's Commission on Migratory Labor. The Commission, among its other duties, was directed to inquire into "the extent of illegal migration of foreign workers into the United States and the problems created thereby" and to ascertain "whether, and in what respect, current law enforcement measures and the authority and means possessed by Federal, State, and local governments may be strengthened and improved to eliminate such illegal migration."

The action of the President in appointing an official Commission to look into the problems created by the presence in this country of a large number of illegal Mexican aliens is indication of a growing concern about the social, economic, and legal consequences of permitting our border counties to be periodically invaded by a vast migration of agricultural and other workers who themselves are not much benefited by being here and whose presence is detrimental to the welfare of large numbers of our citizens. Confined at first to a relatively small number of people in the Southwest, that concern has spread both to a greater proportion of the population of the southwestern states and to individuals and groups, both public and private, in other parts of the nation as they have become aware that the impact of the illegal aliens affects not only those who live along the Mexican border but citizens in many other parts of the nation as well.

Among the groups with the longest history of interest in the problem is the Southwest Council on the Education of Spanish-speaking People. Dr. George I. Sanchez, Professor of Latin American Education at The University of Texas, and President of the Council since its inception, has for years been pointing out the relationship between the presence of large numbers of illegal aliens in the United States and the persistence of problems of health, education, poverty, excessive mobility, and discrimination among Spanish-speaking citizens in the Southwest, and has repeatedly urged that appropriate governmental agencies take steps to ascertain the facts of the situation and undertake such remedial action as may be necessary. In repeated conferences with officials of organizations of Spanish-speaking people, labor leaders, heads of groups dedicated to the preservation and extension of civil rights, government officials, and others interested for one reason or another in the socio-economic problems of Spanish-speaking citizens, Dr. Sanchez has consistently emphasized the need for more information on the numbers, characteristics, living conditions, and relations with local people of the illegal Mexican aliens as a precondition for governmental action on a scale large enough to cope with the problem.

To help meet this need for reliable information, the Study of Spanish-Speaking People of The University of Texas planned and carried out during the summer of 1950 a research project designed to provide factual data about illegal aliens in the Lower Rio Grande Valley of Texas. The study was carried on by Olen Leonard, Professor of Sociology, Vanderbilt University, and Lyle Saunders, Assistant Professor of Sociology, University of New Mexico, with the help of graduate students Bruce Meador and Sam Brewer, of The University of Texas, and Richard Hilbert of the University of New Mexico.

The general purpose of the study was to determine the extent and to outline the major implications of the periodic migration of illegal aliens into the Valley. Particular attention was also given to the following specific objectives:

1. To estimate the number of wetbacks[1] in the Valley at the peak of the cotton harvest season.

2. To discover some of the pertinent characteristics of the wetbacks, including age, sex, marital status, place of origin and residence in Mexico, reasons for coming to the United States, role in the Valley economy, and relations with Valley people.

3. To learn the effect of alien immigration on Spanish-speaking citizens with whom they compete for jobs.

4. To become acquainted with some of the prevailing Valley beliefs, sentiments, and attitudes about wetbacks.

5. To observe and insofar as possible evaluate attempts on the part of people of the United States, both official and private, to inhibit the movement of wetbacks into this country.

6. To gauge the attitudes of Mexican officials toward the migration of wetbacks and to evaluate the effectiveness of any Mexican efforts to prevent or limit it.

No claim is made that we have completely or even satisfactorily achieved these objectives. The problem of the wetback in the

---

[1]Illegal Mexican aliens are referred to in the Valley, and elsewhere in the Southwest, as "wetbacks," a term which undoubtedly derives from the fact that so many of them arrive by swimming the Rio Grande. Throughout the remainder of this report the term "wetback" will be generally used in preference to the longer phrase "illegal Mexican aliens."

Lower Rio Grande Valley is much too complex, much too extensive, to be fully revealed at the conclusion of a single study limited in both time and funds. We do believe, however, that the findings presented in this report illuminate the general situation in the Valley with respect to the wetback immigration, provide the basis for a general understanding of the more important factors involved, and indicate relationship areas wherein more detailed and more intensive studies may profitably be made in the future.

Like all writers, we are heavily indebted to the many persons and organizations who assisted, in one way or another, in the collection of data for our report. The study would not have been possible without the aid of Dr. George I. Sanchez, who not only made funds available from the budget of the Study of Spanish-Speaking People, but who also, through his wide knowledge of the Southwest, was able to suggest numerous sources of information and many valuable lines of procedure. The San Antonio and McAllen offices of the Border Patrol and Immigration and Naturalization Service officials at the Hidalgo bridge generously gave cooperation and assistance without which we could not even have made a beginning on our study in the time we had. Our student assistants, Bruce Meador, Sam Brewer, and Richard Hilbert, did very commendable field work in the Valley and contributed many insights that aided in several of our analyses and interpretations. Thanks are due to the Institute of Research and Training in the Social Sciences of Vanderbilt University for the use of technical equipment and funds for final tabulation of our data and the typing of this report. None of these persons or organizations, however, is responsible for the conclusions and interpretations herein presented. These are our responsibility alone.

Lyle Saunders
Olen E. Leonard

Contents

	PAGE
Editor's Foreword	3
Preface	5
I. An Introduction to the Lower Rio Grande Valley	11

    The Valley—Land, Climate, and Soils
    Industrial and Commercial Resources
    Historical Development
    The People
    Health and Mortality

II. Profile of the Wetback 26
    Age, Sex, Marital Status, and Occupation
    Place of Origin
    Length of Residence in the United States

III. The Problem of the Wetback in the Valley 42
    Economic Effects
    Social Effects
    Health
    Political Effects

IV. The Wetback in the Valley 50
    Relations with Employers
    Relations with Local Spanish-Speaking People
    Relations with Anglos
    Relations with Officials

V. Summary 83
    Number of Wetbacks
    Characteristics of the Wetback
    Impact of the Wetback on the Valley
    Attitudes in the Valley toward the Wetback
    Limitations on Movement of Wetbacks in the United States
    Mexico's Position on the Migration

List of Figures

FIGURE	OPPOSITE PAGE
1. States of Origin of 2,584 Wetbacks, 1920–1950	30
2. Months of Entry Into the United States of 2,584 Wetbacks Apprehended in the Years 1920–1950	32
3. Length of Time Spent in the United States by 2,475 Wetbacks Apprehended in the Years 1920–1950	33

List of Tables

TABLE		PAGE
1.	Estimated Cash Farm Income, 1949, by Counties and by Farm	17
2.	Total Deaths by Age at Death for the Non-Span:sh-speaking and Spanish-speaking Populations of Hidalgo County, 1949	23
3.	Major Causes of Death by Age at Death for the Non-Spanish-speaking and Spanish-speaking Populations of Hidalgo County, 1949	25
4.	Age, Sex, and Marital Status of 160 Wetbacks Deported from Texas in 1950	27
5.	Age Distribution, 2,602 Wetbacks Returned to Mexico Through the Hidalgo Office of the U.S. Immigration and Natural.zation Service	27
6.	Marital Status, 2,351 Wetbacks Returned to Mexico Through the Hidalgo Office of the U.S. Immigration and Naturalization Service	28
7.	Sex Distribution, 2,562 Wetbacks Returned to Mexico Through the Hidalgo Office of the U.S. Immigration and Naturalizat on Service	28
8.	Usual Occupation in Mexico of 160 Wetbacks Deported from Texas in 1950	29
9.	Number of *Hectares* of Land Owned and/or Operated in Mexico by 160 Wetbacks Deported from Texas in 1950	30
10.	State or Other Place of Birth of 2,364 Wetbacks Returned to Mexico Through the Hidalgo Office of the U.S. Immigration and Naturalization Service	31
11.	States of B:rth and Residence of 154 Wetbacks Deported from Texas in 1950	31
12.	Length of Time Spent in the United States by 2,475 Mexicans Illegally Entering the United States from 1920 to 1950	32
13.	Length of Time Spent in the United States by 153 Wetbacks Deported from Texas in 1950	32
14.	The Responses of 136 Wetbacks Deported from Texas in 1950 to a Question Regarding the Time They Had Expected to Remain in the United States	33
15.	The Responses of 160 Wetbacks Deported from Texas in 1950 When Asked (a) Why They Had Come to the United States, and (b) How They Had Learned of Work Opportunities in the U.S.	33
16.	The Responses of 160 Wetbacks Deported from Texas in 1950 When Asked: "If You Could Earn $100 or More in the United States, What Would You Do With It?"	35
17.	The Responses of 160 Wetbacks Deported From Texas in 1950 When Asked: (a) The Number of Times They Had Entered the United States; (b) The Mode of Transportation Used from Residence to the International Boundary; (c) Who Had Accompanied Them to the Border	37
18.	The Responses of 157 Wetbacks Deported from Texas in 1950 When Asked How They Had Crossed the River	38
19.	Tabulation of the Responses of Each of 160 Wetbacks to the Request for the Name, Relationship, Nat'onality, and Language of Five Persons (Other Than Immediate Family) Whom He Knows Best in the United States	40
20.	The Responses of 160 Wetbacks When Asked Whether They Would Prefer to Live in the U.S. or Mexico and Why	41

I
An Introduction to the Lower Rio Grande Valley

Geographically, the Lower Rio Grande Valley of Texas is small. It is largely encompassed within the three counties of Hidalgo, Cameron, and Willacy[1] which lie just north of the Rio Grande where it empties into the Gulf of Mexico at the extreme southeastern tip of Texas. But although small in size and relatively isolated from the rest of Texas by a wide expense of arid, sparsely populated land, the Valley is a focal point of social, political, legal, and economic conditions that have recently and repeatedly attracted national and even international attention. For into this area each year there now pours a stream of illegal Mexican migrants whose presence raises problems that extend far beyond the boundaries of the Valley. Some of these migrants—and nobody knows how large the number may be—move on northward to other parts of Texas and other states where they gradually merge with and become indistinguishable from the general population. Others remain in the Valley to be caught later and returned to Mexico by our Immigration authorities or remain and are absorbed into the local resident population. Most of them stay for brief periods only and then recross the river to return to their homes and families in Mexico.

The impact of these migrants on social, economic, and politcal conditions in the Valley has been tremendous. Accustomed to a low level of living, conditioned by past experiences to exploitation by a wealthy land-owning class in Mexico, desperately poor by our standards, and illegally in the United States, the wetbacks constitute a labor supply whose members are docile and malleable to a degree far beyond that of any group of United States citizens. They accept readily—sometimes eagerly—wages and conditions of work far below those acceptable to citizen workers in the Valley, thus forcing these citizens to migrate periodically or permanently to other parts of Texas or to other states in search of work. They

---

[1]The total land area of the three counties is only 3,019 square miles, which represents about 1.1% of the total land area of Texas. U. S. Department of Commerce, Bureau of the Census, *County Data Book* (Washington: U. S. Government Printing Office, 1947), pp. 354, 360, 372.

create problems for school authorities, for Selective Service officials, for the personnel of both public and private welfare agencies, and for those responsible for the maintenance of public health. They make possible the perpetuation of patterns of ethnic hostility detrimental to the full acceptance of the Spanish-speaking citizens of the Valley. And they cost the taxpayers approximately half a million dollars a year in the Valley alone for Federal efforts to keep them out or at least control their numbers, in addition to the undetermined costs of state and local police action directed towards them.

But at the same time, their presence, coupled with the unusual agricultural fertility and favorable climate of the Valley, has made possible profits in local agriculture and business quite in excess of those that are earned in similar enterprises in other areas of the state or the nation.[2] Furthermore, Valley employers, both in agriculture and other fields, have always at hand an abundant supply of workers for whatever jobs they need to have done, workers for whom they need assume no obligation other than that of paying them when the work is finished, workers who are flexible, mobile, unorganized, and uncomplaining.

Given this situation it is not surprising that there have developed in the Valley many diverging opinions and points of view about the wetback, his relations with other population groups in the Valley, and his effect on local conditions. There are those who believe that the wetback is mistreated and exploited; there are others who insist that the treatment he receives is just and fair and is certainly better than that which he is used to or he would not continue to come. There are those who see the wetback as a major cause of the social problems affecting Spanish-speaking citizens; there are others who see no relation whatsoever between what happens to the wetback and what happens to citizens who culturally resemble him. There are many who maintain that there is no need in the Valley for wetback labor and that they are admitted only for the purpose of keeping down wages and making union organization difficult; and there are others who claim that

---

[2]According to the Bureau of Business Research of The University of Texas, the estimated farm income for the three Valley counties in 1949 was more than $129,577,000, an increase of about 1,000% since 1920. The number of farms in the three counties on January 1, 1945, was 9,611 (*County Data Book*, pp. 357, 363, 375). This would indicate an average farm income of about $13,480, which is 281% of the average farm income of Texas as a whole.

the Valley economy is completely dependent on the labor of wetbacks and that without them the productive level of the area could not be maintained.

The controversy has divided the Valley into three broad groups: those who condemn major aspects of the existing situation; those who deny the more severe criticisms and offer justifications for the milder ones; and those who have no particular feeling one way or the other. At the Brownsville hearings of the President's Commission on Migratory Labor, held in July, 1950, the testimony was at times so conflicting that it was difficult for the listener always to remember that everyone was talking about the same situation. One group of witnesses spoke of exploitation and low wages, of citizens being excluded from jobs for which wetbacks were hired, of inadequate provisions for health and housing, of citizens forced to migrate in search of work at wages which would enable them to live. Another group presented a directly opposing point of view, claiming that the Spanish-speaking citizen "refuses to work at stoop labor anymore," that he "travels about for adventure" and "demands far higher wages than we can afford to pay." This group saw the use of wetback labor as not only necessary but also desirable, since "he is satisfied with the low wages he receives," "isn't worth any more than the wages he gets," and is happy about the whole arrangement because "we treat him better here than his employers do in Mexico."[3]

It is the purpose of this study to explore and report on some of the conditions that underlie this controversy. In so doing we shall begin with a description of the Valley itself, pass on to a statement of the characteristics of the wetback, and then take up the way in which the wetback interacts with the various population groups with whom he comes into contact.

The Valley—Land, Climate, and Soils. The Lower Rio Grande Valley is one of the most productive and prosperous farming regions in the nation. The many varieties of alluvial and loam soils that cover the area, the semi-tropical climate, and the relatively abundant supply of irrigation water have been the bases for its prosperity. These factors, plus a seemingly inexhaustible supply of low cost labor from across the river and modern productive techniques, have all combined into a potential hardly equalled in modern agricultural history.

---

[3]These are not the precise words used, since the report of the President's Commission's hearings was not available until after this was written. The material in quotations, however, does represent the substance of many of the points of view expressed.

About three-fifths of the 3,019 square miles in the three counties in which the Valley lies is classified as farm lands. Of this about 420,000 acres were harvested in 1945.[4] Although largely an agricultural population by occupation,[5] more than half the people of the Valley live in incorporated towns of 2,500 or more population.[6] Towns and villages dot the entire area, with the larger and more important ones being located mainly along U. S. Highway 83 which connects Brownsville and Mission. Others are situated on the many good cross roads that traverse the Valley from north to south. About 400 miles of railroad lines serve the area, and few farms in the irrigated sections of the Valley are more than five miles from a railroad loading point.

There is some evidence to indicate that the Valley has about reached its limit of growth and will not expand much more under existing conditions of water and land. Much of the undeveloped sections of the Valley is a relatively poor prospect for agricultural use. Some of the soils are unfit for profitable farming. And much of the land, particularly that located to the west of the Valley, is owned by Spanish-speaking residents who are not financially able to develop it and who refuse to sell.

Among the more extensive lands generally considered unsuitable for development are those located at levels so far above that of the river that transference of water to them would not be profitable. The lands of northern Starr,[7] Hidalgo, and Willacy counties fall into this category. Several proposals have been made to tap the Rio Grande at points farther up stream than is now being done, but none has, as yet, been acceptable to both the government and the farmers.

---

[4]A total of 1,215,000 acres was classified as farm land on January 1, 1945. This was distributed as follows: Hidalgo County, 670,000 acres; Cameron County, 327,000 acres; Willacy County, 218,000 acres. Croplands harvested the preceding year included 206,000 acres in Hidalgo County; 122,000 in Cameron County; and 92,000 in Willacy County. *County Data Book*, pp. 357, 363, 375.

[5]The proportion of those employed who worked in agriculture in 1940, was: Cameron County 36.4%; Hidalgo County 45.3%; Willacy County 56.7%. By contrast, the leading non-agricultural industry in each of the counties in 1940 employed 6.4%, 10.6%, and 4.8%, respectively. *County Data Book*, pp. 355, 361, 373.

[6]In 1950, 171,254 of the Valley's 305,719 recorded inhabitants lived in areas classified as urban by the Bureau of the Census. For a comparison of rural-urban distribution in the three counties in 1940 and 1950 see Eastin Nelson and Frederic Meyers, *Labor Requirements and Labor Resources in the Lower Rio Grande Valley of Texas*, Inter-American Education, Occasional Papers VI (Austin: University of Texas, December 1950), Table III, p. 14.

[7]Starr County borders Hidalgo on the west. Some observers include Starr County as part of the Valley, but social and economic conditions are so different there that it is doubtful if the inclusion is justified.

In Starr County, in addition to the land in the northern part that is too high for irrigation, a strip of caliche land lying north of Highway 83 and stretching eastward to the Hidalgo County line is unsuitable for crops. A rough estimate of the remaining land in the County shows that, under present conditions of land and water use, only about 34,000 additional acres could be developed for agricultural use. Of these, about half are in the possession of Spanish-speaking citizens who do not wish to sell and who do not have the capital to develop the land themselves. Thus the most productive areas of the Valley seem to be hemmed in on the south and east by the river and the sandy lands of the Gulf coast, on the north by high and arid lands, and on the west by land that is either unsuitable for cultivation or is owned by people who refuse to sell it and cannot develop it.

At present there are about 950,000 acres of land in the Valley suitable for irrigation, 552,000 of which have been under irrigation for the past few years either through the facilities of the 28 major water districts or the more than 120 private irrigation systems that are generally in operation.[8] Thousands of miles of concrete canals, underground pipes, and drainage ditches have been installed, at a total cost of more than thirty million dollars, to carry water to the fields and orchards.

The semi-tropical climate of the Valley permits crops to be grown throughout the year. The average length of the growing season is from 315 to 349 days, depending on the exact location. Killing frosts sometimes occur between December 19 and February 10, but hard freezes, such as that which occurred in January, 1949, are rare. The mean temperatures for summer and winter are 84.1 and 60.7 degees Fahrenheit respectively.[9]

The soils of the Valley, with the exception of the sandy land along the Gulf coast, are generally fertile and suitable for a wide variety of crops. Most of this area was beneath the waters of the Gulf at one time and, consequently, the soils differ somewhat from those found farther up the Rio Grande. Certain sections in the lower parts of the Valley suffer from a high water table which is detrimental to the growing of citrus trees. In much of the area

---

[8]In 1948 there were in the four counties of Cameron, Hidalgo, Willacy, and Starr twenty-seven active irrigation districts, six inactive districts and some 300 independent pumps. Some 552,000 acres were irrigated in 1945, of which about 496,000 were within districts, and 56,000 irrigated by independent systems. U. S. Dept. of the Interior, Bureau of Reclamation, *Plan for Development of Valley Gravity System* (Mimeographed), December 1948.
[9]Data from the U. S. Weather Bureau's mimeographed sheet, *Climatological Data for the Lower Rio Grande Valley of Texas* (undated).

around Brownsville, for example, the land is only thirty to forty feet above sea level, and citrus trees, after a few years of growth, reach the salt water table below and are killed.

A wider variety of crops are grown in the Valley than in any other agricultural area in Texas. Citrus fruits and cotton are the principal cash crops, but there are large annual shipments of tomatoes, cabbage, potatoes, broccoli, beans, peppers, lettuce, squash, eggplant, carrots, peas, okra, cauliflower, sweet corn, and grain sorghums. Vegetable shipments increased from 650 car lots in 1907 to 32,000 car lots in 1945. Citrus shipments increased from a few boxes in 1915 to 72,000 boxes in 1945, and this latter figure does not include nearly 400,000 tons of fruit canned and juiced during that year.

Cotton production has increased fairly steadily during the past twenty years. From 29,000 bales in 1920, cotton production increased to about 80,000 bales in 1930 and to more than 500,000 bales in 1949.[10] Reduced somewhat in 1950, largely as a result of acreage restrictions, cotton production in the Valley may again increase if governmental regulations are relaxed.

Most of the fruits and vegetables produced in the Valley are shipped by express or truck to northern and eastern markets during the winter and early spring months. An increasing proportion is canned or juiced locally. At the present time (1950) there are more than forty canning and quick freeze plants located in the Valley, and others have been projected and are expected to be in operation shortly.

As indicated above (footnote 2), the estimated farm income for the three Valley counties in 1949 was more than $129,000,000, an increase of 1,000% since 1920. This indicates an average farm income of more than $13,400 (using the number of farms in 1945 as the basis of calculation), which is about 280% of the average farm income for Texas as a whole. Probably even more significant is the fact that, although the Valley possessed only 3% of the crop land harvested (1945) it received an estimated 7% of the total cash farm income (1949).

Industrial and Commercial Resources. Although not primarily an industrial area, the Valley has many resources other than those associated directly with agriculture. Its transportation facilities include three main truck highways, four scheduled airlines, two railways, two inter-state and two intra-Valley bus lines, and two

---

[10]Eastin Nelson and Frederic Meyers, *op. cit.*, p. 11.

deep water seaports. When completed the Intracoastal Canal will give two additional communities, Harlingen and Raymondville, water connections with Gulf and Atlantic ports.

TABLE 1

ESTIMATED CASH FARM INCOME 1949, BY COUNTIES AND BY FARM [11]

County	Estimated Income, 1949*	Number of Farms, 1945†	Average Acreage Per Farm‡	Estimated Income Per Farm, 1949§
Cameron	$ 38,536,200	2,943	111	$13,094
Hidalgo	77,728,059	5,616	119	13,840
Willacy	13,312,741	1,052	208	12,654
Total	$129,577,000	9,611	126	$13,482
Percent of Texas total		7%	2.7%	34%	281%

*Estimates of the Bureau of Business Research, University of Texas.
†Apparently taken from U. S. Department of Commerce, Bureau of the Census, *U. S. Census of Agriculture, 1945. Texas.* V. 1, Part 26, Statistics for Counties (Washington: Government Printing Office, 1946), County Table I, part 1, pp. 18–69.
‡*Ibid.*
§Calculated from columns 1 and 2.
A rather tremendous increase in Valley farm income since 1940 can be noted by comparing the above figures with those of the Census Bureau giving the average value per farm of all farm products sold or used by farm households in 1940 and 1945:

	1945	1940
Texas	$2,953	$1,246
Cameron County	5,144	1,567
Hidalgo County	5,314	1,769
Willacy County	4,985	1,477

U. S. Department of Commerce, Bureau of the Census, *op. cit.,* Table IV, pp. 321–345.

With two main ports of entry into Mexico located in the Valley, the tourist trade has added to the income of the Valley business man. Estimates of the Valley Chamber of Commerce place the income from this source at six million dollars for 1949 and the indications are that it will continue to grow. The Valley also benefits from the newly developed agricultural areas just across the border. The close proximity of wholesale sources of supply and the superior mechanical equipment that can be obtained in the United States have encouraged Mexican farmers to buy in the Valley rather than in the interior of their own country, and a substantial

---

[11]Source: The above information is taken, with some modifications, from an undated mimeographed statement entitled *Farm Statistics—Supplemental Page* issued by the Lower Rio Grande Valley Chamber of Commerce. The general sources therein credited are the Bureau of Business Research of The University of Texas and the U. S. Census of Agriculture for 1945. A startling contrast to the Valley is provided by the figures for Starr County as given in this publication where that County is listed as having an average of 553 acres per farm and an average farm income of only $1,006.

proportion of the total wholesale and retail sales of the area are from this source.

In recent years a chemical industry has been developed in the Valley. Three plants for the conversion of natural gas into petroleum and other products have been built near the port of Brownsville with a total investment of over forty-five million dollars.

Canning and food processing plants are numerous and additional units are projected.

The Valley serves as a wholesale center for the surrounding areas on both sides of the border, and retail sales in 1948 were estimated at over $115,000,000, an increase of more than 300% since 1939. The tremendous increase in bank deposits from $15,600,000 in 1939 to almost $128,000,000 in 1949 reflects the prosperity which has come to the Valley in recent years.

Historical Development. If one goes about in the Lower Rio Grande Valley trying to establish definite dates of settlement, two interpretations of his questions become apparent. To one type of informant settlement in the Valley refers to the coming of the Spanish. To another it implies the relatively recent appearance of a varied lot of speculators who came to exploit the economic possibilities inherent in a productive soil and mild climate.

The Spanish occupation of the area dates back to the early part of the 17th century when a few straggling colonists from Mexico were settled there to provide a barrier against the French who were thought to have some designs on the region. This move received both moral and material support from the Catholic Church which was interested in the fact that the sizeable groups of Indians roaming the area had not yet been received into the Christian faith. The early colonists quickly gained a toehold in the area and, although never particularly prosperous, they managed to develop a subsistence type economy, based largely on livestock, which served their major needs, and those of their descendants, until about the beginning of the present century.

With the turn of the century a number of "outsiders," mainly from the north and east, began to appear in the Valley. Some drifted on; others remained to invest money in land and to promote schemes for developing the area as a desirable source of winter crops. Both the climate and the economic promise of the Valley were appealing, and many prosperous northern and midwestern farmers who came to see were convinced and remained to live and to share in the Valley's development. With the completion of the

St. Louis, Brownsville, and Mexican Railroad in 1904, the Valley began to grow rapidly as every run brought prospective settlers from the north with a little money and a large enthusiasm for sharing in the new development. The building of roads and irrigation facilities followed closely the coming of the new settlers, and by 1910 agriculture was flourishing in the Valley.

Many important persons shared in the early development of the area. One of the more important was Thomas Jefferson Hooks who explored the Valley on horseback about 1900 and bought some 25,000 acres of land, some of which he began to cultivate and most of which he devoted to cattle raising. Hooks' success in his enterprises stimulated others to invest. Realizing the value of a railroad to further expansion of the Valley's economy, Hooks and others collectively offered the railroad 200,000 acres of land as an inducement to extend its line from Alice to Brownsville. Hooks himself offered 1,600 acres. The offer was quickly accepted and the line extension built.

During the years immediately following the building of the railroad, a number of land speculators came into the Valley and a considerable number of acres changed hands. A good deal of the land purchased was bought from Spanish-speaking owners. Although the price offered was low, rarely more than a few dollars per acre, the amounts seemed large to the Spanish-speaking owners who were living on a subsistence economy and who, consequently, were not accustomed to dealing in considerable amounts of cash.

The rapid development of the Valley led to the formation of a number of land companies which did a booming business until the depression of the 1930's. Prospective buyers by the hundreds were brought on sightseeing trips to the Valley with all expenses paid.[12] They were wined and dined in royal fashion, exposed to the best that the Valley had to offer and carefully shielded from the worst. The great mansions of the prosperous were opened as showplaces and as examples of what could be done with a few acres of rich Valley soil. Many of those who came to the Valley during this period made sound investments and prospered. Others, however, bought land that proved unsuitable for irrigation, that contained a high salt water table, or that was situated far from any serviceable road. Land prices, of course, were high. As a result the farmers, in order to make a profit on their investment, had to

---

[12] Even as late as the summer of 1949 salesmen living in Austin were offering free air trips to the Valley to prospective buyers of land.

farm their land intensively, not for one crop season a year but all year long.

The nature of the Valley's development has obviously hindered the growth of unity and cohesion among the people in the area. There is little in the way of a pattern or form that may be said to characterize the Valley as a political or social or even economic entity. It is still a mixture of Yankees, Southerners, Midwesterners, and Spanish-speaking Texans, each with their own customs, values, and interests. Any overall unity has been transient and superficial and has generally hinged upon such specialized interests as property or profits. The result has been an individualism that is frequently reflected in the failure of the population to agree on any common issues. There is evidence that this situation has brought difficulties for the least secure elements of the population who have come to feel that their position in the Valley is a purely mechanical one and that their worth lies wholly in their willingness and ability to contribute to the attainment of the twin objectives of the Valley, production and profits.

The People. The Valley is an area of recent rapid population growth. From only 160,000 people in 1930, the population has grown to more than 300,000 in 1950. During the period 1940–1950 the increase was more than 50%. Much of the population growth is represented by an increasing concentration in cities, the urban population having grown nearly 50% faster than the rural during the past ten years.[13]

Perhaps even more significant than the rapid growth and the increasing urbanization is the heterogeneous nature of the Valley's population. For one finds here a differentiation of peoples that would be difficult to duplicate in any other agricultural area of comparable size in the nation. One of the largest of the recognizable divisions is the Spanish-speaking group. With the exception of a few counties in northern New Mexico, there is no place in the country where Spanish is spoken more commonly. But although even the casual visitor to the Valley is immediately struck by the fact that here is a large concentration of natively Spanish-speaking people, no one knows with any considerable accuracy precisely what proportion they are of the population. The standard source of population information, the Bureau of the Census, has done no separate enumeration of them, with the exception of a count of the "Mexican" population in 1930 and a five per cent sample enumeration of mother tongue in 1940.[14] The 1930 tabulation of "Mexican"

---

[13]Nelson and Meyers, *op. cit.*, Table III, p. 14.

population—probably inaccurate because of a tendency to classify all upper and upper middle class people in the "white" category regardless of language spoken or place of national origin and the difficulties of fully enumerating the shifting elements in the Spanish-speaking population—classified more than 50% of the Valley's people as "Mexican." The highest concentration was in Willacy County with 66%; Hidalgo County was listed as having 54% and Cameron just under 50% "Mexican" population.

The 1940 sample tabulations of Spanish mother tongue give no information on the Valley, there being no figures available for political units smaller than states.

Some indication of the present proportion of Spanish-speaking people in the Valley may be obtained from two estimates made in 1949. A U. S. Public Health Service research team, working in the Valley on the general problem of dysentery, went to considerable trouble to get an accurate estimate of the population of Hidalgo County and of the ethnic distribution in that County. They estimated the County population at 150,000 (the 1950 Census count showed 159,994) and the number of Spanish-speaking at 99,500 or approximately 66%. Lyle Saunders, working with the 1948 scholastic census figures and the proportion of Spanish-speaking children in the scholastic population in 1942-43 as counted by Wilson Little,[15] estimated the 1948 population of the Valley as 274,205 and the number of Spanish-speaking as 206,178 or approximately 75%.[16] Whatever the exact proportion, there can be no doubt but that the Spanish-speaking constitute the largest population aggregation in the Valley, and it is also probably true that their number is growing more rapidly than that of any other population group.

---

[14]The Bureau of the Census is intending to make available separate tabulations of the 1950 Census returns for Spanish-speaking people in the Southwest, basing their classification on names. If this is done, there will be, for the first time, something approaching an accurate count of the Spanish-speaking population and much more detailed information on their demographic characteristics than is now anywhere available.

[15]Wilson Little, *Spanish-speaking Children in Texas*. (Austin: University of Texas Press, 1944).

[16]Lyle Saunders, *The Spanish-speaking Population of Texas*. Inter-American Education, Occasional Papers V (Austin: University of Texas Press, December 1949). These estimates do not take into account differentials in birth rate between Spanish-speaking and English-sepaking elements in the population or the presence of a large number of wetbacks who either have no children here or whose children do not get enumerated in the scholastic census. Neither do they allow for the fact that a good many of the English-speaking residents of the Valley are middle aged or elderly people whose children are not living in the Valley. Allowing for these and other factors that might affect the estimates, it is probably safe to conclude that the proportion of Spanish-speaking people in the Valley's population is between 70% and 80%.

In addition to the more numerous English- and Spanish-speaking elements in the Valley's population, there are other sizeable linguistic groups including Italian, German, French, and Japanese. Although here again there are no reliable counts of the size of these groups, cursory examination of the names on rural mail boxes and local telephone directories leads one to conclude that they are fairly large. That the local people are conscious of the numerical importance of these groups was indicated by the repeated cautions made to the authors that the non-Spanish-speaking Valley residents should not be referred to as Anglo, since the group contained substantial numbers of persons speaking a language other than English.

Health and Mortality. One might assume that the high productive efficiency of the Valley would be reflected in a high level of health among the population, since it is generally reckoned that good health, in large part, depends upon the capacity to provide medical personnel and facilities. Such data as are available on the Valley, however, fail to show that this is so. Mortality rates for Hidalgo, Cameron, and Willacy counties, and especially those for the younger age groups, are among the highest in the nation. In 1948, one-seventh of all the dysentery reported for the state of Texas (254 counties) was in Hidalgo and Cameron counties which together include about one-thirtieth of the state's population.[17] And, in addition, the Valley has far more than it proportionate share of tuberculosis, diphtheria, malaria, meningitis, polio, and typhoid.

Unfortunately, data are not available to show the distribution of death and disease among the various elements in the population, but such evidence as is available indicates that the Spanish-speaking population of the Valley, including the wetbacks, have more experience with both than do other segments of the population. The death rate for the Spanish-speaking is undoubtedly higher than that for other groups, although the fact could probably not be documented without extensive and costly research.

In an effort to secure some valid information on the comparative death rates of the Spanish-speaking and other population elements in the Valley, the death certificates for Hildalgo County for 1949 were studied in detail. The results are shown in Table 2.

The total number of deaths among Spanish-speaking in Hidalgo County in 1949 was found to be nearly four times that of the

---

[17]John McCully, "The Spanish-Speaking: North from the Rio Grande," *The Reporter*, 3:25–28, December 26, 1950.

non-Spanish-speaking group. Assuming a two to one population ratio between the two groups (66% Spanish-speaking, 33% non-Spanish-speaking), the death rate among Spanish-speaking is still between one and a half and two times that of the non-Spanish speaking group. Particularly noticeable is the risk of death for children of Spanish-speaking parents. Just less than half (48%) of all Spanish-speaking persons who died in Hidalgo County during 1949 were less than one year old. By comparison, only a little over one-tenth of the non-Spanish-speaking deaths were among those less than a year of age. At the other end of the age scale, only 12% of the deaths in the Spanish-speaking population were among those 65 years of age or over while 53.2% of those dying among the non-Spanish-speaking group had reached or passed the age of 65. Thus, providing these figures represent fairly accurately conditions in the county over a period of years, a

TABLE 2

TOTAL DEATHS BY AGE AT DEATH FOR THE NON-SPANISH-SPEAKING AND SPANISH-SPEAKING POPULATIONS OF HIDALGO COUNTY, 1949

Age Group	Non-Spanish-Speaking			Total Percentage of All Deaths
	Male	Female	Number	
Birth to 1 week	16	10	26	7.1
1 week to 1 year	8	5	13	3.6
1– 4 years	3	0	3	0.8
5–14	3	2	5	1.4
15–34	13	5	18	4.9
35–64	72	34	106	29.0
65 and over	125	70	195	53.2
Totals	240	126	366	100.0

Age Group	Spanish-Speaking			Total Percentage of All Deaths
	Male	Female	Number	
Birth to 1 week	112	73	185	13.4
1 week to 1 year	247	229	476	34.6
1– 4 years	70	88	158	11.5
5–14	17	13	30	2.2
15–34	87	59	146	10.5
35–64	127	91	218	15.8
65 and over	93	72	165	12.0
Totals	753	625	1,378	100.0

Source: Mortality Records, Hidalgo County, 1949.

baby born to Spanish-speaking parents in this part of the Valley has about a 50–50 chance of living beyond the first year, whereas the probability of death for a child born to non-Spanish-speaking parents is about one in ten. Stated another way, there are in Hidalgo County (allowing for the higher proportion of Spanish-speaking people and the probable higher birth rate among this group) not more than three times as many infants among the Spanish-speaking group as in the non-Spanish-speaking, yet the number of infant deaths in the former group in 1949 was *more than sixteen times* that of the latter.

Differences in health and mortality hazards faced by Spanish-speaking and non-Spanish-speaking children in Hidalgo County are also reflected in the data contained in Table 3, which classifies 1949 deaths in the County on the basis of cause. Although it must be admitted that the reporting of deaths, and especially of infant and child deaths, is by no means always based on accurate and detailed diagnosis, there is no reason to doubt that such reporting is sufficiently accurate to depict the general mortality pattern for an area.

The figures in Table 3 indicate the tremendous differences in proper care, sanitary conditions, and medical services available to the children of the two groups. Of all deaths of Spanish-speaking children under five years of age, almost half were the result of dysentery and related diseases which are closely associated with lack of sanitation in food, water, and waste products. Although approximately 39% of all deaths of non-Spanish-speaking children of less than one year of age were from dysentery and related diseases, none from that cause were reported for the group aged from one to four years. Tuberculosis can be seen as a major cause of deaths among the Spanish-speaking population in all age groups but the very youngest, whereas only one death from this cause is reported for the entire non-Spanish-speaking group. For the older people, the causes of death are about the same for both groups; it is the children of the Spanish-speaking group who bear the principal burden of health and mortality risks resulting from the depressed social and economic circumstances under which they live.

TABLE 3
MAJOR CAUSES OF DEATH BY AGE AT DEATH FOR THE NON-SPANISH-SPEAKING AND SPANISH-SPEAKING POPULATIONS OF HIDALGO COUNTY, 1949

Age at Death	Total Deaths in Age Group	Cause of Death (Percentage of all deaths at each age group from the specified cause*)							
		(1)	(3)	(7)	(9)	(11)	(15)	(19)	(22)
Non-Spanish-Speaking Population									
Birth to 1 week	26						100.0		
1 week to 1 year	13		38.8			15.4	7.7	7.7	15.4
1–4 years	3	33.3						33.3	
5–14	5							60.0	
15–34	18				33.3			33.3	
35–64	106			11.3	57.4			6.6	
65 and over	195			11.3	61.5	4.6		3.1	
Spanish-Speaking Population									
Birth to 1 week	185					8.4	64.9		3.8
1 week to 1 year	476		49.2			21.2	3.4		8.8
1–4 years	158		46.2			15.7		7.0	5.1
5–14	30	13.3	6.7			10.0		30.0	
15–34	146	21.9		3.4	7.5			35.6	
35–64	218	17.0		11.5	24.8	3.2		18.8	
65 and over	165	4.9		10.9	40.6	10.3			

Notes: Causes of death accounting for less than 3.0% of all deaths in a given age group have been omitted. 9.6% of all Latin deaths between 15 and 34 were due to homicide. These figures account for over 82% of all Anglo deaths and over 75% of all Latin deaths.

*Key to Cause of Death
1. Tuberculosis.
3. Diarrhea (includes dysentery, enteritis, gastritis, duodenitis, colitis).
7. Cancer.
9. Heart disease (includes vascular lesions affecting central nervous system, chronic heart disease, arteriosclerotic and degenerative heart diseases, hypertension with heart disease, other diseases of the heart, cerebral hemorrhage).
11. Pneumonia and Influenza (includes bronchitis).
15. Birth Injuries and infections (includes congenital malformations, postnatal asphyxia, atelectasis, prematurity).
19. Accidental death.
22. Malnutrition (includes inanition).

Source: Mortality Records, Hidalgo County, 1949

II

Profile of the Wetback

Age, Sex, Marital Status, and Occupation. The most mobile element in any population is usually the young adult group. The Mexican wetback seems to be no exception to this general rule. The wetbacks who come to the Valley are concentrated largely in the ages from 16 to 30, with more in the 20–24 category than in any other.[1] About three out of five of a group of 160 wetbacks interviewed at McAllen were or had been married;[2] about two-fifths of those for whom recorded information was obtained were married at the time of apprehension or had been married in the past.[3] As might be expected, the married group seem to be somewhat older than those who are single, although this group too shows a preponderance in the young adult age categories. A relatively small proportion of the wetbacks are female,[4] and these in general are either children or women who have accompanied their husbands.

Considering the fact that most of the work available to wetbacks in the Valley is in agriculture, it is interesting to note the wide variety of occupations in Mexico from which the wetbacks come. Although the majority of those interviewed were farm operators or farm workers *(ejidatarios* and *jornaleros)*, a good many other types of skilled and semi-skilled work were reported.[5] The fact that many are not familiar with farm work is reflected in frequent statements mady by Valley farmers that the wetbacks are, when

---

[1] See Table 4 and 5. Data for Table 4 were gathered from first hand interviews with wetbacks held in the McAllen Detention Center in July, 1950. No controls were used to assure a representative sample in this group. The information from which Table 5 was compiled was obtained from a random sample of the approximately 380,000 voluntary return cards on file at the Hidalgo, Texas, office of the U. S. Immigration and Naturalization Service. Each of the 478 boxes of record cards was divided into 5, 6, 7, or 8 more or less equal parts (depending on the number of cards in the particular box). Then the second card in each part was selected for tabulation. A total of 3,005 cards was thus selected, of which 2,625 were found to be usable. There is, of course, no practical way to check on the accuracy of the information obtained either through interviews or from the Immigration Service records.

[2] See Table 4.

[3] See Table 6. The discrepancy in this and other tables between data secured by direct interview and that taken from the official records is undoubtedly a reflection of the fact that the latter constitutes a much more representative sample of the wetback group.

[4] See Tables 4 and 7.

[5] See Table 8.

they are first employed, awkward and inefficient in such semi-skilled tasks as picking cotton or working with fruits and vegetables, statements which are often used as justifications of the low wages paid to them.

The heavy dependence of the wetbacks on sources of income other than that obtained from owning or operating farms in Mexico can be seen in Table 9. Judging from the amounts of land reported as being owned or directly operated, most of the wetbacks in this group must devote a considerable portion of their time to working for someone else, either in agriculture or other occupations. And, since most of the land reported as owned or operated

TABLE 4

AGE, SEX, AND MARITAL STATUS OF 160 WETBACKS DEPORTED FROM TEXAS IN 1950

Age Groups	Total		Single		Married		Widowed		Separated	
	Male	Female	Male	Female	Male	Female	Male	Female	Male	Female
0–15	1	----	1	----	----	----	----	----	----	----
16–19	16	3	16	3	----	----	----	----	----	----
20–24	38	5	22	----	15	3	----	1	1	1
25–29	37	2	15	----	22	1	----	1	----	----
30–34	15	1	6	1	9	----	----	----	----	----
35–39	12	1	----	----	11	1	1	----	----	----
40–49	17	3	----	----	17	2	----	1	----	----
50–	8	----	1	----	6	----	----	----	1	----
Age unknown	1	----	----	----	1	----	----	----	----	----
Totals	145	15	61	4	81	7	1	3	2	1

Source: Firsthand interviews with wetbacks held in the McAllen Detention Center, July, 1950.

TABLE 5

AGE DISTRIBUTION, 2,602 WETBACKS RETURNED TO MEXICO THROUGH THE HIDALGO OFFICE OF THE U. S. IMMIGRATION AND NATURALIZATION SERVICE

Age Groups	Number	Percent of Total
0–15	370	14
16–19	401	15
20–24	609	23
25–29	453	17
30–34	235	9
35–39	214	8
40–49	242	9
50–	78	3
Total	2,602	

Source: Records of U. S. Immigration and Naturalization Serivce, Hidalgo, Texas, 1950.

is not irrigated,[6] the areas would seem to be much too small to produce more than a few vegetables or a few kilos of beans or corn for family consumption.

TABLE 6

MARITAL STATUS, 2,351 WETBACKS RETURNED TO MEXICO THROUGH THE HIDALGO OFFICE OF THE U. S. IMMIGRATION AND NATURALIZATION SERVICE

Marital Status	Number	Percent of Total
Married	902	38.37
Single	1,417	60.27
Widowed	32	1.36
Totals	2,351	100.00

Source: Records of the U. S. Immigration and Naturalization Service, Hidalgo, Texas, 1950.

It will be observed that eleven *ejidatarios* or persons operating land portioned out to the people in the form of community grants, were included among the 160 wetbacks interviewed. Unfortunately, it was not possible to learn the size of units operated by these persons on their *ejidos*. Most of them, however, held the opinion that the parcels of land available to them were not large enough to support their families and that it was necessary for them to do supplementary work.

TABLE 7

SEX DISTRIBUTION, 2,562 WETBACKS RETURNED TO MEXICO THROUGH THE HIDALGO OFFICE OF THE U S. IMMIGRATION AND NATURALIZATION SERVICE

Sex	Number	Percent of Total
Male	2,150	83.92
Female	412	16.08
Totals	2,562	100.00

Source: Records of the U. S. Immigration and Naturalization Service, Hidalgo, Texas, 1950.

Place of Origin. In 1930, Manuel Gamio, a distinguished Mexican anthropologist, published the results of an extensive study of Mexican immigration to the United States.[7] Among the more

---

[6]Untabulated interview data.
[7]Manuel Gamio, *Mexican Immigration to the United States* (Chicago: University of Chicago Press, 1930).

striking features of Gamio's study was the finding that these immigrants came largely from deep in the interior of Mexico. Previous to this work the general assumption seems to have been that they came from those states located along the United States-Mexico border.

TABLE 8

USUAL OCCUPATION IN MEXICO OF 160 WETBACKS DEPORTED FROM TEXAS, 1950

Occupation	Males	Females
Jornalero	70	---
Unpaid family worker	4	6
Bricklayer	9	---
Farm operator	8	---
Truck driver	7	---
Carpenter	5	---
Ejidatario*	4	---
Mechanic's apprentice	4	---
Domestic servant	---	4
Miner	3	---
Salesman	3	---
Factory worker	2	1
Helper on a truck	2	---
Weaver	2	---
Welder	2	---
Chauffeur	2	---
Seamstress	---	1
Barber	1	---
Tree grafter	1	---
Railway worker	1	---
Painter	1	---
Wood seller	1	---
Shoemaker	1	---
Miller	1	---
Butcher	1	---
Policeman	1	---
Blacksmith	1	---
Taxi driver	1	---
Waitress	---	1
Tractor driver	1	1
"Repairman"	1	---
No information	5	1
Total	145	15

*It seems probable that some *ejidatarios* were lumped together with the *jornaleros*.

Source: Firsthand interviews with wetbacks held in the McAllen Detention Center, July, 1950.

Information gathered in this study, although limited to the Lower Rio Grande Valley of Texas, substantiates the earlier findings of Dr. Gamio.[8] Although more wetbacks seem to come from

---

[8] See Table 10 and Figure 1.

the border state of Nuevo León than from any other single state, about 65% of the total sample group were from the interior of Mexico.[9] Nearly a third were from the two states of Guanajuato and San Luis Potosí, while Jalisco, Michoacán, Zacatecas, and Durango were also represented by sizeable proportions. Gamio explains the large migrations from Jalsico, Guanajuato, and Michoacán by the fact that conditions there are difficult for agriculture and that the land is largely concentrated in the possession of a few families.[10] To the extent that this explanation holds today, it would also apply to San Luis Potosí and, to a somewhat lesser extent, to Nuevo León.

TABLE 9

NUMBER OF *HECTARES* OF LAND OWNED AND/OR OPERATED IN MEXICO BY 160 WETBACKS DEPORTED FROM TEXAS IN 1950

Number of Hectares	Number of Men* Owning Given Number of Hectares	Number of Men* Operating Given Number of Hectares
None	117	105
One	1	1
Two	1	2
Three	1	3
Four	4	7
Five–nine	---	6
Ten–fourteen	3	4
Fifteen–nineteen	---	1
Twenty–twenty-four	2	1
Twenty-five–twenty-nine	1	1
Thirty–forty	2	---
Ejidatarios	11	11
No information	2	3
Total	160	160
Total *hectares* owned—192		
Total *hectares* operated—180		

*The fifteen women included in this sample are lumped with the men under the category "None."

Source: Firsthand interviews with wetbacks held in the McAllen Detention Center, July, 1950.

About the same distribution of birthplace was found among the 160 wetbacks interviewed in 1950 as among the 2,364 for whom information was obtained from the records of the Immigration

---

[9] Information secured in interviews with 160 wetbacks at the McAllen Detention Center would lead to the belief that a large proportion of those giving their birthplace as Nuevo León come from Monterrey and nearby places which are located a considerable distance from the border.

[10] *Op. cit.*, p. 23.

Figure 1 – States of Origin of 2584 Wetbacks, 1920-50, Sample Study

Service. The majority of these were from Guanajuato, Jalisco, Michoacán, and Nuevo León, and most of them, at the time of the interview, claimed as their residence the state in which they were born.[11] Thus it would seem that, throughout the twenty-year

TABLE 10

STATE OR OTHER PLACE OF BIRTH OF 2,364 WETBACKS RETURNED TO MEXICO THROUGH THE HIDALGO OFFICE OF THE U. S. IMMIGRATION AND NATURALIZATION SERVICE

State or Other Place	Number	Percent of Total
Nuevo León	530	22.3
Guanajuato	430	18.2
San Luis Potosí	328	13.9
Jalisco	198	8.4
Michoacán	182	7.7
Coahuila	177	7.5
Tamaulipas	156	6.6
Zacatecas	119	5.0
Durango	103	4.4
Distrito Federal	36	1.5
Vera Cruz	25	1.1
Aguascalientes	23	1.0
Others	57	2.4
Total	2,364	100.0

Source: Records of the U.S. Immigration and Naturalization Service, Hidalgo, Texas, 1950.

TABLE 11

STATES OF BIRTH AND RESIDENCE OF 154 WETBACKS DEPORTED FROM TEXAS IN 1950

States	Number	States of Birth Percent of Total	Number Residing in Same State as Born in	Percent of Those Born in Each State Residing in Same State
Guanajuato	28	18.2	27	96.4
Jalisco	24	15.6	22	91.7
Michoacán	21	13.6	19	90.5
Nuevo León	17	11.1	17	100.0
Zacatecas	14	9.1	10	71.4
San Luis Potosi	11	7.1	10	90.9
Coahuila	10	6.5	8	80.0
Durango	8	5.2	7	87.5
Other	21	13.6	16	76.2
Total	154	100.0	136	88.3

Source: Firsthand interviews with wetbacks held in the McAllen Detention Center, July, 1950.

[11]See Table 11.

period since Dr. Gamio's study was made, the greatest source of population movement from Mexico to the United States has been the states occupying the central plateau in the interior of Mexico.

Length of Residence in the United States. The transient nature of the wetback's residence in the United States is clearly illustrated in Tables 12 and 13. Of the sample of 2,475 wetbacks on whom information was available, 351 (14.2%) had been in the United States less than five days, and 1,075 (43.5%) had been here less than a month. Of the 153 wetbacks from whom first hand information was obtained, 40 (25%) had been in the United States less than five days and one hundred (63.3%) had been in this country a month or less.[12]

TABLE 12

LENGTH OF TIME SPENT IN THE UNITED STATES BY 2,475 MEXICANS ILLEGALLY ENTERING THE UNITED STATES FROM 1920 TO 1950

Length of Time	Number	Percent of Total
Under one day to four days	351	14.2
Over four days and less than one month	724	29.3
Between one and six months	1,026	41.4
Between six and twelve months	161	6.5
Between one and five years	182	7.3
Between five and ten years	22	0.9
Over ten years	9	0.4
Total	2,475	100.0

Source: Records of the U S. Immigration and Naturalization Service, Hidalgo, Texas, 1950.

TABLE 13

LENGTH OF TIME SPENT IN THE UNITED STATES BY 153 WETBACKS DEPORTED FROM TEXAS IN 1950

Length of Time	Number	Percent of Total
Under one day to four days	40	26.1
Over four days and less than one month	60	39.2
Between one and six months	42	27.5
Between six and twelve months	4	2.6
Over one year	7	4.6
Total	153	100.0

Source: Firsthand interviews with wetbacks held in the McAllen Detention Center, July, 1950.

---

[12]It should be remembered, however, that all our information pertains to wetbacks who had been apprehended by the Immigration Service. How many are not caught and remain here indefinitely, it is impossible to say.

FIGURE 2

Months of Entry into the United States of 2,584 Wetbacks Apprehended in Years 1920 to 1950.

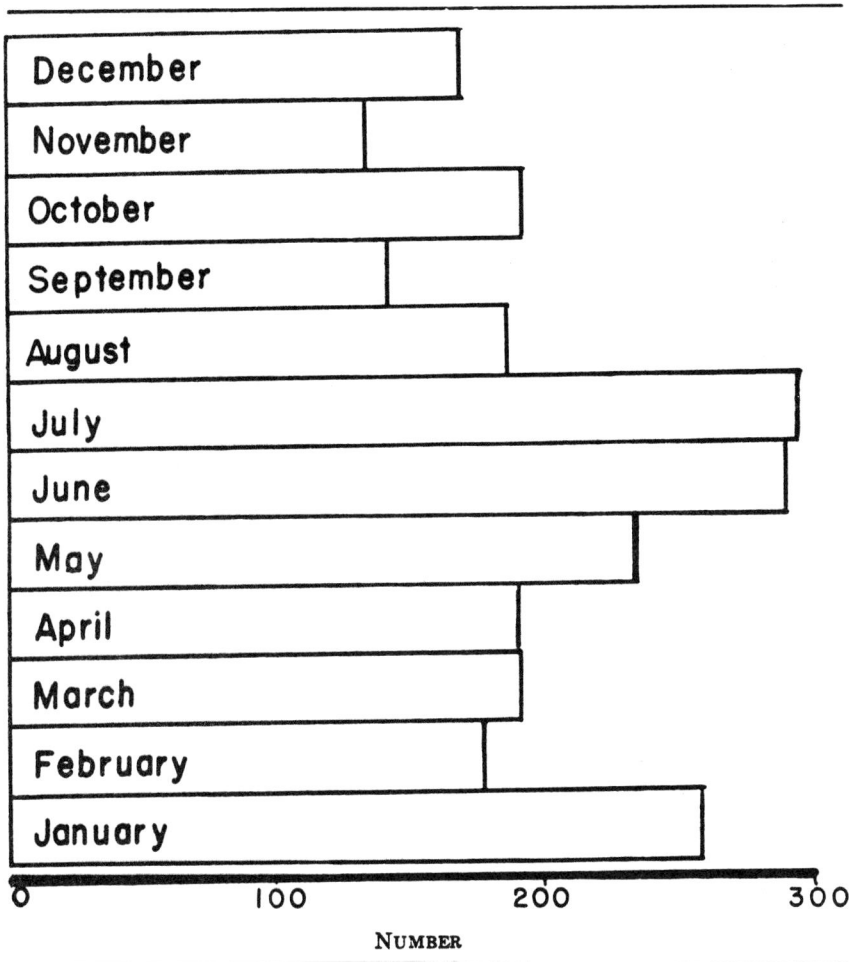

Source: Files of United States Immigration and Naturalization Service.

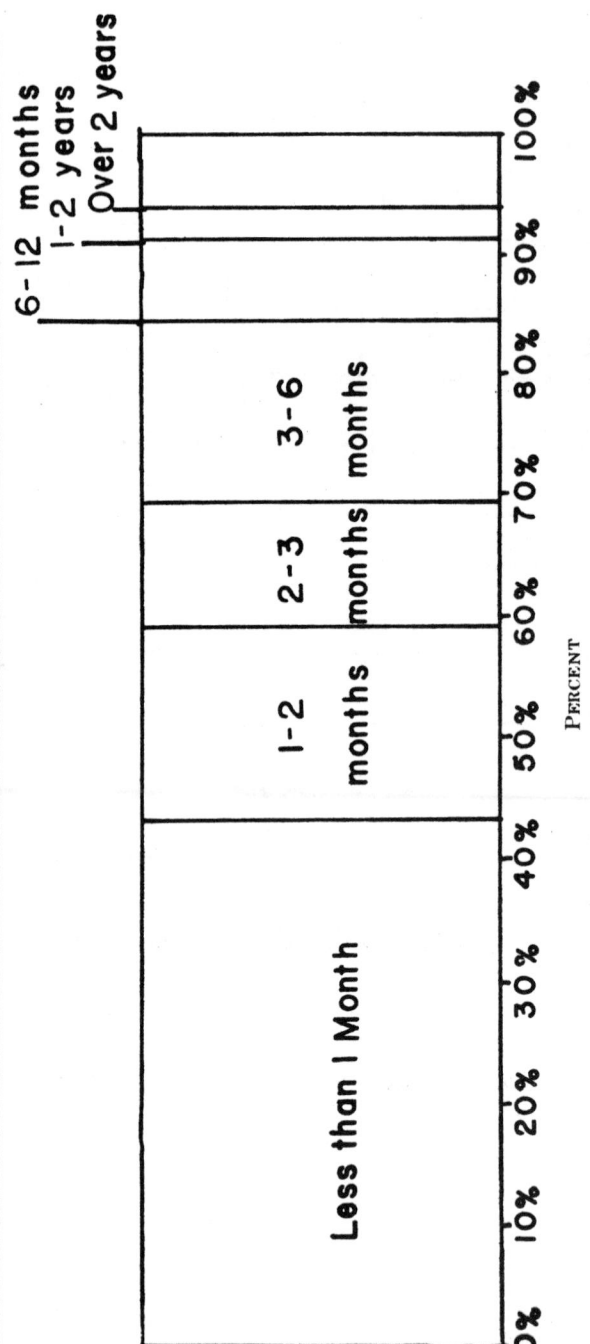

FIGURE 3
Length of Time Spent in the United States by 2,475 Wetbacks Apprehended in Years 1920 to 1950.

Source: Files of United States Immigration and Naturalization Service.

TABLE 14

THE RESPONSES OF 136 WETBACKS DEPORTED FROM TEXAS IN 1950 TO A QUESTION REGARDING THE TIME THEY HAD EXPECTED TO REMAIN IN THE UNITED STATES

Time Expected to Remain	Number	Percent of Total
Only during the cotton harvest	41	30.1
"A few weeks"	23	16.9
"A few months"	51	37.5
A year or more	2	1.5
"As long as possible"	10	7.4
"As long as work lasts"	6	4.4
Long enough to earn a specified amount of money	3	2.2
Total	136	100.0

Note: Twenty of this number expected to re-enter the United States as soon as possible, while 92 stated that they did not expect to re-enter. Twenty-four were undecided.

Source: Firsthand interviews with wetbacks held in the McAllen Detention Center, July, 1950.

TABLE 15

THE RESPONSES OF 160 WETBACKS DEPORTED FROM TEXAS IN 1950 WHEN ASKED (a) WHY THEY HAD COME TO THE UNITED STATES, AND (b) HOW THEY HAD LEARNED OF WORK OPPORTUNITIES IN THE U.S.

Response to (a)	Number	Percent
Little work in Mexico	64	43.5
Better wages in the United States	50	34.0
Adventure, travel, to escape job, wife, etc.	13	8.8
"Poor crops at home"	7	4.8
Seasonal work in Mexico is over	5	3.4
"It's easier to live in the U.S."	4	2.7
To get in the U.S. Army	2	1.4
Husband or father is on contract	2	1.4
Total	147	100.0

Response to (b)	Number	Percent
Word of mouth	116	81.7
Had been to the United States previously	20	14.1
Newspapers	4	2.8
Radio	2	1.4
Total	142	100.0

Note: Of the total sample of 160, 13 failed to reply to question (a) and 18 to question (b).

Source: Firsthand interviews with wetbacks held in the McAllen Detention Center, July, 1950.

Many of the wetbacks, however, remain in the United States for relatively long periods without being picked up by the authorities. Of the larger sample, 213 (8.6%) had lived here a year or more. Nine of them had been here over ten years, and three of these had been here more than twenty years. These numbers would undoubtedly be much larger if it were possible to locate and interview wetbacks who had managed to escape being caught.[13]

It is quite probable that a process similar to the "passing" of Negroes into the white group occurs in the Valley and in other areas where the wetbacks can live among natively Spanish-speaking residents. A wetback newly arrived from Mexico is, of course, quite conspicuous. One who has managed to avoid being caught begins after a time to blend into the human landscape. He learns new social habits and takes on new linguistic ways. His clothing and his mannerisms change subtly. The longer he stays, the more he becomes like the group he lives among. The longer he stays, the harder he is to detect visually, and the greater are his chances of escaping apprehension.

According to the wetbacks' own stories, most of them who enter the United States wish to remain for brief periods only. Of 136 who gave information on the subject, 115 (84.5%) planned to remain only a few weeks or a few months.[14] Since these informants were interviewed during the cotton picking season, it is probable that most of them had come with the intention of remaining only during the harvest season. Furthermore, all of those interviewed were persons who had been apprehended by the Border Patrol and who were somewhat disillusioned about the economic possibilities of the "Magic Valley." Some of them indicated that they intended to re-enter the United States as soon as they could; twenty-four were undecided. The majority, however, claimed that they were not interested in coming back in view of the limited opportunities for earning much and the ever-present possibility of being promptly caught and sent out again.

It is generally assumed that wetbacks come to the United States for the higher wages that they can earn here. Attention is seldom

---

[13]Some indication of how large the number might be can be seen in figures recently released by the Study of Spanish-Speaking People which show that of 16,782 Spanish-speaking residents of Hidalgo County, 31.4% of the total group and 53.8% of that portion of the group 21 years of age and over had been born in Mexico. Since the rate of naturalization and the numbers admitted legally for permanent residence are very low, it is probable that a good proportion of those born in Mexico are former wetbacks who have avoided apprehension.

[14]See Table 14.

directed to the fact that many of them come from overcrowded rural areas of Mexico where available manpower is disproportionately high in relation to its demand. In many sections of rural Mexico little work is to be had during certain seasons. This is particularly true in the states of Michoacán, Jalisco, and Guanajuato.

The push and pull factors in the wetback migration can be seen in Table 15. While slightly more than one-third of the wetbacks interviewed gave "better wages" as their reason for coming to the United States, nearly half reported "little work in Mexico" as their reason for leaving. A few of the others seem to be the adventure seekers and travel lovers that one hears so much about in the Valley.

Since the most commonly given motivation for coming to the Valley seems to be of an economic nature, it might be thought that most of the wetbacks would have definite plans as to how they

TABLE 16

THE RESPONSES OF 160 WETBACKS DEPORTED FROM TEXAS IN 1950 WHEN ASKED: "IF YOU COULD EARN $100 OR MORE IN THE UNITED STATES, WHAT WOULD YOU DO WITH IT?"

Responses	Number	Percent
Buy food, clothes, etc., for family in Mexico	33	20.6
Buy land in Mexico	17	10.7
Send it, or part of it, to relatives in Mexico	16	10.0
Set up a business in Mexico	14	8.9
Buy farm animals in Mexico	11	6.9
Attempt to legalize status in the United States	9	5.6
Buy or make the initial payments on a house in Mexico	8	5.0
Buy food, clothes, etc., for self	8	5.0
Establish an occupation in the United States	7	4.4
Save most of it for future needs	5	3.1
Put it in the bank "to make interest"	5	3.1
Pay debts in Mexico	3	1.9
Buy beer, whiskey, etc.	3	1.9
Don't know	2	1.2
Make improvements on house and land in Mexico	2	1.2
Provide a better education for the children in Mexico	2	1.2
Buy an automobile and take it back to Mexico	2	1.2
Others and those who did not reply	13	8.1
Total	160	100.0

Source: Firsthand interviews with wetbacks held in the McAllen Detention Center, July, 1950.

would spend any money earned in the United States. A good many apparently do, although many of those interviewed were somewhat vague about any proposed expenditures involving anything beyond the acquiring of more or better food, clothing, and shelter for themselves and members of their families.[15] A few, however, had definite plans for buying additional land, acquiring farm animals, or setting themselves up in some sort of small retail business in Mexico. The majority were seeking merely enough money to provide a few more of the immediate necessities for living, while only a small number had any clear ideas about using their earnings to increase their future security in Mexico.

Most of the wetbacks interviewed had heard of work opportunities in the United States through the "grapevine." Twenty had been in the United States in other years and presumably had some fairly clear notion of what conditions were like here. Relatively few had learned of opportunities through the formal channels of communication.

The proportion of wetbacks who were repeaters was high in both samples used. Slightly more than half admitted crossing the river more than once,[16] and some had crossed as many as six times or more. It is quite likely that there is some bias in these answers, although there seems to be no way in which the exact amount could be accurately determined.[17]

Almost all of the wetbacks interviewed had come to the international border by bus or train, paying the required fare out of their meager capital.[18] One of those interviewed claimed to have walked the entire distance; one other hitch-hiked. The wide, arid expanse of land that separates the interior of Mexico from the Rio Grande represents a formidable barrier for any but the most

---

[15] See Table 16.
[16] See Table 17.
[17] No tabulations were made of the information regarding number of illegal entries for the sample for whom information was obtained from the files of the Immigration Service. Observation of the situations in which this information is obtained and recorded led to the conclusion that it is probably highly inaccurate. For the most part, wetbacks admitted to two or three previous crossings when questioned by Inspectors of the Border Patrol. To claim less would result in their not being believed; to admit to more could result in their being held for formal deportation proceedings. Some few records, however, were found in which as many as twenty or more illegal entries were admitted.
[18] See Table 17. Many of these workers had liquidated almost their entire capital in order to buy tickets, and thus arrived at the border without means for securing either food or lodging. Such persons, if apprehended immediately after crossing the river, were frequently in desperate circumstances, facing a police barrier on one side of the river and no work and little opportunity to secure food on the other.

hardy, or perhaps foolhardy, to attempt crossing without transportation.

While the majority of wetbacks interviewed came to the border with friends or relatives, about two out of five reported that they came alone.[19] This, according to their explanation, gave them freedom to move about from one place to another and from job to job. More came with friends than with relatives, although many of the friendships admittedly were established with persons contacted somewhere along the road. Family groups, including frequently some combination of fathers, sons, uncles, nephews, and brothers, were observed to be fairly common, and not infrequently families consisting of husband, wife, and children are apprehended

TABLE 17

THE RESPONSES OF 160 WETBACKS DEPORTED FROM TEXAS IN 1950 WHEN ASKED: (a) THE NUMBER OF TIMES THEY HAD ENTERED THE UNITED STATES; (b) THE MODE OF TRANSPORTATION USED FROM RESIDENCE TO THE INTERNATIONAL BOUNDARY; (c) WHO HAD ACCOMPANIED THEM TO THE BORDER

Responses	*Number*	*Percentage*
Responses to (a)		
Once	69	44.0
Twice	43	27.4
Three times	26	16.6
Four times	9	5.7
Five times	4	2.5
Six times	3	1.9
"Many times"	3	1.9
Total	157	100.0
Responses to (b)		
Bus	82	53.9
Train	58	38.1
Bus and train	7	4.6
Car	2	1.3
Truck	1	0.7
"Hitch-hiked"	1	0.7
On foot	1	0.7
Total	152	100.0
Responses to (c)		
Came with friend(s)	64	41.8
Came with relative(s)	30	19.6
Came alone	59	38.6
Total	153	100.0

Source: Firsthand interviews with wetbacks held in the McAllen Detention Center, July, 1950.

[19] See Table 17.

and sent out. Such family groups usually remained intact even when work for all at the same place became difficult to obtain. The return of entire families, particularly those with children, was often complicated by the fact that the family unit, particularly if it had been here for some time, had acquired dishes, utensils, bedding and other household articles too awkward or too heavy to be easily carried.

The hazards involved in crossing the border at points other than the international bridges are well recognized in the Valley. Almost any week, one can read one or more articles in Valley newspapers describing deaths incurred by wetbacks in the attempt to cross the Rio Grande. Several unidentified bodies are taken from the river each week. So commonplace has this practice become, that only the most cursory inquiries are made into the cause of death or the circumstances surrounding the death. Many of the bodies are never identified, and the cause of death is not always accurately determined. Undoubtedly many of the deaths are from drowning, for the Rio can be treacherous when high and is full of deep holes even when the water is low, but enough probably occur from other causes to give some credence to the stories of violence meted out to returning wetbacks for the purpose of stealing the money they earned in the United States.

TABLE 18

THE RESPONSES OF 157 WETBACKS DEPORTED FROM TEXAS IN 1950 WHEN ASKED HOW THEY HAD CROSSED THE RIVER

Method of Crossing	Number	Percentage
Swam	48	30.6
Waded	81	51.6
Boat or "launcha"	19	12.1
With the aid of an inner tube, tree trunk, etc.	5	3.2
Over the bridge in Laredo with falsified papers	4	2.5
Total	157	100.0

Note: The cost of the trip across by boat was usually 10 pesos; one person paid 8 pesos, three paid 7, four paid 5, and one paid 3 pesos. Ten paid 10 pesos.
Two of those who came across by miscellaneous methods paid nothing, one paid 8 pesos, one paid 10 pesos, and one paid 20 pesos.

Source: Firsthand interviews with wetbacks held in the McAllen Detention Center, July, 1950.

Of the 157 wetbacks who gave information on their method of crossing the river, 129 (82.2%) either swam or waded.[20] Both practices are dangerous because of the unpredictable currents and the many holes in the bed of the stream. The remainder came by the relatively safer methods of rafts, boats, or some lighter-than-water objects such as boards or paper bags filled with air.[21] Since the stream is quite wide at some points and swift at times elsewhere, and since many of the wetbacks are not good swimmers, the wonder is not that so many drown but rather that so many get across safely.

Table 19 provides a limited amount of information on the extent to which the wetback in the Valley remains apart from or participates in the major facets of local life. Almost one-fourth of those interviewed claimed to know no one in the area. On the other hand, only slightly more than one-fourth claimed to know as many as five persons. Even here, a substantial proportion of the "persons known" were employers or foremen with whom relations were generally formal and limited.

Some wetbacks had relatives in the Valley, and thus were often able to establish a fairly well-rounded set of contacts with local people. These relatives were Spanish-speaking, and included local citizens as well as alien Mexicans. Language, of course, was a major barrier to the establishing of either economic or social relationships with the people of the Valley since almost none of the wetbacks interviewed knew any English and perhaps an even smaller proportion of the English-speaking people of the Valley know Spanish.

Evidence secured in the study indicates that most of the wetbacks who enter the United States are interested in remaining only for short periods. Of 152 who replied to questions about where they would prefer to live, 97 (60%) indicated a preference for Mexico.[22] That the choice is of an emotional rather than a rational nature is indicated by the fact that almost half of the 97 gave as their reason for preferring Mexico the simple explanation that "it is my country." Mexico for this group provides an environment with which they are familiar and to which they know how to respond. Mexico is a place in which they are socially comfortable.

---

[20]See Table 18.
[21]The common practice of those who cross in fairly deep water is to tie their clothing into a bundle which is then carried on the head. This leaves hands and feet free for swimming or propelling a raft or other conveyance and the clothes get only slightly wet.
[22]See Table 20.

This is a point that is frequently overlooked by many persons in the Valley who are genuinely interested in improving inter-group relations in the local situation. Many fail to understand that the wetback, when he arrives in the Valley, is in an environment with which he is not familiar, and that he may easily violate customs, modes of behavior, or regulations which he does not fully understand and frequently cannot learn about because of his inability to communicate with those who do not speak his language.

TABLE 19

TABULATION OF THE RESPONSES OF EACH OF 160 WETBACKS TO THE REQUEST FOR THE NAME, RELATIONSHIP, NATIONALITY, AND LANGUAGE OF FIVE PERSONS (OTHER THAN IMMEDIATE FAMILY) WHOM HE KNOWS BEST IN THE UNITED STATES

Number indicating that they knew no one in the U. S.	39
Number indicating that they knew only 1 person in the U. S.	33
Number indicating that they knew only 2 persons in the U. S.	23
Number indicating that they knew only 3 persons in the U. S.	13
Number indicating that they knew only 4 persons in the U. S.	10
Number indicating that they knew five persons in the U. S.	42
Total	160

Relationships

	Person #1	Person #2	Person #3	Person #4	Person #5
Friend	59	48	39	36	25
Employer	34	24	16	7	8
Relative	25	12	7	4	4
Priest	---	1	---	---	---
No information	3	3	3	5	5
Total	121	88	65	52	42

Nationality

	Person #1	Person #2	Person #3	Person #4	Person #5
U. S.	66	51	38	28	25
Mexican	54	37	27	22	15
No information	1	---	---	2	2
Total	121	88	65	52	42

Languages

	Person #1	Person #2	Person #3	Person #4	Person #5
English	17	9	7	4	2
Spanish	103	77	57	46	39
Italian	---	1	---	---	---
No information	1	1	1	2	1
Total	121	88	65	52	42

Source: Firsthand interviews with wetbacks held in the McAllen Detention Center, July, 1950.

It is perhaps revealing to note that only one wetback preferred the United States because "I like the people here." Here is negative evidence of the deep underlying current of misunderstanding, frustration, and even covert conflict and animosity that flows beneath any large-scale contact of the "foreign" Mexican with the "efficient and practical" Anglo, even though the situation is such that on the surface such relationships appear placid and unruffled.

TABLE 20

THE RESPONSES OF 160 WETBACKS WHEN ASKED WHETHER THEY WOULD PREFER TO LIVE IN THE U. S. OR MEXICO AND WHY

Would prefer Mexico	97
"Because it is my country—"mi tierra"	45
"There are many difficulties in the U. S."	11
Because of family and friends in Mexico	29
"There's little work and it's too expensive to live in the U. S."	5
"One may live peacefully in Mexico"	2
"Mexico is higher, cooler, prettier"	1
"Living is just as good in Mexico"	1
No reasons given	3
Would prefer the United States	55
"More work, better living"	28
"I like the life in the U. S."	7
"The U. S. has a just government, protects workers, provides better education"	5
"It costs less work to live here"	5
"One can live well and dress well"	2
"Steady work is possible"	1
"I like the people here"	1
No reason given	6
Undecided or no preference given	8
Total	160

Source: Firsthand interviews with wetbacks held in the McAllen Detention Center, July, 1950.

III

The Problem of the Wetback in the Valley

The problems created or augmented by the large numbers of wetbacks who pour into the Valley each year[1] are many and have numerous ramifications. Some of them are major problems; others are relatively insignificant. A few of the broad areas affected by the presence of wetbacks are touched upon in this section.

Economic Effects. The economic consequences of the wetbacks' role in the Valley are generally complex, although some of them are much more tangible and measureable than others. Clearly, one of the more obvious is the effect on profits in agriculture. Since labor in agriculture, as well as in other types of industry, constitutes the major production cost, large agricultural units, of which there are many in the Valley, can reduce production costs tremendously through the use of an accessible, adequate, and tractable supply of labor willing to work at low wages.[2] Unfortunately, there is no fully satisfactory means of calculating such savings or gains in the Valley for an entire year because of the varied types of work involved and the lack of detailed records kept by farmers with respect to the amounts of labor used during the various seasons. A consideration of cotton production, however, indicates something of the potential. During the summer of 1950, the approximate differential in the amount paid for picking 100 pounds of cotton in the Valley and elsewhere in Texas was from one dollar to a dollar and a half. This means an increased return of from $15 to $22 on each bale of cotton. If the minimum

---

[1] In the period July 1, 1949–June 30, 1950, the Border Patrol apprehended 221,418 aliens in the McAllen sector alone. The McAllen sector extends roughly from Brownsville to Roma.

[2] The President's Commission on Migratory Labor found that an inverse relationship exists between the number of wetbacks and Mexican contract workers in an area and the wage rate. In a comparison of cotton picking rates in California and Texas in 1945 and 1949, the Commission reported that in the latter year "Texas, with its large supply of wetback and contract labor, reduced its wages 11 per cent; California, with little contract labor and a relatively smaller wetback saturation, raised its wages 15 per cent." The conclusion of the Commission was that in agriculture "foreign labor has detrimentally affected the wages of domestic labor." *Migratory Labor in American Agriculture. Report of the President's Commission on Migratory Labor* (Washington: U. S. Government Printing Office, 1951), pp. 58–59.

differential is used as a basis for calculation and the 1950 production of the Valley estimated at 350,000 bales,[3] the saving for cotton picking alone can be figured at $5,250,000. Even for the small grower who produces only fifty bales a year, the saving on labor costs may amount to as much as $1,000.

The same situation exists in other areas of both agricultural and nonagricultural employment. The prevailing hourly wage paid to wetbacks in the Valley is 25c, a wage that has become highly standardized. The minimum acceptable to local citizen labor is 40c per hour.[4] No complicated calculations are necessary to demonstrate the financial gain accruing to those who use large numbers of wetbacks. For the Valley as a whole, the figure must be tremendously large.

It should be kept in mind that there are also economic advantages in the employment of wetback labor other than that derived from low wage rates. In some kinds of employment no strict accounting of hours need be kept since the employee is paid by the day,[5] which may involve as much as twelve hours of work. There is little or no responsibility for injury or accident, since the wetback is an alien who is here illegally and who came presumably at his own risk. No effort was made in this study to evaluate the economic advantages resulting from this situation, but its exploitive possibilities can hardly be overlooked. Furthermore, the employer is under no compulsion, legal or otherwise, to provide his employees with health, medical, or sanitary facilities or even decent housing. What the wetback receives, including the amount of wages paid, is largely determined by the employer's conscience and the opinions of similarly situated friends and neighbors.[6] The alternative facing the wetback who refuses to accept a given set of conditions is either

---

[3] More than 540,000 bales of cotton were produced in the Valley in 1949. Acreage and production were both down in 1950, but the figure of 350,000 bales probably represents a conservative estimate.

[4] In the summer of 1950 skilled construction workers—carpenters, plumbers, painters—were being employed in the Valley at wages of from 50c to $1.00 an hour. Unskilled workers were in some instances receiving as little as 30c an hour, even though working at jobs in which the legal minimum is 75c. Extensive documentation of agricultural wage rates as low as 20c an hour will be found in the stenographic report of the Brownsville hearings of the President's Commission on Migratory Labor.

[5] $2.00 and $2.50 were figures frequently reported by those working by the day in the summer of 1950.

[6] It should be pointed out that it is extremely difficult for any single employer, however altruistic he may be, to extend economic benefits to wetbacks greater than those generally given by all employers. To do so would not only be to be placed in a disadvantageous position in the competitive struggle, but also to be subject to strong pressures to conform exerted by relatives, friends, and business associates.

to remain unemployed, which he cannot long afford, or face deportation.

Fruit and vegetable packing plants—of which there are over 300 in the Valley—are able, by virtue of a special ruling which classes them with agriculture, to hire wetbacks without regard to the provisions of the Federal minimum wage law. Thus, these plants are able to recruit the bulk of their labor at rates ranging from 25c to 40c per hour[7] instead of the 75c per hour required under the Federal law. Again there is no way in which the saving to the Valley through this means can be calculated, but if the average difference were only 25c per hour, the total would be a sizeable one for the thousands of workers who are employed in the packing plants for several months of the year.

An indirect effect which the wetbacks' presence in the Valley has upon local wages and salaries can be seen in the wage rates for clerical and skilled labor, particularly those of native Spanish-speaking citizens.[8] The amount of this saving too would be difficult to measure precisely, but some idea of its magnitude can be gained from comparing wage rates for skilled or clerical workers in the Valley with those in other parts of the state.

The implications of a competing, cheap source of labor for the local labor force were vividly revealed in testimony given by witnesses appearing before members of the President's Commission on Migratory Labor in Brownsville during the latter part of July, 1950. Individual workers, members of labor organizations, and union officials repeatedly and sometimes vehemently pointed out the deleterious effects for them of the presence in the area of a throng of wetbacks willing to work for almost any wage.

One of the more serious by-products of the presence of wetbacks in the Valley is the huge annual migration of local citizen workers to other parts of Texas and other areas in the United States. Local explanations of this migration, based largely on the assumptions

---

[7]The Executive Manager of the Texas Citrus and Vegetable Growers and Shippers, Assn., in testimony before the House Committee on Education and Labor early in 1949 stated that "Our wage scale in the packing house runs from 40 to 65 cents per hour. In the vegetable sheds where more roustabout, or trucking, or common labor type is needed, approximately 60% of the labor draws 40 cents an hour." U. S. House of Representatives, *Hearings Before the Committee on Education and Labor, House of Representatives, Eighty-First Congress, First Session on H. R. 2033* . . . (Washington: U. S. Govt. Printing Office, 1949) vol. I, p. 626.

[8]Craft union officials in the Valley say that wage rates there are considerably under those in many other parts of Texas. And an employee of the Texas Employment Commission, who makes many referrals for skilled, semi-skilled, and clerical jobs pointed out to the authors that Spanish-speaking people are consistently paid less for comparable jobs than are Anglos.

that the local Spanish-speaking citizens "like to travel" and "refuse to work in local agriculture," lose considerable weight, however, in the light of knowledge that many of the workers travel over the same routes each year (and thus see nothing new) and that a majority of those who leave continue in agricultural jobs. The logical explanation, and the one given by many local people, is the wage differential—they simply earn more money elsewhere for the same type and amount of work. Although the full extent of the seasonal migration is not known, it has reached such proportions that one does not find in the fields during the summer months any considerable numbers of local workers, and those who are there are largely women, children, and others who for one reason or another are not able to leave.[9] It is perhaps significant that the migration comes at the time when, according to Nelson and Meyers,[10] the Valley is moving towards its peak demand for agricultural workers.

Social Effects. Many social effects of the wetback labor supply in the Valley are becoming visible. They are frequently overlooked, however, in evaluating the situation. No attempt is made here to analyze the range of social consequences produced by the wetback, but a few of the more prominent aspects can be pointed out.

The social isolation in which the wetback coming into the Valley lives is not difficult to perceive. Anticipating only a brief stay in the area, he is not interested in constructive participation in the life of the community into which he comes. He has no interest in or intention of establishing himself there, and, therefore, is not concerned about his own behavior, except to see that it meets the minimum requirements of his employer and enables him to work without serious interruption. His real concern is centered in Mexico where his family lives and to which he expects to return as soon as he has accumulated enough money. He establishes few or no intimate ties of friendship—except occasionally with other wetbacks—and has human contacts only with the group with whom he works and lives and with the employer or foreman who hires him. As a result of his position, his contribution to a community is more likely to be negative than positive. In other words, to the extent

---

[9] A random check of fourteen fields located in the vicinity of Raymondville in July, 1950, and including a total of some 700 workers, showed only seven out of every hundred workers were citizens and that far more than half of these were women or children. An unpublished survey made by the Study of Spanish-Speaking People in 1948 and 1949 revealed that about 8,000 out of a total of slightly more than 16,000 Spanish-speaking residents of Hidalgo County migrated northward one or more times during a two-year period.

[10] *Op. cit.,* p. 29.

that he does not become an integrated element in the local life, he is likely to behave in a way that will serve to increase the problems of the community, especially in the field of minor crimes and delinquencies. And, since the wetback is often identified with the Spanish-speaking citizen population, the latter suffers any stigma resulting from such behavior.

The impact of a large number of wetback children—and the migration of citizen children resulting from the presence of wetback competition for their fathers' jobs—upon the public school system is obviously great.[11] The problem is probably less serious in the small rural schools, since the numbers involved are smaller, but even here the presence of wetbacks and their effect on the behavior patterns of citizens raises serious administrative problems. Enrollments are unpredictable. A school may have few or no children when school opens and be overcrowded several months later. Attendance is irregular. The health of children is frequently poor; their rate of learning is consequently retarded. Disciplinary problems are intensified. The difficulties of teaching the English language are increased. School facilities and services are required for children whose parents pay no taxes for the upkeep of schools. School supplies, especially books, are lost when wetback children are suddenly returned to Mexico.

The school problem is rendered particularly acute in some areas by the fact that throughout the Valley the Spanish-speaking and English-speaking elements in the population live in separate areas. Wetbacks, when they live in town, tend to live in the Spanish-speaking sections. The result is a concentration of wetback children in those schools attended predominantly by Spanish-speaking children. Their presence is undoubtedly an important element in the fact that some of these schools in recent years have at times been so crowded that they have had to operate in two shifts.

Another way in which the wetback migration is influencing education in the Valley is in its effect on the Spanish-speaking children who leave the Valley each spring and summer and return in the fall after the school term has begun. Many of the children involved in this migration are able to attend school only for a few months out

---

[11]The average daily attendance of all children in the three counties of the Valley in 1949–50 was 57.2 per cent of those enrolled. In the common school d'stricts of all three counties it was less than 50; in Hidalgo common school districts it was 28. For trends in selected years since 1935, see Nelson and Meyers, *op. cit.*, Table IV, p. 15. These figures are for larger areas and do not reflect the fact that average daily attendance is probably much lower in schools attended by Spanish-speaking children than in those whose students are mainly children of English-speaking parents.

of each year. Their school progress is thus retarded, and often from two to three years is required for a child to complete a single grade. Soon the chronological age of the child is out of line with his grade status, and many drop out in preference to remaining in class with a group much younger than themselves.[12]

Since the Catholic Church is relatively strong in the Valley, the religious needs of the wetback, who is almost always Catholic, are perhaps more nearly met than are others of his social needs. Church leaders, however, do not always have the means for getting in touch with the wetbacks, and it is quite probable that many of the illegal aliens are not as closely related to the Church here as are citizens or as they perhaps would be in Mexico. Special efforts have been made, particularly by the Bishops' Committee on the Spanish-speaking, to provide for the religious needs of wetbacks, but because of the great mobility of the wetback group, the task is a most difficult one.

Observations throughout the Valley lead to the conclusion that there are practically no recreation facilities available to wetbacks other than the numerous small *cantinas* and cabarets that seem to spring up near the centers of any wetback concentration. Since the migrants are largely men, there is a Saturday and Sunday influx of wetbacks into the border towns on the Mexican side, where a wide variety of entertainment is provided at almost any level of cost to the consumer.[13] One result is an increase in the incidence of venereal and other contagious diseases in the Valley. There are no precise data available on the extent to which disease in the Valley results from this practice, but anyone who has observed the Saturday night activities in a border town could hardly escape the conclusion that it is considerable.

---

[12]The direct and indirect effects of the presence of wetbacks on the educational attainments of the Spanish-speaking population of the Valley are sharply revealed in unpublished survey figures of the Study of Spanish-Speaking People based on data gathered by the U. S. Public Health Service from 16,782 residents of nine towns in Hidalgo County. According to these tabulations, 53.0% of the group had no schooling; 79.8% had four years or less; 89.4% had six years or less. Of that portion of the group who were 21 years of age and over, and who, therefore, might be expected to have completed their schooling, 44.7% had not been to school; 77.8% had completed four years or less; 2.1% had completed high school and only 0.2% had ever attended college. It is interesting to note that 68.0% of those over 21 who had had no schooling were born in Mexico. Many of them are undoubtedly wetbacks.

[13]There is a considerable illegal traffic across the river on every week end during the summer, particularly in areas near such large towns as Matamoros and Reynosa which specialize in the provision of entertainment for unattached males.

Health. Little information is available on the health of the wetback as a separate group in the Valley. One can be certain, however, that the medical or other health services available to him on either side of the river are quite limited. Serious cases of illness are sometimes handled by local health organizations, although there seems to be a tendency to deport such cases as quickly as possible. The employer group, of course, has no legal responsibility toward the workers who are not citizens. The policy of the Mexican government has been to insist that workers under contract receive protection from the effects of illness or injury, but it is doubtful if the policy has had much effect on the condition of the wetback. One frequently hears in the Valley that some employers of large numbers of agricultural workers furnish certain medical facilities to their workers in mild cases of illness, but no precise information is available on the extent to which this is the practice. For every employer who so provides for the health of his workers, there are probably several who do not. During the summer of 1950, the authors heard a good many accounts, pro and con, about the health conditions among and services available to wetbacks. They ranged from the quite callous account of one farmer who playfully chased a wetback with a tractor, crushed his foot, and then turned him over to the Immigration Service for return to Mexico, to the humanitarian behavior of an employer who paid medical bills averaging two hundred or more dollars each month for the care of his wetback employees.

On the whole, the health conditions of the wetbacks are probably not good. Poor housing, a lack of sanitary facilities, improper and inadequate food, and few or no medical services probably combine to produce in the wetback group a state of health that results in their contributing far more than their proportionate share to the generally poor health picture of the entire Spanish-speaking group.

The situation seems to be one in which a minimum of health services for wetbacks are available; in which officials of both public and private agencies and organizations are trying to stretch their services and facilities to the point where they will meet the needs of citizens; and, in which, judging from the high mortality rate among local children, their efforts are not conspicuously successful. Funds available in the Valley for health services are apparently inadequate to care for citizen needs, and when these funds are diverted, even in part, to meet the needs of aliens, the result is the condition which now exists—poor health for a large segment of the population and one of the highest infant mortality rates in the nation.[14]

Political Effects. The extensive and highly profitable nature of agricultural operations in the Valley has been one factor in the development of a strong economic and political block, which is becoming increasingly effective. Through commercial associations of packers, canners, farmers, shippers, and other organizations there can be presented a united front against any challenge to the local economic structure. Several factors have operated to increase the power of this group far out of proportion to its numerical strength in the Valley. One of these is the financial position of members of the group; another is its isolation from similar and competing areas. It is probable that the general public of the United States and even much of the population of Texas is not much aware of the conditions which exist in the Valley or of the problems involved in the relatively unchecked migration of illegal aliens.[15] And it is likely that even many of those who are aware of the situation still see it as of no concern to the whole of Texas or the United States. These factors, and the absence of any sustained or organized interest in the problems of the Valley, either from local groups or those representing larger areas, have made it fairly easy for Valley political forces to keep the situation well under control and to resist successfully the few efforts that have been made to deal with the wetback problem in that area.

---

[14]"If you ask me, the cause of a good deal of the polio and dysentery in the Valley is wetback children. If a wetback child gets sick, it doesn't get to a doctor; and if it dies, it is put in a box and taken out in an orchard and buried without anybody knowing about it but the family. People say the wetbacks don't have polio because they don't ever hear about a wetback sick with it, but that is not because they don't have it, but because it doesn't get into the records." Comment of a Border Patrol Inspector, June 20, 1950.

[15]The recent report of the President's Commission on Migratory Labor, an article in *Time* for the week of April 9, 1951, and a series of five articles by Gladwin Hill in the New York *Times*, March 25-29, 1951, are, however, indication of an increasing national interest in the Valley.

IV

The Wetback in the Valley

Once he has crossed the river, the wetback faces an uncertain future. What will happen to him is largely dependent on the kinds of people he comes in contact with and what their attitudes towards him are. If he is very lucky, he will meet an employer who will hire him at wages much higher than he could earn in Mexico. He will work for a few months, regularly sending a share of his earnings to relatives or friends on the other side. And, in time, he will return to his own country, where he may live for six or eight months on his accumulated savings. If he is very unlucky, he will be apprehended almost immediately by U. S. Border Patrol Inspectors and taken to one of their detention stations in the Valley. There he will be detained for a day, questioned, written up on official forms, and finally sent to Edinburg, where he will remain in the county jail until the next session of the District Court in Brownsville. There, if his bad luck holds, he may be sentenced to from sixty days to a year in a federal prison.[1] If, on the other hand, his luck is average, he will work a little while, earn a little money, enter into limited relationships with local citizens, and ultimately be permitted to return voluntarily to Mexico, neither much better nor much worse off for his experiences.

There are, in broad terms, four categories of people with whom the wetback is likely to come in contact. They are: employers, native Spanish-speaking people, Anglos in general, and public officials. That is to say that the kind of relationships established with any one on this side of the river and the kind of treatment received by the wetback from any individual or group on this side will be determined largely by two sets of factors: the ethnic affiliation of the person or group with whom he interacts (i.e., whether they are "white" or "Mexican") and the nature of the relationships entered into (e.g., employer-employee, immigration official-alien; landlord-renter; storekeeper-customer, etc.). These four broad categories are not mutually exclusive, nor are they the only possible ones which might be used in describing the roles and

---

[1]His luck would have to be almost incredibly bad if he did not receive a suspension of sentence.

relationships of wetbacks in the Valley, but they do have the advantage of separating out groups of people whose attitudes towards and relationships with wetback differ in ways that can be both readily observed and easily described.

Relations with Employers. The immediate objective of the wetback once he is in the United States is to find a job. How quickly he succeeds, what kind of job he is able to get, and how much he is paid depends on his own aptitudes, interests, or skills; the existing labor situation; the season of the year; and a number of other factors over which he has little control. There are quite a number of possibilities open to him. He may work in town or on farms, alone or in groups, on tasks requiring considerable skills or those demanding muscles only. In the summer he picks cotton; in the winter he harvests citrus fruits and vegetables or works with them in packing and canning sheds. Between seasons he may be employed to maintain orchards, to irrigate land, or to prepare fields for the next crop. At all times he can find work as a cook, yardboy, dishwasher, or as a railway or construction worker. He may, if he has the necessary skills, become a painter, a carpenter, an electrician, or a truck or tractor driver.

Between the employer and the wetback there is at least one bond of common interest. The employer wants work done, usually at the lowest possible price. The wetback wants an opportunity to earn money. This common interest forms the basis for a relationship from which both benefit. The employer finds in the wetbacks an abundant and flexible supply of cheap, willing labor for which he need assume no responsibility other than to pay for it. The wetback finds in the employer a source of income, sometimes, but not always, greater than he could earn in Mexico.

There is no formal channel through which the wetback finds his way to the employer's factory or fields. Field offices of the Texas Employment Commission will accept applications from wetbacks and make referrals to jobs, but seldom are asked to do so. For the most part, wetbacks seeking agricultural employment approach the farmers where they find them, whether along the roads, in the towns, or in the fields. Farmers who need a supply of workers quickly may drive a truck along the river roads and either wait until wetbacks come along or patrol the roads in search of them.

Sometimes the task of recruiting workers is given to truckers who nearly always are natively Spanish-speaking citizens. The truckers are particularly active during the cotton picking and fruit and vegetable harvesting seasons. For cotton, the farmer arranges with a trucker to pick his fields, the two fixing a price at which it will be done, i.e. the price per hundred weight. The trucker then recruits the workers, transports them to and from the field, weighs and hauls the cotton, and keeps records of the amount each worker picks. For this he receives 50c a hundred pounds[2] which is deducted from the amount paid by the farmer. The balance goes to the worker. This year (1950) there has been a widespread tendency to eliminate the trucker from the cotton picking picture. Farmers have recruited their own workers and have used trailers of their own or trailers borrowed from gins to haul the cotton. The resulting saving, if any, has not gone to the pickers in the form of higher prices for their work.

A certain minimum of housing and services are provided the wetback hired to do agricultural work. He must have a place to sleep; he must have food to eat and water to drink. If he has no money, credit is extended to him until such time as he can pay. Shelter of a sort is usually furnished the worker, although in harvest seasons when the number of wetbacks is large, many of them live in the open.

Shelters vary in quality from one farm to another, but generally provide nothing beyond the bare minimum. The most common type is a single room shack, seldom larger than 8' x 10' or 10' x 12'. The better ones are constructed of eight or ten inch planks nailed on to a 2 x 4 frame. The rare new or nearly new ones may be painted. Most are old, weatherbeaten, dark, and draughty. There may or may not be a plank floor; in most cases there is not. Many of the shacks are built of palm fronds; others are thrown together from parts of old packing cases, scraps of tin or galvanized roofing, pieces of brush, or whatever else may be handy. Some few growers supply tents during the harvest seasons. A few provide large open sheds which serve as dormitories. Most of the shacks have a single door and a single window, both unscreened. Some have no windows. There is rarely much furniture. Cooking is done over an open fire kindled in a tub, bucket, or pan which has been filled with ashes. Clothes are hung on nails driven into the walls. The floor serves as chair, table, and bed. Some of the larger growers who use wetbacks the entire year provide somewhat better living quarters, but even the "better" furnishings seldom include more than a small, portable kerosene stove; a few orange crates nailed to the wall to serve as

---

[2]This price may vary a little from time to time, but it seems to be highly standardized.

shelves; a table; a chair or two; and, perhaps, a battered iron cot, without mattress.

The density of wetbacks per room is generally high. It is seldom less than three per room and may be many more. Sometimes individual families are given shacks, sometimes not. One shack on a farm visited by the authors held two women and five men; another one woman and four men. In another lived a woman and five children. One of the children, a daughter of 13, spoke good English and had just finished the sixth grade in the local school. On another farm we saw a one-room shelter containing two beds. In this one room lived three women and eight men. These observations could easily be duplicated in almost any part of the Valley.

No brief description could adequately portray wetback housing in the Valley. There is too much variety, too many small yet important differences. But it can be said that, judged by any standard of health and decency, wetback housing is inadequate. Materials and construction vary; furnishings may be different from one shack to another; but it can be said without exaggeration that almost all are small, bare, dark, untidy, under-furnished, and overcrowded.

The water supply of the wetback constitutes one of his most omni-present hazards of contagion and disease. Most of it comes from ditches and canals—the same ditches and canals in which he and others bathe, swim, wash clothes, and dump their waste. It is drunk directly from the canal or carried to the shelter in old pots, cans, or cooking utensils.

Privies for the wetback are the exception rather than the rule. Men, women, and children simply retire into the brush.

Food, clothing, and such other necessities as may be required are usually purchased from a commissary or store operated by the grower or from traveling peddlers who visit the wetback camps regularly. Sometimes the truckers either bring out the supplies or transport the wetbacks into towns to make their purchases. In any case prices paid under these conditions are likely to be considerably higher than those charged local residents for the same commodities.

Credit is frequently necessary, since the wetback is likely to arrive with little or no money. If credit is extended, an additional charge is frequently made. Periods for payment are short, usually not more than a week. If the credit is given by the grower, the amount of the debt will be deducted from the wetback's pay. If an account is owed a store, it usually must be paid at the end of the week before another week's credit will be granted. The credit system in the Valley frequently serves to reduce seriously the small amount of cash that the wetback earns. Under the system he starts in debt and can remain so unless his earnings are more than enough to retire his last week's obligations. Some of the creditors lose money on the system occasionally when wetbacks who are in debt are picked up by the Immigration Inspectors or voluntarily return to Mexico. But the system as a whole seems to be profitable. The proprietor of a small store west of Mission remarked that, "Wetbacks come with nothing and we give them credit to help them through the first week before they can get paid. Then they pay their bill and don't have enough left to carry them through the next week, so we give credit for that. As a result, a running account, usually paid every Saturday, is established. Sometimes when a wetback leaves or is deported, he forgets to pay his account. Sometimes he comes back later and pays it. Sometimes we have to charge it off as a bad debt."

A few of the larger Valley employers make some provision for recreation for their wetbacks; others give limited medical care. A farm near McAllen had a couple of battered pool tables. Some of the commissaries provide juke boxes and pin ball machines. A large cotton producer was reliably reported to have paid a doctor bill of more than $200 a month for services rendered his employees and an additional sum for the care of two or three women who gave birth to children during the 1950 cotton season. On the other hand, it can hardly be doubted that most employers are little concerned with the health or welfare of their workers. It is likely that for each owner who is genuinely interested in the health of his wetbacks another can be found who refuses to accept any financial responsibility for them. In the newspapers, from the files of public agencies, and from the lips of reliable local residents one can find stories such as the one of the Japanese farmer near Rio Grande City who had his bracero contract abrogated because he "pistol-whipped" one of his workers. One hears too of a wetback, "an old man," who was picked up on a road near McAllen and brought to the detention center. He was ill and was taken to a hospital where he died a few hours later. The *Valley Monitor* reported that a contributory cause of his death was malnutrition.

The wetback who finds agricultural employment in the Valley frequently does not have an enviable lot, even in terms of local standards. His hours are long, his wages low. He is likely to be employed on a piece-work basis, picking cotton or harvesting fruits or vegetables. On such a job he may lose many hours waiting for good working conditions or in going from one field to another. His work day may vary in length from eight to twelve hours. His time is completely at the disposal of the employer. His productivity, hour for hour, is probably less than that of citizen laborers, but he will work longer and more steadily than citizens. He is usually afraid to protest against working conditions and will accept fairly low wages without comment. He seldom bargains for his services, but accepts the rates offered by the employer. He can make few demands on his employer. It is a common belief among those familiar with working conditions in the Valley that it is the wetback's docility, even more than the low wages he work for, that makes him so attractive as a worker. At least it can be stated with assurance that the illegal status of the wetback in the United States provides a powerful club that can be brandished over his head at any time. And, it is not difficult for an employer to see that a recalcitrant wetback is rapidly deported to Mexico.

For a ten or twelve hour day, the wetback who is regularly employed in agriculture will ordinarily receive about $2.50, but may receive as little as $2.00. Some, working in the Mission area, reported earnings as low as $1.50, although this wage was not verified. A few truck or tractor drivers in that area were reported to receive $3.00. If he picks cotton, he receives $1.25 per hundred pounds (1950 rate), or rarely $1.50 a hundred pounds. The same price is paid (1950) for repeat pickings as for the first time over the field. An average wetback can pick 200 or 250 pounds a day, which means that if he works full-time seven days a week, his maximum earnings are about $26.25. Few actually earn more than a fraction of this amount. Most of the wetbacks interviewed had earned just about enough to pay for their food.

At a meeting of the local citrus workers' union in Mission on July 11, it was reported that 75c a hundred was being paid for picking cotton in the Mission area at that time. Other reports were received of $1.00 being paid in that area. A letter received by the Border Patrol on July 12, signed by a Spanish-speaking citizen, claimed that he had applied for and been refused work at _____'s place, between Mission and McAllen, because "we can get more workers than we can use for 20c an hour." One wetback, an inexperienced picker, worked three days in the cotton fields before being picked up by the Border Patrol and earned only enough to pay for the food he had eaten. A father, mother, and two children interviewed at the McAllen detention center July 12 said that they had all worked for four days and had received a total of $6.50. A good many who gave themselves up to the Border Patrol said they wanted to go back to Mexico because they could not earn enough here.

The International Agreement between the governments of Mexico and the United States, dated August 1, 1949, and providing for a program of contract labor to be supplied by Mexico, had little effect on the Valley. Local farmers were not much in favor of a contract arrangement, and there were a number of provisions in the International Agreement which they did not like. Some examples include: the requirement that recruiting be done in cities back from the border, the necessity of providing a bond guaranteeing the return of the worker to Mexico, the agreement to pay 40c an hour even to "inexperienced" workers, the payment of travel costs by the employers, and a stipulation that no contract could be of less than four months duration (changed by special agreement beginning January 1, 1950, permitting Valley farmers, for a period of 90 days, to make six-weeks contracts). Under the terms of this agreement wetbacks illegally in the Valley could have their stay legalized at a processing center established in Harlingen, provided their families returned voluntarily to Mexico. A number of workers were so legalized; many others continued to work without benefit of contract.

The participation of Valley growers in the contract arrangement was not great. *The Valley Evening News* reported on January 18, 1950, that Valley farmers would not contract braceros at recruiting points in Mexico, and would accept contract wetbacks processed here only. The U. S. Employment Service reported that by March 20, requests for only 1,500 braceros to be recruited in Monterrey had been received from Valley farmers. An official of the Texsun Citrus Exchange at Weslaco wrote on April 17 that only 415 employers in the Valley had contracted braceros during 1949 and that this number included quite a few packers and canners, so that the number of growers using contract labor must have been considerably less.[3] The small effect of the bracero program on wetbacks can be seen in the fact that between July 1, 1949, and June 30, 1950, a period during most of which the bracero agreement was in effect, more than 220,000 wetbacks were returned to Mexico by the Border Patrol from the McAllen sector alone (Roma to Brownsville).

Probably the largest single source of non-agricultural employment for wetbacks is in the packing and canning sheds, located

---

[3]There were in 1945 about 10,000 farms in the Valley.

mainly along the highway from Mission to Harlingen. During the peak of the vegetable and fruit harvest seasons many thousands of workers are employed in these plants, a good proportion of whom are wetbacks. A number of employers are said to prefer wetbacks in their plants because they are easier to handle and make no complaints about the wages paid them. Others apparently hire whoever comes along, making no inquiry about citizenship. We found no one who expressed preference for citizen labor.

The Citrus Cannery Workers and Food Processors Union, AFL, which has been attempting to organize packing sheds and canneries in the Valley, is much concerned about the preference of employers for wetbacks. The secretary of the union, speaking at a union meeting at Weslaco on July 13, 1950, reported talking that day to a man who had driven more than 500 miles seeking work but who had repeatedly been told that he could not be hired because he was a citizen. Members of the union present spoke of having had similar experiences. One reported that he had gone to a plant at Weslaco some time earlier to apply for work. The foreman, he said, picked out a portion of the waiting group to be hired and dismissed the others. The union member (who was among those selected for work) walked up to the foreman and asked, "How much are you paying?" He was told to "get the hell out of here; we don't want any smart .... who want to know how much we're paying." Another member told of being in the same plant when a foreman separated out all the citizens from the aliens, then dismissed the citizens and put the aliens to work.

An organizer for the AFL, who has been working in the Valley for four years, feels that plant officials, whenever possible, refuse to employ local labor. The local plants in and around Raymondville employ wetbacks, he said, as do the cotton gins there. He cited a total of some several hundred jobs that are being filled by wetbacks, including janitors in schools, other city and county laborers, workers for the International Boundary Commission, and employees of water districts.

There is a widespread feeling among union members and officials that the Border Patrol co-operates with packers and canners to facilitate the employment of wetbacks. It is unlikely that there is much real foundation for the belief, except possibly in isolated instances, but it continues to be strong local opinion. The AFL organizer, for example, thinks the patrol tips off the canneries before a "raid," for he has noted that when he turns in a list of employed wetbacks to the Patrol, there is a period of about a day before any investigation is made and then some signal is usually given which enables the wetbacks to hide before the Patrol Inspectors can get to them. Similar reports are given by union members and officials in other parts of the Valley.[4]

Certainly employers do, at times, help wetbacks escape the Border Patrol. The treasurer of the Citrus Workers' Union at McAllen spoke of one plant at Raymondville that had a concealed opening in the floor through which the wetbacks could escape if the Patrol approached. In other places, he said, workers, with the knowledge and sometimes the co-operation of the employers, hide behind machinery, in lofts, under tables, or anywhere they are likely not to be found. In one plant this same informant stated that Patrol Inspectors called to pick up three aliens who had been reported as working there, and the employer informed them that the aliens were gone although they were actually in the shed at the time. Under existing law there is no penalty for harboring or concealing an illegal alien. Thus employers take no risk in helping employees escape.

A good many of the jobs in packing sheds and canneries (especially the latter) are covered by the provision of the Social Security Act. For these jobs workers need social security cards,[5] and are entitled to have established a social security account to which both laborers and employers contribute. Those responsible for administering the Social Security Act are not authorized to inquire into citizenship, but must set up an account for any employee, alien or citizen, whose job is covered by the Act. Consequently, many wetbacks in the Valley have social security cards or social security accounts set up for them. Some, according to local Social Security officials, have several cards and several accounts as a result of their working under different names at different times. Social security payments can be made to aliens living abroad, but apparently few wetbacks ever get any return on the contributions they make, since they seldom work long enough to become eligible for benefits or, if they do, they do not know how to apply for them.

Even so, the wetbacks complicate greatly the administration of the Social Security program. The seasonal nature of their employment, the rapid turnover, the use of various names by the same person, the failure by many aliens to make application for social

---

[4]Our personal obeservation of the work of Patrol Inspectors did not reveal any examples of this type of co-operation between Patrol Inspectors and the local growers.

[5]The cards are merely a convenience to facilitate bookkeeping; actually social security accounts may be set up without them.

security numbers—all add to the work of the Administration and increase its cost far out of proportion to the relatively small number of wetbacks involved.

Canneries and juicing plants come under the provisions of the Federal Wage and Hour Law[6] which calls for a minimum wage of 75c an hour. Many of the canneries undoubtedly pay this minimum, but there are current stories and rumors that others find ways of evading it. One union official described a popular method of evading this law by paying in cash by the day and keeping incomplete records. Several persons informed us that some plants required their wetback workers to sign receipts for wages of 75c an hour but actually paid them only 40c.[7]

Union officials have been fairly successful in organizing the packing and canning sheds. An official of the AFL claims that about 35% of the packing and canning employees of Mission and about 75% of those of Donna and Elsa are organized. The union has won NLRB elections in four or five plants and during the summer of 1950 was negotiating its first contract with a shed in Donna. Several other contracts were to be negotiated when the plants open in the fall.[8]

The investigators were told by a number of persons that the unions admit wetbacks as well as citizen labor, and preliminary checks show that there is some truth in the story. The vice-president of a Mission local said that a few aliens had been admitted to the union in Mission. He thought some of them joined because they felt that union membership would somehow permit them to remain in the Valley. According to his story, the wetbacks were told that the union did not want them, could not help legalize their status, and that after paying their membership fees and due they might still be apprehended at any time and sent back to Mexico. If, after hearing this, they still wanted to join, they were accepted. The secretary of a Valley union said that as far as he knew, there were no recent wetbacks in the union, but that a number of non-citizens

---

[6] Packing sheds, for some reason classified as agricultural, are generally exempt.

[7] Most of the Valley's plants were shut down during the summer months the authors spent in the Valley so that there was no opportunity to verify the existence of this practice.

[8] A recent (February, 1950) NLRB election at the Texsun plant at Weslaco was declared invalid in July because of interference by company officials and a new election ordered held. Union officials claim local police patrolled inside the plant grounds on the day of the election and that on the morning of that day a straw vote was taken using ballots printed by the company. This vote, it was claimed, was not secret, and each employee was required to fill out his ballot and hand it open to an official of the company, who then read it.

of long residence had been admitted. An AFL organizer for the Valley, stated that most of the few aliens who wanted to join were former members of labor unions in Mexico, who were likely to have somewhat radical views, and who were not looked upon as assets to the union here.

Aside from the packing sheds, there are many sources of non-agricultural employment open to wetbacks. Cafes employ them as cooks, waiters, and dishwashers; laundries employ the girls, as do tortilla factories; filling stations use them to wash cars; a good many of them find work on construction jobs, either as unskilled helpers or as skilled mechanics. One painting contractor informed the authors that wetbacks frequently are hired for painting and other construction in McAllen and other Valley cities for both skilled and unskilled work. The wage rate for citizen mechanics is $1.75 an hour, we were told, while wetbacks who are employed as skilled mechanics are sometimes paid as much as $1.00 an hour but generally less. Unskilled wetbacks received 30c to 50c an hour.

The minimum legal wage is 75c an hour, but, according to this informant, employers may, and sometimes do, evade the law by paying 30c or 50c and having the employee sign a receipt for 75c. He cited the case of one contractor who took the job of building a local apartment on a cost-plus basis. He was able to receive reimbursement at the rate of $1.75 and $1.00 an hour for skilled and unskilled labor, respectively, but he used wetback labor at the rate of $1.25 and 50c an hour and pocketed the difference. The competition of wetbacks is so great in construction work, our informant said, "that a white man just can't earn a living here." He has been in the Valley 15 years, but says that the competition is now so tough that he plans to move.

Some corroboration of the points of view expressed by this contractor-informant was obtained through information supplied by wetbacks. An example includes three aliens found working on a construction job on Ivy Street in McAllen. One was a painter, another a carpenter, and the third a carpenter's helper. The painter informed us that he was receiving $4.00 for an eight-hour day; the carpenter said he was paid $6.00 for eight hours; and the helper said he got $3.00 for an eight-hour day. Others working for unlicensed contractors frequently receive no more than $2.50 for eight hours of work.

Evidence collected in the Valley shows conclusively that the minimum wage law is often violated there. Extensive investigations in this phase of the study revealed that laborers in the Valley, including both local and foreign, are much more likely to work for less than 75c an hour than to receive that much or more.

Although no systematic check was made of this, it is probable that a majority of business establishments of any size in the Valley, as well as many private residences, employ wetbacks in one capacity or another. The manager of a motel at which our group stayed for a time said that eleven were working at the lumber yard next door (at which he was also employed) and that almost all business houses in the immediate area used them. He himself kept one to irrigate the motel lawn. He spoke of the yard man at one of the more lavish homes of the Valley who, he said, was operating a sort of wetback hotel on the family's farm and who could supply workers at any time and in about any number.

For the employer or prospective employer the wetback is an established source of labor. Whatever needs doing, there is always a wetback to do it, and cheaply. It may not always be done well. A local woman who operates a farm told of a wetback who was sent out to plow her cotton field, but who innocently plowed up her cotton instead. However, if one can supervise their work, most jobs can be and many are satisfactorily done by wetbacks.

Relations with Local Spanish-speaking People. There is a certain amount of integration of the wetback and the local Spanish-speaking population—an integration that is facilitated by the fact that the two groups speak a common language, have many other cultural traits in common, and the fact that they are generally thought of as constituting a single group by the English-speaking people of the Valley. In a strange land where the dominant customs and language are different from those of his own country, the wetback finds it easier to establish contacts with those most like himself. He does his shopping in the "Mexican"[9] section of town. If he lives in town he occupies a rented shack on the back of a lot owned by a Spanish-speaking family. He turns to Spanish-speaking truckers for employment, patronizes *cantinas* and pool halls in the "Mexican" area, and attends social affairs and *bailes* with the Spanish-speaking people. He may even court or marry the daughter of a Spanish-speaking family. It is in the "Mexican" areas, nearly always separate from "Anglo" areas in the Valley, that he lives; it is there that he establishes whatever portion of normal, everyday, human relations he achieves.

[9] The term "Mexican" is frequently used in the Valley as a somewhat derogatory expression to designate any Spanish-speaking person, regardless of national origin, who works with his hands.

The native Spanish-speaking people of the Valley generally resent the presence of the wetback. They seldom, however, feel any particular rancor towards wetbacks as individuals. They will exploit them economically if the opportunity arises; and, on the other hand, they will offer them shelter or food or other assistance if necessary. As one Spanish-speaking citizen said, "They are people like us, members of the same race, and we want to help them if we can." This undoubtedly expresses the general feeling of the local Spanish-speaking people of the Valley toward the wetback even if his presence has caused them considerable financial and social loss.

Businessmen in the Spanish-speaking centers derive considerable economic benefit from the business of the wetback. One of them frankly stated that he liked having wetbacks around because of their influence on business. In his own words, "The more there are around here, the more business I do." This group, however, is in the minority and its opinions would, by no means, represent those of all the local Spanish-speaking population.

The economic contribution of the wetback to the Valley is complex and many-sided. Many local Spanish-speaking people derive substantial incomes from renting to wetbacks shacks they have built on the back of the lots where they live. Such places may rent for $3.00 or more a week, and a single family may rent as many as four or more, thus substantially adding to its income. Local truckers frequently earn sizeable incomes from the wetbacks by providing them with jobs and transportation, by selling them food and clothing, and by hauling the cotton they pick. Stories are widespread that many truckers charge the wetbacks excessive prices for goods, give them short weights on the cotton they pick, and underpay them for harvesting cotton, fruits, and vegetables. It is these and similar practices, which many of the Spanish-speaking people will admit go on, that give substance to the often-heard assertion of the English-speaking group that, "Their own people are the ones who really exploit them."

Some of the local professional people take advantage of the wetbacks by charging excessive prices for professional services. One wetback, picked up by the Border Patrol in McAllen, proudly displayed a receipt for aid in completing a form for suspension of deportation request. He had given a local Spanish-speaking lawyer $80 for it. The form is a simple one, and any Immigration Service employee or Patrol Inspector will help complete them without charge. Birth or baptismal certificates of local deceased citizens frequently find their way into the hands of wetbacks who use them, when questioned by the Border Patrol, to substantiate false claims to citizenship. Some of these papers are undoubtedly sold by Spanish-speaking people; others are given to wetback relatives, friends, or acquaintances. One girl to whom we talked at the McAllen detention center had the baptismal certificate of her cousin who had been born in McAllen and had died in infancy.

By no means all of the relations between local Spanish-speaking people and wetbacks are exploitive. Some of the citizens go to considerable trouble to aid individual wetbacks. A business man who operates a small store in a community a little west of Mission is perhaps typical of this group. Not only does he extend easy credit to wetbacks, but he also has a number of shacks on a large lot east of his home which he loans or rents to wetbacks, depending on whether or not they have funds. In addition, he engages in many other activities which bring him no immediate profit. He has, for example, helped a good many wetback couples living in consensual unions to marry legally in order that their children may enjoy citizenship rights. He persuades wetbacks to put their children in school and keep them there. Frequently he expends considerable effort and time to procure midwives to assist wetback women in childbirth. At some expense to himself he has helped a number of wetbacks legalize their status here.

Quite a few complaints are received by officers of the Border Patrol from Spanish-speaking people who want particular wetbacks picked up and returned to Mexico. In most cases the motive seems to be jealousy or friction between women living too close together. When the complaint involves women, it often carries the charge that the woman is noisy, quarrelsome, and entertains men in her shack. Most of these complaints are investigated by Patrol Inspectors who find, in many cases, that the person against whom the complaint is made is a citizen or an alien legally here.

Another class of complaint received by the McAllen Border Patrol unit from local Spanish-speaking citizens involves charges that wetbacks have replaced local people in jobs. On July 6, 1950, for example, two Spanish-speaking women came to the McAllen detention center to complain of working conditions in a gin near Pharr. Their husbands had been employed there, they said, but had been replaced by wetbacks. According to the women, all of the new employees of the gin were wetbacks. It was observed that this complaint was not written up in the Patrol record book and a check made during the next few days failed to reveal that the incident had been investigated.

On July 12, 1950, the following note, written in Spanish and signed by a citizen, was received at the McAllen detention center. The translation is as follows:

Gentlemen, Immigration Inspectors at the bridge;
I wish to tell you and to make known to you of a ranch located at *tirlo* route on the street where the office of Mr. _____ is. To the south side there is an entrance. This entrance leads us to where there is a bunch of "wet" people. There are about 90 in men and women. Even the gardeners of the _____'s are "wetbacks."
This report I make because I went there to look for work and they refused me (and) said they had too many people willing to work for 20 cents an hour. Go at 6 pm or later so you will get them all.

This complaint was not investigated.[10]

The local Spanish-speaking people are obviously aware of their disadvantaged economic position as a result of competition with the wetbacks. They speak frequently, and sometimes bitterly, about the low wages that they are offered; the number of times they are refused work because they are citizens; the necessity they have for going north during a part of the year because of their inability to obtain work in the Valley at wages on which they can live; and the educational handicaps placed on their children as a result of this migration, which, for many, starts before school is out in the spring and ends long after it has started in the fall. Many of them are also aware of the effect of their migration on workers in other parts of the country. One tells of an experience he had in Oregon where he went to pick fruit one summer. Asked there why so many Spanish-speaking people were coming, he answered, "We have no choice; we must live and we cannot compete with the wetbacks." "But," protested the Oregonians, "you are doing the same things to us that the wetbacks are doing to you." "And they were right," the Valley man said; "but what can we do?"

"We know the wetback has nothing in Mexico," many Spanish-speaking people told us, "and we would like to help them. But it is not fair for them to come here and take jobs at wages so low that we can't compete with them." One citizen, a young veteran, told us of his brother-in-law who had lost his house through inability to pay taxes when he could find no work in the Valley. The same story —that local Spanish-speaking people are not paid enough to enable

---

[10]"If wetback bankers and mayors and lawyers and doctors started coming over and taking the jobs of the ones here, we'd soon see an end to this coming of wetbacks. But as long as only our jobs are taken, nobody seems to care about it." Statement of a Spanish-speaking union official in Mission, July 13, 1950.

them to keep up with their taxes—was related by a Spanish-speaking employee of the U. S. Public Health Service and many others. And yet many of the local governmental units—counties, towns, the Boundary Commission, the Water Districts, etc.—do hire wetbacks in jobs that could be filled by local Spanish-speaking citizens if the wages were only a little higher.

Relations with Anglos. The wetback, for the most part, must rely for jobs on the English-speaking citizens, the economically, socially, and politically dominant group in the Valley. They are, to a larger extent than any other group, responsible for conditions in the Valley. They own the bulk of the land and most of the businesses; they hold the important political offices; they make up the staffs of governmental agencies. Many of them want wetbacks and are determined to keep them coming. And, unless something should happen to change local political control, they probably can.

There is a definite pattern of uniformity in the attitudes of English-speaking people towards wetbacks of the Valley.[11] An elaborate system of rationalizations has been built up to explain why they are needed and why they are present. And, so often are these rationalizations heard that a good many of the English-speaking group firmly believe them. Almost any Anglo that one talks to in the Valley can discourse at length on the characteristics of "Meskins" and why they are and must remain an inferior race. The indisputable evidence most frequently offered for these conclusions is that the "Anglo" has lived here many years and has had innumerable opportunities to know "Mexicans" intimately.[12]

The myth of the Mexican, as told by Anglos to each other and to outsiders, varies somewhat in details, but is usually consistent in theme. At one extreme it holds that the "Mexican" is somehow biologically inferior and is simply not capable of absorbing a highly complex civilization. A somewhat more widely held view is that he is an irresponsible child who must be looked after and protected by his wiser and presumably more responsible fellowmen. At no time does the prevalent stereotype elevate the Spanish-speaking person to the status of a responsible, adult human being capable of looking after his own interests.

The belief of many Anglos that they know and understand the characteristics of "Mexicans" underlies and supports many of the

---

[11] And by extension toward local Spanish-speaking people.
[12] This is the same tendency on the part of a dominant group to feel that it understands a minority people that was noted by Gunnar Myrdal in relations between whites and Negroes in the South. See Gunnar Myrdal, *An American Dilemma* (New York: Harper and Brothers, 1944), pp. 657–659.

attitudes and practices affecting the Spanish-speaking population of the Valley, both wetback and citizen. It enables the rationalization of the raw, sometimes vicious, sometimes paternal exploitation of wetback labor with the statement that "they never had it so good in Mexico"; it justifies the hiring of aliens in preference to citizens with the explanation that local citizens won't do agricultural work. It minimizes the often difficult position of the wetback by calling attention to great opportunities he enjoys there that presumably are not available to him in Mexico. It justifies the $2.00 and $2.50 a day wetbacks are paid in the Valley by comparing them to the five or ten pesos they might earn daily at home. It lends credence to the feeling that "A Mexican who has become Americanized is ruined"—meaning that he then wants adequate wages, decent working conditions, and other privileges enjoyed by American citizens. It provides a reason for residential, recreational, and other types of segregation, and at the same time allows the admission to the select society of the "whites" of a few Spanish-speaking citizens whose membership in old families, business skills, economic standing, or ability to compete successfully are such as to make it difficult to group them with the wetback or "the lower class Meskins."

The complete story of the development of Valley attitudes toward the wetback and the association of those attitudes with the native Spanish-speaking population would be long and difficult. Something of their general nature, however, can be depicted in an account of three fairly typical interviews on the matter in the Valley.[13]

The first was with a Valley politician, a current member of the Texas legislature. His statement was as follows:

The local situation is not so bad. It works out to just about the best advantage of everyone. The farmers need labor; the wetbacks need work; and the local Spanish-speaking people have a gypsy spirit which makes them want to travel. They just can't resist going north each year, and it is fortunate that there are wetbacks around to take their place. Then, too, the local Spanish-speaking people are tending to leave agriculture. They don't like the hard work. They are beginning to want to get white collar jobs. A few of them are going to school where they are being trained for non-agricultural work. So again, it is a good thing there are wetbacks around.

Relations in the Valley between English-speaking and Spanish-speaking people are good. The people eat together and visit together. They don't intermarry much. Although there is no discrimination in the Valley, of course there is segregation in a few

---

[13]These are not verbatim accounts, but rather summarized reports of points of view expressed in interviews lasting from one to three hours.

things, but that is for hygienic, not racial reasons. Spanish-speaking people live in their own part of town and have their own businesses. They prefer it that way. They are excluded from swimming pools and barber shops. The exclusion from pools is because it is not possible to tell the clean ones from the dirty, so we just keep them all out.[14] We just can't have all those dirty, possibly diseased people swimming with our wives and children. Recently a group of Mexicans here working on food-handling jobs were found to be suffering from syphilis. One had a leg that was just a mass of sores. Mexicans are excluded from barber shops because of the fact that 80% of them have lice in their hair or scalp diseases.

Another resident whose attitudes reveal other aspects of the local stereotype of the Spanish-speaking group is quoted at length below. He is an employee of the Texas Employment Commission and has a Master's degree awarded on the basis of a thesis written on education in Mexico. This academic work and the fact that he had lived for 35 years in the Valley gave him, he thought, deep insight into the "nature" of the local people.

The Mexicans are creatures of impulse. They don't think with the cold, hard-headed logic of Anglos, but always act hastily in accordance with emotions and without considering consequences. Mentally they are all children. Oh, there are a few exceptions, of course, but I am talking about the lower class Mexicans. They have behind them five hundred years of burden bearing and animal-like living and just can't adjust to civilization in the way a white man does. They are extremely lazy and won't work, even for 50 or 60 cents an hour. The City of Edinburg has to hire wetbacks because it can't get citizens who will work steadily on the job. All the governmental agencies have to hire them (wetbacks) if they want to get any work done. Good Mexicans, however, are the best people in the world. They are hard working, docile, and very loyal. One of them will do anything for you. But the majority aren't worth much.

Mexican children don't get any training and they are allowed to do just about what they please. I've seen them in public places, doctors' offices, bus stations, and the like, where I wanted to get up and smack them one—kicking their parents, yelling, tearing things up, and the parents sitting calmly letting them do it. By the time they are twelve they all carry knives. They'll cut up anybody. They're just creatures of impulse. Human life doesn't mean a thing to them. Of course they're all cowards. Even a Mexican's dog won't attack a white man. By the time they're grown up something happens to them. They develop a strong loyalty to their family. If a man has six or seven kids working, he takes their pay and sits in the shade all day claiming he is 'seek.' That's what a Mexican lives for—to get a bunch of kids that he can put to work so that

---

[14]In reply to a question, the informant said that dirty Anglos are also excluded, implying apparently that one can separate dirty from clean Anglos, but not dirty from clean Mexicans.

when they are ten or twelve he can retire. A grown man, even if he's married, has to ask his father's permission to do anything. And anyone of them is likely to quit a good job at any time just to come back and be with his family. They have no sense of responsibility. I (Texas Employment Commission) got twelve Edinburg boys jobs in a Boeing plant in California during the war. None of them had ever made $10 a week in his life before, and at Boeing they were paid $300 a month. But in a couple of months they were all back. Just because their mother got a cold or somebody in the family died they quit a good job and came running home.

The working class of Mexicans are all dirty. And they have a smell, a peculiar Mexican smell. Sometimes I have to back away from this counter they smell so bad. It hurts my nose if I stay close. It is a different smell from that of dirty Anglos or Negroes. It's a sort of sour, acid smell. A Negro, now, smells like a goat, but the Mexicans smell even worse. About 80% of them have lice in their hair, the women especially. They believe that lice help them have babies, and the one thing a Mexican woman lives for is to please her husband by presenting him with a baby every ten or eleven months. One of the main forms of recreation of Mexican women, especially those who live on farms or in small towns where there isn't much to do, is to sit around picking lice out of each other's hair. Sometimes when a Mexican woman is brought into the hospital at Edinburg, her friends or relatives smuggle in some lice to replace those the nurses take out of her hair when they clean her up.

Mexicans don't want to learn English and don't want their kids to know it. They keep the kids in school until they reach the third grade and then yank them out and put them to work. If a family has enough of them working, the father can retire and take things easy. They ought to be forced to learn English. We ought to have a law saying no one could work unless he learned English. Of course, those that do know English aren't much better off. They don't get any better jobs than the others.

Around here Mexicans get paid about 20% lower than whites for the same kind of work. They just have no sense of responsibility and can't do good work. They have to be supervised all the time. Housemaids get $10–$12 a week for about 48 hours. Some women pay less. And they have to watch the Mexicans all the time to see that the work is done right. Good Anglo secretaries get about $150–$250 a month; the average is around $167. Good Mexican secretaries, even those who have the advantage of being bilingual, get $100–$150. The difference lies in the fact that the Mexican girls just aren't capable of holding the better jobs.

A third illustration of the attitude of Valley Anglos towards "Mexicans" (whether alien or citizen) is a report of a conversation with a Valley farmer, a man who has owned a large acreage located west of Mission. Our research group had been his guests at dinner and afterwards we were discussing the perennial topic of conversation in the Valley—the wetbacks. Our host began:

The wetback comes into the Valley because the local people won't work. They're all inherently lazy and they just can't be persuaded to work, especially in agriculture. They lack initiative and ambition; they are content to go north and earn some money during the summer and then return here and live on it the rest of the year. They've been spoiled by too many advantages; too many welfare, educational and other services. If you give a man something for nothing, you ruin him. And the local Mexicans know they can get services whether they work or not. As soon as you begin to Americanize a Mexican he's no longer any good. He just won't work any more.

Why is it, we asked, that all the people we see doing hard work in the Valley are Mexicans?

That's town work, he said, yard work, filling station work, construction work and stuff like that.

But hard work, we asked, it is hard work, isn't it?

Yes, but for that they get six or eight dollars a day.

Would they work in agriculture for six or eight dollars a day? They might.

What *would* they work for in agriculture?

I don't think they'd work at any wage.

Would they work for, say, $15 a day?

Yes.

Ten dollars a day?

Yes.

Eight dollars a day?

Yes, they would.

Five dollars a day?

No.

Then they would work if the wages were from five to eight dollars a day?

No, they won't work in agriculture. We had a few working on our farm. They wouldn't do an honest day's work. When we leased the farm, the man we leased to had to let them go and get wetbacks. Wetbacks are good workers. We get a lot of them. Some of them have been with us for years. There are a couple of places on our farm where they cross over. They come by the hundreds. They've worn a sort of road up from the river. They come in a pitiful condition, with nothing, and we give them work at good wages, much better than they'd get in Mexico. I've got four boys working on my farm who have been with me for five years. Their home is about forty miles across the border and they go back every once in a while. But they always return. They're clearing a bit of land for themselves there. They're hard-working boys. And very dependable. One time their father came over. He told me that if his boys didn't do what they were told, just to let him know. We've got some other families on the farm that have been there a long time. They have a house to live in and have managed to buy some small furnishings. Their children are in school. They have been picked up by the Border Patrol two or three times, but they always come back. We pay the men $2.50 a day. We've got four boys on the farm that we pay $26 a week rain or shine. And one boy who takes care of the irrigation who gets $30 a week rain or shine. But we don't hire local Mexicans. They just don't work.

Valley farmers just can't afford to pay higher wages. Of course we get a good year now and then, but we also get bad ones. Labor costs run about 60% of our total production costs, and if they were higher we'd go out of business in a bad year. And you won't solve this problem by destroying the men who provide the work. We pay the highest wages we can. The wetback comes over and tells us what he'll work for and we pay it. And for six months or so after he comes he doesn't know anything and we pay him twice what he's worth.

Would it, perhaps, not be more economical in the long run, we asked, to hire dependable, skilled, local people at higher wages than the wetbacks get?

The local Mexicans are no good. They've been ruined by being partly Americanized. They've been spoiled by the unions with their talk of a forty hour week and security for everybody. What a man needs is to get out and work and earn his own security. You can't give him anything without ruining him. I know, because I've ruined some Mexicans by being too good to them. I sent eleven to school, and almost all of them turned out to be no good. The ones I gave the least to turned out the best. There was one I helped a little by loaning him money to get to school. I made him sign notes for it. When he got out I gave him a job as a roughneck. In a year he had paid off all his debts to me. Today he's worth a million and a half dollars. No, sir, the local people are just no good. It will take generations to raise them up to our level. And they'll have to do it themselves. But they won't. If a man is born without initiative, without ambition, he just won't get ahead. And that's how the Mexican is.

In the Valley no careful distinctions are made between illegal aliens and local citizens of Mexican descent. They are all lumped together as "Mexicans" and the characteristics that are observed among the wetbacks are by extension assigned to the local people. And since the wetback, for reasons explained in a previous section of this report, is hardly representative of the best of Mexican culture, the characteristics believed to be those of local Mexican people are not such as to inspire in the Anglos any great liking for the group.

A "Mexican" in the Valley, it sometimes seems, is not so much a person as a commodity. Wetback or citizen, he is something to be used when needed and otherwise ignored as much as possible. One does not find in the Valley the same pride in elements of Mexican culture as would be found in San Antonio or Albuquerque. There is little or nothing observable along the main highway or in the central business sections of the towns that would indicate to a casual traveler that more than half of the population of the area is Spanish-speaking. In all the towns, and in the rural areas as well, the Spanish-speaking population lives apart, separated from the Anglos by a highway, a railroad, a canal, or just an imaginary line. Between the two groups there is little or no meaningful communication. Few Anglos speak any Spanish; a considerable proportion of the Spanish-speaking group either do not use English or are hesitant to do so.[15] It could be argued with considerable reason that most of the Anglos fail to see the problems of the Spanish-speaking people as human problems. These problems are, unless they seem likely to affect the welfare of the Anglos, considered with the same detachment as one would have toward the ills of a cow or other farm animal. The obviously inadequate living conditions of the wetbacks, for example, are justified on the grounds that they are better than those the wetbacks were accustomed to in Mexico and in any case are all the wetback expects or wants. That local, Spanish-speaking citizens, because of the low wage scales and the competition of wetbacks, are required to live under the same conditions is given scant consideration. Spanish-speaking citizens who refuse to work for $2.50 a day or who balk at a 12-hour work day are regarded as "ruined" or "spoiled" and are accused of stepping out of the role assigned to them, or of having "forgotten their place." A "Mexican" is expected to be passive, docile, industrious. He should take what is given to him and be grateful for it. He should make no complaints and, above all, no demands. He should work hard and long because that is what he is best fitted for. And when he is not wanted, he should remain quietly in the background until a demand for his labor again arises.

Of course one can find many examples of kindness towards both Mexicans and Spanish-speaking citizens in the Valley. Their medical expenses may be paid by an employer who has no legal responsibility to pay them. Money may be loaned or given to them in slack times or for the purpose of buying needed things or for sending children to school. An old man, long employed by one family, may be given a small weekly grant for food after he is no longer able to work. But the feeling that almost always motivates these kindnesses is paternalistic. The attitude behind such actions is generally akin to that which must have been held by a feudal lord toward his slaves

---

[15]Unpublished tabulations of the Study of Spanish-Speaking People show that out of a group of 16,782 Spanish-speaking residents of Hidalgo County, 67% of these over 21 years of age do not know English.

or vassals. Not much is given because the Spanish-speaking person has earned it, has a right to it, or because he is felt to be a fellow human being in difficulty. One might say that what is given is given as charity, but charity without compassion, without understanding, and with little human warmth. And in return for these acts of kindness, not only the recipient, but all Mexicans are expected to be overtly grateful.

A Federal employee recently described the Valley as a "colonial empire." It is so in many respects, and the attitudes between ethnic groups that have developed here are the attitudes one would expect to find in a colonial area. The major or key configuration of the Valley is certainly the economic welfare of the producer. Other factors are secondary and minor. Institutions, agencies, and services, both governmental and private, are evaluated in terms of their contribution to economic ends. Governmental regulations that enhance the economic position of the owners—such as price supports for agricultural products, etc.,—are sought; those that operate to improve general welfare—minimum wage laws, *bracero* contract agreements, fair employment practice regulations, etc.—are opposed or at least ignored. Several instances were reported to us[16] of farmers who contracted alien workers at 40c an hour under the terms of the 1949 International Agreement and then paid them 25c. The workers were told, our informants said, that if they complained, they would be released and sent back to Mexico. Then, if they wished to come back and work, they could only cross the river as wetbacks, in which case they could earn no more than 25c an hour and that without the safeguards provided for laborers under contract. The workers saw the point and remained to work at the 25c per hour rate.

The International Executive Agreement of August 1, 1949, provided (Article 23) that permission to contract workers should not be granted to employers continuing to use illegal aliens and that any employer who so continued after arranging for contract workers should have his contract arrangement terminated. It is a matter of common knowledge in the Valley that many of the growers who used contract workers at the same time used wetbacks[17] yet we

---

[16]These, it should be noted, are second-hand reports which should not be given too much credence. We were unable to verify them by any first-hand statements either of farmers or wetbacks. These are the type of rumor stories one would expect to find being passed around in a situation like that of the Valley. They are also, in the light of our observations of other practices in the Valley, quite believeable.

[17]We have been present on many occasions when Border Patrol Inspectors picked up wetbacks in fields where *braceros* were also working.

were not able to trace a single case where a contract has been broken in the Valley for this reason.

The very use of wetback labor is certainly a violation of the intent and spirit if not the letter of the Federal law covering the harboring and concealing of illegal aliens.[18] But the employment of wetbacks is so commonplace in the Valley that no stigma of any kind attaches to it. It is recognized as the thing to do. And everyone is amiable about the whole business. The wetback beams at the Patrol Inspector who apprehends him, knowing that the worst that is likely to happen to him is a day at the detention center (with no lunch provided), a free trip to the bridge, and a long walk back. The employer, if he doesn't exactly beam, is placidly philosophical about the matter and cheerfully pays off the worker, knowing that he will likely return after a short time. And the Patrol Inspector carries out his part of the ritual pleasantly enough knowing that if he chose to take the trouble, he could probably come back to the same place the next day and pick up the same alien again. The whole thing has many characteristics of a game in which the alien tries to escape capture as long as he can (but without suffering any real penalty if he is caught), the employer helps him to avoid the Patrol, and the Patrol Inspectors try to capture enough to run up a respectable daily score and keep up the reputation of their sector for apprehending and returning more aliens than any other. The spirit of the thing is illustrated by an incident which occurred while the authors were with the Border Patrol on a trip to pick up the workers of a large Valley farmer. A couple of our research group had been asked by the Patrol Inspector to watch a group of aliens while he rounded up some more. While he was absent, the grower appeared, asked what we were doing there, and when he learned we were not with the Border Patrol officially, he told his aliens to ignore us and run. When the Inspector came back, they all were gone. The farmer protested to the wrathful Inspector, "These men aren't Border Patrol. Why do you bring them in here. *You aren't playing fair.*"

To a newcomer in the Valley the situation seems unreal, with many

---

[18]The weakness of the present law is that it is so worded that one violates it only if he can be proved to have aided an alien to cross the border. The President's Commission on Migratory Labor, in reporting on problems encountered in enforcing the immigration law, point out that the present law is not adequate against those who harbor or conceal illegal aliens. "The Supreme Court (*U.S. v. Evans*, 333 U.S. 483, Mar. 15, 1948) held that, because of lack of a penalty in the statute, the Immigration Act does not make it a punishable offense to conceal or harbor aliens not entitled to enter the United States. New legislation is needed which will penalize the acts of transporting, harboring, and concealing of illegal aliens." *Migratory Labor in American Agriculture. Report of the President's Commission on Migratory Labor* (Washington: U. S. Government Printing Office, 1951), p. 86.

of the elements of a musical comedy plot. If one cares to look under the surface, however, many elements of a real life tragedy can be found.

Relations with Officials. The official group with whom the wetback has the most numerous contacts is the U. S. Immigration and Naturalization Service, particularly the Border Patrol. He may come into contact with public health or welfare workers, local police officials, educators, Social Security or Internal Revenue employees, or almost any other public official, but the ones with whom he is most concerned and who are most interested in him are those mentioned above.

Aliens here illegally may pass back across the border in any one of several ways. They may return, as they came, either by wading, swimming, or in a boat. Or they may present themselves at one of the international bridges, in which case they are likely to be permitted to cross with no other record being kept than a count of the total number who so cross. If they are apprehended by the Border Patrol they may be permitted to return voluntarily to Mexico or may be detained for further proceedings leading to formal deportation or possible imprisonment.

Technically, any alien here illegally is guilty of violating a Federal statute and is subject to penalty. Any who return after having been formally deported are subject to possible imprisonment. But, because of the enormous numbers who are apprehended or voluntarily return from the Valley area,[19] the majority are permitted the privilege of voluntary return without penalty.

Wetbacks apprehended by the Patrol in the McAllen area are taken to a detention center located about a mile south of McAllen, near the airport. Here a record card is filled out on each one, giving the number of times previously sent out, name, age, birthplace, date of entry into the United States, occupation, and the name of his father and mother. A good deal of the information so obtained is inaccurate, either because the alien does not understand the questions as asked in the somewhat sketchy Spanish of most of the Patrol Inspectors, because he does not remember accurately, or because he deliberately gives false information for the purpose of obscuring the number of times he has previously been in the United States. Most of the aliens who have repeatedly crossed the river will admit two or three previous returns. But with the increased efforts made in the summer of 1950 to determine those with repeated

---

[19]More than 221,000 during the twelve months ending June 30, 1950, in the area between Brownsville and Roma alone.

crossings on their record, the proportion who claim never to have been returned before increased considerably as apparently did the proportion of those giving false names. Some few admit to seven or eight crossings. Our investigation of one man's record showed that he had been returned twice in a single day, June 15, 1950. These records of the Border Patrol, incomplete as they are, show a considerable number who have been returned ten or more times and a few with thirty or more apprehensions.

After an information card has been filled out for an alien, he signs it, indicating his willingness to be considered as voluntarily returning to Mexico. It is doubtful if many know what they are' signing. Some cannot write, in which case a notation is made on the card that they are illiterate. If money is due the wetback, or if he has clothing or other belongings at the place he was working, he is taken by the Patrol to pick them up or his employer is notified to bring them to the center. The Patrol Inspectors feel that a good many who have money, clothing, or other possessions here do not admit it because they intend to return and do not want to be bothered carrying their belongings on the long walk back. The Patrol cannot compel the co-operation of the employers but most of them willingly bring to the center any money owed to the wetbacks who are apprehended. Some, however, do not,[20] in which case the Inspectors may take the alien out to the place of employment so that he can collect. The refusal to "come down and pay off" may, some of the Inspectors feel, be a way of assuring that the employee will return promptly. If the wetbacks have families here who have not been apprehended, and so tell the Patrol, the families will be brought down to the center and returned also. Here again, the Inspectors feel the aliens generally deny having relatives here because they intend to return immediately.

Aliens are kept at the Patrol detention center until a fairly large number is at hand[21] and then, at the convenience of the Patrol, they are transported in buses to the Hidalgo bridge. Here, those having records of several previous crossing or other charges against them are processed further, and the remainder are permitted to walk across the bridge. If they admit having any money, they pay the 10c for pedestrian crossing. If they do not, the fee is paid by the Government.

---

[20]One Patrol Inspector said about 40%.
[21]They are seldom detained more than a day, since food and lodging at government expense must be provided for those held overnight. Ordinarily no meals are provided those held in the detention center during the day, although there are machines from which cold drinks and candy bars may be purchased by those having money.

Once in a while, aliens, after getting on the bridge, fail to cross over to the Mexican side. They go out on the bridge a few yards, climb over the bridge railing,[22] drop down to the river bank, walk down the bank a short distance, and then go back to their jobs. This may occur in plain sight of the Immigration authorities, but they are usually too engrossed in other matters or too short handed to do anything about it other than to notify the Border Patrol, who will then attempt to pick the aliens up again.

Since about August, 1949, the volume of wetbacks returned has been so great that the Immigration Service has established a new category—Aliens Leaving without Record. This group consists of those who are not apprehended by the Border Patrol but who voluntarily present themselves at a bridge and request to be sent back to Mexico. A large proportion of this group, it is believed, consists of aliens who have been working in the United States during the week but who return to Mexico for the weekend. Others are undoubtedly wetbacks who are returning to Mexico because they failed to find work.

Technically, all illegal aliens apprehended are subject to prosecution and punishment, but the large numbers in which they now come make such prosecution all but impossible. Consequently, only a few of those with many recorded voluntary returns are selected each day from among all persons apprehended. Figures compiled by the head of the Immigration Service in the McAllen area, show that for a sample month in 1948 the percentage held for prosecution was only .0018% or 18 per 10,000 of the total number returned. A 1949 sample month count showed the proportion to have increased to .0025%. In the spring of 1950, as a part of an intensification of the efforts of the Border Patrol, a somewhat higher proportion was selected for prosecution. The ideal in the summer of 1950 was to prosecute all who had three or more verified voluntary returns and, of course, all those who had been formally deported previously. Actually, however, the numbers were still too large for this ideal goal to be realized. In fact, on June 28, 1950, the District Attorney at Brownsville asked that, because of pressure of work in his office and crowded jail facilities, a policy be temporarily instituted of not referring any wetbacks for prosecution.[23] Apparently this news reached the wetbacks very quickly. A group was in the detention

---

[22]Considerable effort is spent in maintaining the fence which is supposed to eliminate this practice.

[23]A Patrol Inspector, hearing of the request, said bitterly: "The Detroit papers used to advertise that Detroit had the highest paid bus drivers in the world. It isn't true. The highest paid ones are in the Border Patrol. All we can do now is give these tonks free rides to the river."

center the day after the request came through. They were noticeable restive (those detained are usually very quiet and docile) and as one said, "in a hurry to get back to Mexico so they could return to the Valley and get some sleep." One of the authors rode down with them on the bus to the bridge. As they got off, he said to a group, "Hasta mañana." One replied, grinning, "No mañana, esta noche" (not tomorrow, but tonight).

Those who are singled out for prosecution seldom receive more than a token punishment. They are generally detained a few weeks in jail or until the Federal District Court is able to handle their cases. And that is about all that happens. Five hundred forty-nine of them came up for mass trial on July 11, 1950. All were given suspended sentences with the provision that they not return to the United States within the next five years. We were not able to check the records, but it is quite probable that there were some in the group who had previous suspended sentences.

Despite the large numbers of aliens apprehended, it is obvious, even to a casual observer, that the McAllen unit is not doing as complete a job as it could. Patrol Inspectors frequently complain that they don't have enough men or equipment to do a thorough job, but it can easily be noted that the men and equipment they do have are not always most effectively used. In the middle of July, 1950, when cotton picking was getting well underway, nearly half the McAllen unit were on annual leave and several others were detailed to help build a water filter in the yard of the main office. An order had been issued forbidding annual leave between August 1 and September 15 because of the cotton season, but from the amount of cotton picked in June and July it was apparent that the greater part of it would be picked before August 1.

The Patrol Inspectors usually work in pairs, driving around in sedans. This, obviously, is not an effective way to transport large numbers of wetbacks, since it is necessary to make frequent trips back to the center to unload.

The use of small cars for patrolling makes it virtually impossible for the Inspectors to do much raiding of farms, unless they wish to arrest only a part of the farmer's workers and let the rest go. The cars simply don't hold enough people. Consequently, the larger farms usually are not raided except occasionally when one or two of the Inspectors decide to use a bus.

The Patrol Inspectors of the McAllen unit, when patrolling, do not cover any definite route, nor do they attempt any regularity in their cruising. For the most part they cruise the roads between Highway

83 and the river, picking up such aliens as they happen to spot. They know a good many of the crossing places and the roads most frequently used by wetbacks coming up from the river and are thus able to pick up considerable numbers with relatively little effort. Occasionally they cruise in towns, paying particular attention to alleys and small houses on the backs of lots in the area inhabited by Spanish-speaking people, watching for "wooly heads sticking around the corners of the cardboard shacks." There is no assignment of territory, and each Inspector goes where he chooses. As a result two or three cars may be going down the same road a few minutes apart while other areas remain unvisited for relatively long periods.

The various Patrol units in the Valley seem to operate in such a manner that a good many gaps are left where no Inspectors go. For example, the San Juan and Alamo area is between the Weslaco and McAllen units and neither seems to make much effort to cover it. The north side of the main highway (U. S. 83) is less well-patrolled than the southside;[24] east-west roads are less well-covered than north-south roads. And with the exception of the efforts of a few of the Inspectors who "like to pick up townspeople in order to be fair to the farmers," establishments in towns are not visited much.

In talking to one of the Inspectors about means for increasing the efficiency of the Patrol, it was suggested that it might be desirable for a while to visit some of the larger users of wetback labor each day or every other day in order to make it so inconvenient for them to use wetbacks that they would begin to employ local labor. "We tried that," said the Inspector. "There was one man who owned a farm down near the river, about a hundred acres. When I was patrolling some time ago, I raided his place consistently day after day, hauling out all the wetbacks he had each time. At first we found some every day; then the proportion of citizen labor began to increase; finally we weren't picking up any wetbacks at all and it wasn't worth our while to go down there any more. But, as soon as we stopped coming, he went back to wetbacks." The same tactics, the Inspector said, were tried in the packing sheds. The immediate result was an increase in the proportion of citizen labor. But, as soon as the raids stopped, the number of wetbacks again increased.

If the point of view expressed by this Inspector represents that generally held by members of the Patrol, it would seem that the group is much more interested in palliative than in preventive or remedial measures. The emphasis is on picking up wetbacks, not on

---

[24]This is based on observation in the territory of the McAllen unit and may not hold true for other units.

taking steps which might discourage their coming and their being hired in preference to citizens. The nuisance value of systematic raids was demonstrated, but they were stopped "because it wasn't worth our while to go down there any more" just at a time when they were most effective and when those particular fields could have been kept free of wetbacks with a minimum of effort.

Patrol Inspectors are left fairly free to conduct their work as they see fit (subject to occasional suggestions from Inspectors in Charge) as long as they "keep out of trouble." "Trouble," as one Inspector defined it, "means anything that gets in the newspapers or that causes a complaint of any kind to be lodged against you."

New Inspectors assigned to the area are sent out for a while with "old hands" who "know the ropes." From the "old hands" they learn that one occasionally picks up workers in the fields, but largely confines his attentions to wetbacks walking along the roads. No official word is given that the farmers are to be left alone, but the Inspectors soon learn that they are apt to be called up before some kind of investigating board if they are too zealous in doing their jobs. Actually very few such investigations are ever held, but the fear of "trouble" is real enough to have an adverse influence on the work of Inspectors. Young Inspectors who take their jobs seriously, one of the "old hands" told us, are likely to get frustrated with the way in which they don't seem to get anywhere. But he and the older hands have adjusted. They can pick up only a limited number of wetbacks in a day anyway, so they get their quota mainly on the roads. Since the wetbacks on the roads are likely to be looking for work, there is no need to carry them about to get paid or to pick up clothes and, perhaps even more important, the loss of these potential workers will not "antagonize" the farmers.

When a concerted drive is on, such as that represented by the "task force" operation in the spring of 1950, when additional men and equipment were sent in and the area systematically combed for wetbacks, local employers have shown themselves capable of retaliating with pressures of their own. The most frequent, and probably the most effective, measures are the spreading of rumors or making of complaints that the Border Patrol Inspectors are mistreating wetbacks. An example is the publicity given a case in the spring of 1950 when an Inspector exploded several firecrackers under a packing shed at Raymondville in order to get wetbacks to show themselves. There was much newspaper space devoted to the "shooting of wetbacks," many charges and countercharges were made, and finally at least two hearings were held to "get at the facts." All this, of course, diverts the Inspectors from their work and makes them much less likely to continue "interfering" with working wetbacks when there are so many unemployed ones to pick up along the roads.

Between the farmers and the Patrol Inspectors there exists a considerable amount of informal co-operation from which both benefit. The Inspectors are able to apprehend wetbacks with a minimum of resistance from the farmers, and the farmers, in turn, are permitted to use wetbacks fairly freely and are not molested when immediate work needs to be done.

One Inspector, for example, stated that he never picks up a wetback engaged in irrigating. "To take the men away then," he said, "would ruin the fields." One of the older Inspectors has a policy of not picking up anyone who is working or who is carrying any agricultural implement that would indicate that he had been working. Farmers whose wetbacks are taken are allowed to come to the detention center at their convenience to pay off their hands. The latter wait patiently, sometimes a whole day. One Inspector cited the case of his stopping a truck belonging to a big Valley farmer. There were only three aliens on the truck and they were going for a load of fertilizer. The grower said that these were the only aliens he had at the time. So the Inspector let them continue, saying that he would be back to pick them up later. In this way, he said, he would remain on good terms with the farmer and would be able to pick up more wetbacks on his place. His rationalization was that "a good Patrol officer has to use diplomacy."

In spite of this obvious pattern of informal co-operation, the Inspectors feel that their interests and those of the farmers are opposed. They point out that "only a handful of Border Patrol officers want to get rid of the wetbacks." The farmers, they think, earn high profits and could well afford to pay good wages. Most feel that there would be plenty of labor without wetbacks and that the practice is unfair to citizens who cannot afford to work for "wetback wages." But, they realize that the Border Patrol is a governmental agency, and, like all such agencies, is subject to political pressures of various kinds. They also are aware that the growers and business people who use the wetbacks are precisely the ones who can bring pressure to bear on the agency.

Each of the Inspectors in the McAllen area has his own methods for dealing with wetbacks. All speak Spanish, although some of them do not speak it very well. Some of the men occasionally slap or push the wetback around although that is strictly against regulations. Still less often a wetback may be lightly kicked. On the whole, however, there is little of what might be termed harsh treatment of the wetback. The main cause, when it does occur, seems to be the result of exasperation at being "lied to" or loss of patience with the more dull among the wetbacks. Several of the Inspectors frequently yell at wetbacks, and some of them seemed to be unnecessarily severe and loud in their routine questioning at the McAllen center.

There is little evidence that the Inspectors understand very well the people they deal with. One, who has been in the service on the border a long time, sees the presence of so many Mexicans in Texas as a "danger to Anglos" and offered his opinion that "even children born here should be sent out." "We're just sitting by and watching them take over political control." One, fairly new on the border, admits that he knows little about Mexicans. He speaks of Mexicans and whites and makes no particular distinction between wetbacks and Spanish-speaking citizens, except that he feels the latter are a bit more lazy. He is fairly genial, doesn't believe in using violence, but is somewhat erratic in his methods of dealing with the wetbacks. One was born on the border and has a fairly typical south Texan attitude. One is a firm believer in the "stupidity of all Mexicans." When told by us that we were interested in getting some intelligence test results from wetbacks, he said that from most of them we would get "only a blank piece of paper." He thinks that "a few ha.. some brightness, but about the same level of intelligence that one would expect from a reasonably bright dog."

There is little to show that any of the local Inspectors has any appreciation or understanding of the deep cultural differences between the Mexicans and themselves or of the different value systems each accepts. As one of the Inspectors said, "They are generations behind us in their development." Little distinction is made between wetbacks themselves; in dealing with them they are all lumped together: the bright, the dull, the foolish, the shrewd, the rascals, and the simple, hard working and poor who constitute the bulk, certainly, of this sometimes miserable lot of humanity.

There are no native Spanish-speaking Inspectors in the area stretching from Roma to Brownsville.[25] There was one recruit, a young man from Arizona, but he was released in July, 1950. He had passed his written tests (his grades were not very high, except in Spanish) but was given a low efficiency rating and his dismissal was recommended by the three senior Inspectors in Charge. He felt

---

[25] As of August, 1950.

that there had been a little unfairness to him because he is a "Mexican" and that a part of his low rating may have been due to prejudice on the part of one of the seniors.[26] Even to an outsider, however, it was apparent that his work was not of top quality, and it would be difficult to judge whether or not or to what extent prejudice may have contributed to his dismissal.

The Patrol has no objection to hiring "Mexicans" if they are good, we were told by one of the higher officers in the local unit. But there is no particular advantage, he felt, in hiring Spanish-speaking inspectors in this area, and some possible disadvantages. "Some of the farmers don't like Mexicans coming on their place and picking up their workers."

Everything considered, the Border Patrol is probably doing as good a job as could be expected from any similar group of men in their position. Most of the Inspectors would like to do a better job, but they see no point in "knocking themselves out" when they can, under the best of circumstances, pick up only a small fraction of the aliens here;[27] when they see those that are apprehended return almost immediately; and when they realize that almost no one in the Valley is sympathetic to or willing to support their efforts to keep wetbacks out.

The border could be effectively closed to wetbacks—nearly all Inspectors agree to that. But it cannot be closed without strong support and backing of their efforts on either the state or national level and at least a minimum of co-operation from local people. The role of the Border Patrol at present is like that of a balance wheel. They let in enough wetbacks to do the local work quickly and cheaply; but they send out enough to prevent serious overcrowding. One Inspector laughingly tells of the reaction of a local farmer to his suggestion that the Border Patrol retire a hundred miles north and allow wetbacks free access to the Valley. "Don't do that," the farmer said. "In a week they'd be overrunning the place, camping on our lawns, swarming everywhere. And there wouldn't be enough local police to handle them. What we want of the Border Patrol is to let in enough wetbacks for us to get our crops harvested and to keep the others out."

And that is about what they get.

---

[26]One of the Seniors did say to the authors on one occasion that "on this part of the border there is no place for a Mexican in the Patrol."

[27]Individually the staff of the Border Patrol are as honest, conscientious, and hard working a group as one could find in government service anywhere. They could, and probably will, handle the wetback problem efficiently if given adequate facilities and support.

V

Summary

Number of Wetbacks. Utilizing such available sources of information as the number of daily and weekly deportations by the Immigration and Naturalization Service, the amount of cotton picked per day in the Valley, and sample counts in a number of fields, it can be conservatively estimated that more than 100,000 illegal alien laborers were in the three counties of Hidalgo, Cameron, and Willacy during July, 1950. This gives a ratio of about one wetback for every three Valley residents, including men, women, and children. Compared on an adult male basis the two populations are probably about equal.

The *Valley Monitor* for July 16, 1950, carried a story giving estimates by an official of the Texas Department of Agriculture that about 10,000 bales of cotton were being picked daily at that time in the Valley, with each requiring the labor of about ten pickers. This would mean some 100,000 pickers steadily employed. However, the authors know from observation and from interviews with wetbacks that relatively few were steadily employed at cotton picking at that time, so that, had all the cotton been picked by wetbacks, the number here must have been considerably greater than the 100,000 working on any given day. Of course, not all cotton pickers in the Valley are wetbacks, but it is probably a conservative estimate that not more than 10% of those so employed in July, 1950, were local residents.[1] Thus it is quite likely that there were in the Valley, on any given day in July, 1950, a hundred thousand illegal aliens in agriculture alone, and an undetermined number—possibly as many as ten thousand—who were either seeking work or working at non-agricultural jobs.

Between July 1, 1949, and June 30, 1950, there were in the McAllen sector—an area including about 125 miles of border—more than 221,000 aliens returned to Mexico. This does not mean that 221,000 different individuals were apprehended, since many who

---

[1] A random check made on July 20 of fourteen fields in the Valley, in which there were a total of some 700 pickers, showed only about seven citizens for each hundred pickers, and those mostly women or children. The authors have been present on many occasions when fields were raided by Border Patrol Inspectors and have observed that only infrequently were citizens found among those picking cotton.

are returned to Mexico immediately come back, and some of them certainly appear in the records more than once during a given year. A good many show up two or three times, and a few have records showing that they have been picked up and sent out as many as twenty or more times over a period of years. Furthermore, it is known that many use different names at various times, so that the same individual may appear in the records at a number of places. However, the figure 221,000 averages out to about 600 apprehensions a day during the year, and, from our observations of the activities of the Border Patrol, it appears unlikely that more than 1% of the wetbacks in the area on any given day were apprehended. This would mean that there are in the McAllen area on an average day about 60,000 wetbacks. This estimate is given some support by the fact that during an intensive campaign to clear the area of wetbacks, carried on during February, 1950,[2] by an augmented Border Parol force, more than 40,000 apprehensions were recorded. The campaign was successful to the point where those who were present in the Valley at the time spoke of the wetbacks as being "somewhat scarce" and "not so often seen on the streets," but no one to whom we talked, including members of the Patrol who participated in the campaign, indicated any belief that all those in the Valley had been caught.

Everything considered, it is probable that at any given time, depending on the season and job opportunities open, there are from 15,000 to 125,000 wetbacks in the three Valley counties. And these are only three of the many border and near-border counties in Texas, New Mexico, Arizona, and California where wetbacks are used.

Characteristics of the Wetback. Although the wetbacks are by no means a homogeneous group in every respect, there are certain attributes that tend to characterize them as a body. Preliminary analysis of our data shows that the wetback is likely to be male and from 18 to 30 years of age. The chances are about even that he is married and has one or more children. Only a few come from those Mexican states bordering on Texas;[3] many came from the central and southern parts of Mexico, especially from the states of Guanajuato, Jalisco, San Luis Potosí, and Michoacán. They are,

---

[2]It should be remembered that February is by no means a peak month for agricultural labor in the Valley.

[3]With the exception of Nuevo León. Most of those born in Nuevo León whom the authors interviewed came from those parts of the state quite distant from the border.

almost invariably, farm laborers in Mexico although many own or rent small parcels of land which is cultivated in their absence by other family members. They come for relatively short periods ranging from three to six months. The peak of the migration is in the Valley cotton picking season which begins about July 1 and usually ends not later than September 1.

The wetbacks are lured to the Valley through real and mythical rumors of possibilities for quick economic gain. Such rumors travel through the medium of the "grapevine" from persons who have had work experience in the United States either as wetbacks or as volunteers recruited during the war to relieve acute labor shortages in Southwestern and far Western United States. Some of the stories are factual; others are exaggerated. Almost all depict possibilities for earning from four to six or seven dollars per day—fantastic sums to the Mexican laborer whose daily wage ranges from 3 to 5 pesos (36 to 60c U. S. currency). Conversations with the wetbacks indicate that this wage differential is not interpreted in terms of wide differences in the cost of living or the fact that sizeable transportation costs separate the Valley from the interior of Mexico.

A small but significant proportion of the workers come to the United States in the hope of earning and saving enough money to purchase land or establish a small business in their home communities. Most of them, however, expect to earn only enough money to supplement their production in Mexico and thus to achieve a slightly higher level of family living and comfort.

Almost all the wetbacks who enter the United States are empoyed in unskilled jobs. Relatively few achieve positions involving skills unless, of course, they are able to remain unmolested for a period long enough to enable them to learn a skilled occupation through apprenticeship and to master the fundamentals of English. Predominantly their jobs involve arduous, stoop, manual work such as picking cotton and cultivating and harvesting vegetable and citrus crops. Probably their nearest approach to performing skilled work is in irrigation work, which most of them learn in Mexico. Such work is considered unskilled or at most semiskilled in the Valley, however, and is paid for accordingly.

The use of wetback labor on Valley farms has become thoroughly rationalized in the thinking of the Valley farmers. Ample moral and ethical, as well as economic, justification is found for the low wages paid the wetback. Economic justification hinges upon "the many cash expenditures" involved in Valley agriculture including cost of irrigation water, mechanical equipment, and excessive shipping costs. Moral and ethical justification is found in the fact that "he still receives higher wages than in Mexico" and "here he can learn how to do scientific agriculture."

Impact of the Wetback on the Valley. This, obviously, is a complex category involving innumerable factors. Here, attention is devoted only to the more important and tangible factors that affect the two major social groupings of the Valley, the Anglo and the Spanish-speaking. This is not to imply that the Anglo-Spanish-speaking classification is altogether a satisfactory one, since there are Spanish-speaking employers as well as Anglo employers and Anglo laborers as well as Spanish-speaking laborers; but, by and large, local land and capital are in the hands of the former while the latter, both citizen and alien, furnish the needed labor. This major, if incomplete, division of the local population provides the basic classification of this section of the report.

Relations of the Anglo with the wetback are limited to those of an economic nature. The two groups are in contact only in the fields or in business; never or almost never do they meet socially except in the case of the few wetback children who attend the public schools. Thus, for the Anglo producer, the wetback is merely a cog in the production machine—serving as a source of cheap labor and returning to Mexico when the need for his labor ceases. The picture is somewhat different for the Anglo businessman who, to be sure, shares in the benefits to be derived from cheap, wetback labor, but, at the same time, loses to the extent that much of the money earned by wetback labor is returned to Mexico and not spent locally. This is a factor frequently ignored or overlooked by the businessman who defends the use of wetback labor.

The entrance of wetback labor into the United States affects the bulk of the Spanish-speaking people in the Valley in various ways. First they must compete with the wetback for jobs. This, obviously, applies mainly to the relatively unskilled, semi-skilled, and clerical jobs. Most of all, however, it applies to jobs of an agricultural nature, including the harvesting and packing of both fruit and vegetables, their canning and processing, and the picking of cotton. Since the fruit and vegetable seasons reach a peak during the winter months when other agricultural labor is not available elsewhere, many of the local Spanish-speaking people remain in the Valley to compete with the wetbacks. During the cotton picking season, however, there is agricultural work to be had elsewhere and native workers leave the Valley in large numbers. The seasonal migration of native labor from the Valley is generally considered to begin in April, however, with the migrants going first to north Texas and then into the beet fields of Michigan and other areas. Near the end of July, 1950, a sample census through a number of Valley towns indicated that more than half the local, Spanish-speaking people were temporarily away from the Valley. Local Spanish-speaking residents consider this estimate too low. A labor union in Mission claimed that only about 30 of its winter membership of more than 600 have remained in the Valley through the summer. Although no check was made on the statement, one might well expect that a greater percentage of such a group would migrate than would be true of the general or total population. At any rate almost none of the Valley cotton picking was in 1950 being done by citizen labor. Another random check in the Valley, completed on July 20, showed that practically all workers in the Valley cotton fields were wetbacks, and that the few citizens who were working were women, children, and old people who could not migrate.

Another area in which the influence of the wetback has been enormous is in the retarding effect it has exerted on intergroup relationship, especially those between the Spanish- and English-speaking groups. This is obviously a difficult factor to measure, but its significance is evident on every hand. It is most visible in what might be called the power structure or hierarchy in the Valley, i.e., the subordinate economic and political position of the Spanish-speaking population as compared with that of the non-Spanish-speaking or Anglo.[4] These positions have been buttressed in the past by differences in educational and employment opportunities between the two groups. Justifications or rationalizations for these differences that are current in the Valley include much-worn ideas regarding the difference in the standards of the group, e.g., "the Mexican doesn't want a good house, a variety of foods, and education for his children" and the notion that to pay a Spanish-speaking person more money is merely to increase his indulgence in leisure-time activities and idleness.

[4]Information received from the State Employment Commission in Edinburg indicated wide discrepancies between wages paid to local Anglo and Spanish-speaking employees. An Anglo stenographer, for example, receives $20 per month and up more than a Spanish-speaking stenographer for the same work. Clerks in the stores are mostly Spanish-speaking because they will work for lower wages, etc.

It is clear to anyone who makes an objective observation in the Valley that the local Spanish-speaking people have done much during recent years to undermine the above rationalizations. Some of the more tangible evidence for this is found in the increased enrollment of Spanish-speaking children in the higher grades[5] and in a slow but fairly steady response to their demand for a wider range of employment eligibility and a decrease in the historical wage differential that has existed in the Valley.[6]

The importance of the wetback migration on this situation is obvious. The wetback, first of all, is a real caricature of the Valley "Mexican" stereotype. He is illiterate, unable to speak English, and visibly poor. His historical status as a peon on the landed estates of Mexico has done little to establish in him values and attitudes in keeping with those generally believed to characterize a society of individual initiative and free enterprise. And, regardless of whether he is in the Valley a few weeks or a few years, he is able to raise himself but little from this unenviable level. This, of course, reflects back upon the native Spanish-speaking group, since society at large tends to label the entire Spanish-speaking population in terms of those characteristics possessed by a few. Hence the native Spanish-speaking people in the Valley, with the exception of the few who are accepted in the Anglo society, are classified as "Mexicans" with no differentiation being made between them and the *bona fide* nationals of Mexico.

Attitudes in the Valley Toward the Wetback. The attitudes of the Valley people toward the wetback migration vary strikingly from one group to another. Farmers and growers, be they English-, Spanish-, or German-speaking, maintain consistently that wetback labor "has made the Valley" and that Valley agriculture could not long exist should it be prohibited. As indicated in an earlier paragraph, the use of wetback labor has its ethical and moral justifications also. These, in general, revolve around such judgments as "the native people won't work," or "the native people are becoming urbanized—are leaving the farms for the cities," or "the native laborer is not satisfied to remain in one place but wants to travel about and visit other parts of the country." Some of the local growers seem to feel that this migration stems from a desire on the part of the local people to "punish"

---
[5]The Regional Junior College at Edinburg for the summer of 1950 enrolled more Spanish- than English-speaking students.
[6]This obviously does not apply, or applies hardly at all, to the upper-class Spanish-speaking people of the Valley who are in secure financial positions and who identify their interests with those of the dominant Anglo.

the grower, although most of them would seem to believe that the Spanish-speaking people regard these migrations as "we do a vacation." Evidence of these attitudes can be had from interviews with the growers, businessmen, and from careful scrutiny of local publications.

The experience of the Valley has been such as to enable the growers to gauge their needs for wetback labor rather accurately. Obviously the optimum number would be just enough to fulfill employment needs with only a slight surplus. This balance is generally attained through the activities of the United States Immigration and Naturalization Service. Unrestricted migration would quickly result in a surplus of idle labor which would offer a real threat to the area in terms of order, and the stealing and pilfering of crops, especially in the citrus and winter vegetable season. Even under the fairly well-controlled situations that have prevailed during the past few years many small farmers complain of damage to their orchards and gardens by camps of wetback labor housed on the larger units near them.

Attitudes of the local Spanish-speaking people, and especially the laboring class, toward the entrance of wetback labor is in definite contrast to that of the Anglo. The difference, of course, is rooted in the economic competition provided by the wetback and in the social and political problems already mentioned. Citizen labor will not, except where special circumstances force them to do so, work for the same pay and under the same conditions of housing, sanitation, etc., as the wetback. The acceptance of such conditions by the wetback is thus resented by the local Spanish-speaking people, a resentment that is increased by a failure on the part of many elements of the community to differentiate one group from the other. Even so, the attitudes of the local Spanish-speaking people toward the wetback are frequently ambivalent, and especially so among those who have recent and strong ties with Mexico. Then too, the cultural similarity that characterizes the two groups results in a mutual understanding and sympathy.

The total set of Valley conditions which foster identity between the wetback and legal Spanish-speaking residents of the Valley tends to bring the two groups together at various levels as well as to separate them at others. Wetbacks who drift into the towns looking for work always settle or locate in the Spanish-speaking sections of the town where they are able to rent rooms or small houses that frequently have been constructed for this purpose. This physical proximity in living has resulted in the attendance of children of the two groups in the same schools, and in the development of visiting and fraternizing relationships that frequently lead to intermarriage. Thus the attitudes of the native toward the wetback are dual and frequently conflicting, the antagonistic ones deeply rooted in economic competition, and the sympathetic ones in the sharing of many elements of a common culture, and a common set of values and standards. Conflicts imbedded in these attitudes come quickly to the surface if and when the local people are questioned about "why, if you are opposed to the entrance of wetback labor, do you rent them houses and rooms?" Obviously the easiest and most direct response to this question is, "It's business; we make a little money out of it," but some frankly admit that "they are our people and we feel sorry for them when they come to us without a place to sleep and with nothing to eat." The importance of this mixed situation is generally overlooked by those working towards solutions of attendant problems. Its recognition and effective utilization must come before any satisfactory and permanent solution of the problem can be realized.

Limitations on Movement of Wetbacks in the United States. Since the wetback is illegally in the United States, certain limitations exist to restrict his moving about from one place to another. Some of these are rationally designed and executed. Most of them, however, are of an informal nature and have grown out of convenience and preference rather than efficiency and reason. Among Federal officers, whose duty it is to prevent illegal entries, many informal controls exist, including a general tendency to restrict apprehensions to the main roads, in certain streets in the towns, and at certain points along the river. There is a strong general tendency on the part of these officers to apprehend anyone who is idle and to leave those who are working, especially in the fields. There are, of course, observable differences in the approaches of individual officers, from those who consciously refrain from apprehending anyone working on a farm to those who will, on occasion, interrupt agricultural operations in the field. The latter practice, however, is less common and such behavior definitely has a negative effect on the officer's status in his own organization. The result of all this is that certain "types" of wetbacks are apprehended more frequently than others, including those who do not know their way around, those who are least sophisticated in dealing with the police, and those who become lost or confused in the new and strange surroundings. Some of the local people maintain that those apprehended are the less energetic since the main roads and trails are easier to travel and are the most direct routes to farms.

Mexico's Position on the Migration. Such evidence as is available (largely from newspapers and conversations with both Mexican and United States Government officials), would indicate that Mexico maintains a dual position on the wetback situation, an official position formally established and proclaimed, and an unofficial one, under which the present migration of wetbacks actually functions. The official stand opposes the migration on the grounds that the workers are needed in Mexico, that they leave Mexico and enter the United States illegally, that frequently they are exploited in the United States by unscrupulous employers, and that they create problems for Mexico in the defense of their rights in the United States and the re-establishing of those who return from the United States in destitute circumstances. This attitude is reflected in the placing of many legal obstacles in the path of the migration and in the signing of various agreements by Mexican and United States officials.[7]

On the other hand one can find convincing evidence of the existence of an opposed informal policy that largely ignores or actually abets the migration. This policy is based upon the belief that temporary work in the United States, even if illegal, relieves part of the unemployment and underemployment that chronically exists in much of Mexico. There is no reason to believe that officials and others in Mexico are not aware of the worth of the many dollars these workers send or carry back. Whatever the reason, one can easily observe the failure of the Mexican Government to punish those who illegally cross the river and to provide any substantial means to prevent their doing so. Unwittingly, perhaps, the Mexican Government has magnified the opportunity for illegal migration to the United States by an extensive campaign for workers in the cotton fields south of the river between Matamoros and Reynosa, a campaign that quickly produced a huge surplus of workers in the summer of 1950, not only for the

---

[7]It should be remembered that the wetback traffic is in violation of the emigration laws of Mexico as well as immigration laws of the United States. In the International Agreement of August 1, 1949, both governments acknowledged the illegal nature of the wetback migration and agreed "to take all measures necessary to suppress radically the illegal traffic of Mexican workers." The same agreement, however, provided for the legalized contracting of aliens illegally in the United States and for giving them preference in contract jobs over other Mexicans who had not violated the United States immigration laws. For a discussion of this ambivalence in the Agreement see *Migratory Labor in American Agriculture. Report of the President's Commission on Migratory Labor* (Washington: U. S. Government Printing Office, 1951), pp. 52–54.

Mexican cotton fields but for the Valley as well. This observation was given prominent space in the Monterrey newspaper *El Porvenir* on July 13, 1950, in an article stating that the volume of the migration had been so great that "the railroad companies between Monterrey and Matamoros have been ordered to increase the number of coaches used in both day and night trains in order to transport, as quickly as possible. the number of workers who are arriving (in Monterrey) from the centrally located states of the republic." These workers, in large part, were headed for the Lower Rio Grande Valley.

The effectiveness of this campaign was evident a week later when apparently more workers were returning from the Rio Grande area than were entering it. The story on all sides was then that of too many workers. Wetbacks began to file into the local deportation centers in the United States and nearly all reported "too many workers" and "impossible to find work." And this at the peak of the cotton picking season. On July 19 the same Mexican newspaper, *El Porvenir*, pictured the current reversed in an article labeled "The Sad Return of the Workers from Tamaulipas." "Thousands of citizens," so the article read, "are returning to the southern states of Mexico, repeating in the central railroad station the same crowded scenes that transpired on their leaving . . . the workers are traveling with their families, including children in the younger age groups. . . ."

Lack of men and materials prevent Mexican officials from completely controlling the situation on the Mexican side of the river. Conversations with members of the Mexican Patrol on July 25, 1950, revealed that the Mexican Patrol Service then had 16 men employed to work the territory from the town of Camargo to Rio Rico, a distance of approximately 60 miles and several times that distance if one follows the banks of the winding river. The transportation facilities for these men, according to the Patrol chief, consisted of a single jeep. Under such handicaps these men have been able to do little more than look for boatmen who frequently make a profitable business out of ferrying the wetbacks across the river. On neither side of the river, however, is there evidence of maximum effort to apprehend all who cross. One could hardly expect more than token effort where little or no punishment is meted out to violators and where the officers know that any who are deported will likely return in less than 24 hours. A local patrolman illustrates the situation by a parable of the simpleton who went to the seashore to dig a hole and as he threw one shovel full out two more were washed in to replace it. To the conscientious Patrol officer on either side of the river it is almost as hopeless as that.

What Price WETBACKS?

American G. I. Forum of Texas

Texas State Federation of Labor (AFL)

Austin, Texas

WHY THIS SURVEY

This is a report on wetbacks.

It is not offered as an exhaustive report on all the effects that the wetback, the Mexican alien illegally in this country, has on the economy, the national security, the health and the living and working conditions of the United States. Much more detailed reports on most phases of the problem have been published heretofore by The President's Commission on Migratory Labor, the University of Texas' Study of Spanish-Speaking People, and other groups, as listed in the bibliography in the back of this report.

This report has two goals: To re-emphasize the importance of the wetback problem and to refute those who contend that the stories about wetback wages and housing and health and exploitation are untrue. To that end, actual interviews with wetbacks and pictures of wetbacks and the conditions under which they live and work are used throughout the report. Getting these pictures and interviews in the hands of people who will do something about the siutation is our primary purpose.

The idea for this report on wetbacks was conceived by people who got tired of hearing defenders of the wetback system claim that the dangers of the wetback system, the housing and sanitary conditions under which wetbacks live, the threat to the health of American citizens, the displacement of American citizen labor, the many other evils—that all these are the imaginings of outside agitators, that no such conditions exist.

We, as Texas citizens of the United States, living in the midst of the disrupted economy of the border area, seeing wetbacks daily, watching our neighbors depart on their annual migration as a result of the wetback invasion, decided to make a report to the American people on what we saw happening around us. Perhaps, with our on-the-spot interviews with wetbacks, we can help awaken the people of America to the danger of this wetback invasion. Perhaps with pictures showing the wetbacks and the conditions under which they live, we can convince the skeptics that there actually are wetbacks and that they actually are a threat to our health, our economy, our American way of life.

When we made our survey during May and June, 1953, we did not anticipate that before our findings were made public U. S. Attorney General Herbert A. Brownell, Jr., himself, supported by President Eisenhower, would spotlight the wetback problem as a national issue. We are glad that they have done so. We sincerely hope that the Attorney General and the President make good their pledge to stop the wetback traffic.

The field investigators for this report were Ed Idar, Jr., executive secretary of the American GI Forum of Texas, and A. C. McLellan, a businessman of Rio Grande City. The survey and report are sponsored by the American GI Forum of Texas, an organization of veterans of World War I, World War II and the Korean War, most of them of Latin-American descent, and by the Texas State Federation of Labor (AFL), the state organization of American Federation of Labor union organizations in Texas.

In this report are the results of many interviews with wetbacks, a survey of bracero conditions, a brief description of the life of the migrant American citizen farm worker, who has been forced on the road by the wetback, and a discussion of the effects of the wetback on the lives and economy of American citizens. The living and working conditions of the wetbacks on the farms described are no worse—and no better—than the conditions on many other farms along the border. The point is that wetbacks do exist, that they are employed by otherwise law-abiding citizens, some of them of great prominence, and that wetbacks are a problem and a threat to our security and standard of living. And most important, there are numerous pictures to back up the report.

The authors of this report vouch for the accuracy of their statements and for the true reporting of interviews and the reporting of information compiled from other sources. They feel that the situation they expose herein is attributable not to the Mexican national, either as wetback or bracero, nor to the American of Mexican descent, but to the many governmental agencies and public officials who thus far have made no all-out effort to solve this problem. The American of Mexican descent forms the second largest minority group in this nation and one-fifth of the population of Texas. His contribution to our welfare and progress as a nation would be many times what it now is were he given the means to climb above the morass of infantile mortality and disease and lack of economic and educational opportunity. It is the sincere desire of the authors that their work in exposing the conditions detailed in this report will awaken the American people and their elected officials to the need for giving the citizens of Mexican descent a square deal—one which they will never get as long as the wetback system is kept alive.

ACKNOWLEDGEMENT

It would have been impossible to complete this study without the cooperation of a number of Federal, State, County and City agencies. In practically every area of operation during the survey, cooperation was given wholeheartedly, indicating that all agencies concerned were not only in accord with the purpose of the survey but were honestly and actively seeking an anwser to a grave problem. So, to the officers of the U. S. Immigration and Naturalization Service and the U. S. Border Patrol, the United States Employment Service compliance officers and officials, other law enforcement agencies, school officials, retail businessmen, labor organizations, farm groups, church organizations and others who made our task in the field easier by their courtesy and cooperation, we extend our sincere thanks.

Time and finances were limited, and no attempt was made to duplicate the work done by previous surveys, some of the findings of which are incorporated in this report. We give full credit to the sponsors and writers of those reports for their invaluable contribution to our own effort.

AMERICAN GI FORUM OF TEXAS

The American GI Forum of Texas is an independent veterans' organization open to all honorably discharged veterans from either of the two World Wars or the Korean War. Its entire program, however, is aimed at improving the status of the Spanish-speaking population of the Southwest, and for that reason its membership is almost wholly made up of veterans of Mexican or Spanish-speaking descent.

Founded in Corpus Christi, Texas, in March, 1948 by Dr. Hector P. Garcia, a Corpus Christi physician, the organization is now found in every part of Texas with substantial concentrations of Spanish-speaking citizens, and in New Mexico and Colorado as well. In its short history it has devoted itself strictly to problems affecting the Spanish-speaking veteran and his family. It has yet to go on record as seeking special privileges for the veteran or for the Spanish-speaking population. Its whole program is aimed solely at lifting the status of this minority to the same level enjoyed by other population groups.

The many local GI Forums, Auxiliaries and Junior GI Forums are encouraged to sponsor back-to-school drives at the opening of every school year, as well as poll tax and get-out-the-vote drives at other times during the year. Its officers and members, as individuals, are encouraged to take part in political activity both as candidates and as voters, but the organization itself is non-political and its name cannot be used in support of any candidate or party.

It is active also in the protection of civil rights from violations by law enforcement officials and in ending segregation of Spanish-speaking children in the public schools.

It is interested in the wetback problem because it considers this the fundamental problem facing the Spanish-speaking population in the Southwest. For this reason, the organization from its inception has been an ardent advocate of a border barred to illegal aliens, of stronger immigration laws, and of more personnel and facilities for the U. S. Border Patrol.

TEXAS STATE FEDERATION OF LABOR

The Texas State Federation of Labor, founded in 1900 and chartered by the American Federation of Labor, is the state organization of A. F. of L. union locals and organizations in Texas.

As the representative of all A.F. of L. union members in Texas, with a primary responsibility to union members and a fundamental responsibility to look out for the interests of all working people in Texas, the State Federation has a basic interest in the wetback problem, not only because it affects union members but also because it affects all the people of Texas.

ED IDAR, JR.

Ed Idar, Jr., executive secretary of the American GI Forum of Texas and a member of the investigating team for this report, was born in Laredo, Texas. His family is well-known throughout the South Texas area. His grandfather, the late Nicasio Idar, was a printer and newspaperman, justice of the peace and deputy United States Marshal in Laredo. His father, the late Eduardo Idar, was also in the printing and newspaper business and was one of the founders of the League of United Latin-American Citizens (LULAC), an organization of Spanish-speaking citizens in the Southwest.

After graduating from high school and serving for one year as secretary to the school's principal, Idar became a civilian employee at Duncan Field in San Antonio, Texas. In August, 1942, he volunteered for service at an installation of the Eighth Air Force in England. While there he married Miss Joan Stringer of Cadishead, England, who came with him to the United States in 1944. They have a four-year-old daughter. Idar was inducted into the Army in April, 1944, and served until June, 1946, being discharged honorably as a Technical Sergeant. His service in the Army included duty in India and China. He holds the Bronze Star Medal, the Army Commendation Ribbon, and several area service ribbons.

In September, 1946, he entered the University of Texas at Austin where he graduated with honors in August, 1949, with a bachelor of journalism degree. He was elected to membership in Sigma Delta Chi, honorary journalism fraternity, and to Phi Eta Sigma, honorary freshman fraternity. He re-entered the University in September, 1953, and is now working toward a law degree.

Idar became active in the GI Forum in June, 1950, when the Austin GI Forum was organized, and a year later was elected State Chairman. He served in that capacity until August, 1953, when he was elected executive secretary, and City Commissioner Chris Aldrete of Del Rio succeeded him as chairman. As an officer of the Forum, Idar has travelled some 50,000 miles throughout Texas and the Southwest during the past two years and knows intimately the situation of the Spanish-speaking population in the area.

ANDREW C. McLELLAN

As a resident of the Texas border country since 1936 and a student throughout that period of the people and problems of Mexico and of Latin-Americans in Texas, Andrew C. McLellan was well-qualified to be a member of the survey team. And as an amateur photographer of several years' experience, he fitted naturally into the photographic slot, along with the gathering of other material for the report.

Born and educated in Scotland, he moved to Canada at the age of 15, came to the United States in 1934. After two years as an investigator and reporter in Rhode Island, he went to South Texas to make his permanent home. A businessman in Rio Grande City on the U. S.-Mexico border in Starr County, he has devoted considerable study to the field of human relations, particularly the relations between people of Latin descent and the non-Latins. He speaks fluent Spanish, equally as well as English.

McLellan has been politically active with Latin-American groups throughout South Texas and has an extensive knowledge of grass-roots politics in the area. He has a wide knowledge of Mexico and the Mexican people and has spent considerable time in that country in both official and unofficial capacities. Most recently, he spent two years, from 1949 to 1951, with the Joint U. S.-Mexico Commission for Eradication of the Hoof and Mouth Disease. He had served in similar work in 1940-41.

Following four years' service in the U. S. Army during World War II (two of them in the Pacific Theater), McLellan started his own personal research program on the problems of the wetback and the Bracero Program. He has compiled what is probably one of the most comprehensive files of information on the subject in existence. In the course of his study, he has followed the migrant trails of the domestic farm workers in many states of the U. S.; and he has travelled along the hundreds of miles of the Texas-Mexico border country as well as through practically every state in Mexico.

THE WETBACK

Crossing the Rio Grande

Caught by the Border Patrol

Ready for Deportation

THE WETBACK

In the grey light of dawn on May 20, 1953, three figures came out of the brush across the Rio Grande River in Mexico. They ignored the bridge a little way up the river at Eagle Pass, Texas, obviously preferring the simpler—and illegal—crossing of the nearly dry river, away from the eyes of immigration officers.

There was no hesitancy even when they sighted the men on the American side of the river waiting for them. They posed for pictures, if not willingly, at least without strong objection. And while they talked, a fourth "visitor" from Mexico—a girl—came across the sands of the Rio Grande by the same route.

They were Jose Martinez of Piedras, Negras, Joe Sanchez of Guadalajara, Julio Ortega of Guadalajara, Olivia de la Rosa of Musquiz—all wetbacks who scarcely got their feet wet. One moment they were free citizens of the Republic of Mexico. The next they were fugitives without recourse to the protection of the laws of either of the two great neighbor nations on the Rio Grande.

Martinez was traveling alone. Sanchez and Ortega, the latter 15 years old, were together; and the girl was on her own. She claimed she had no job, but her neat dress and appearance indicated she probably was on her way to her daily work as a maid in an Eagle Pass home.

Sanchez and Ortega wanted work in the onion fields near Eagle Pass at the prevailing rate of 10 cents per sack of onions sacked. Between them they had earned $2.55 in the course of eight hours the day before. Two days before that they had earned 80 cents apiece. They would have liked to be working legally as braceros, but they said that recruiters were charging 200 to 300 pesos just to get into the recruiting centers in Mexico.

The newly-arrived wetbacks went their way that morning, only to be caught and shipped back to Mexico before the day was over. But the next day Ortega came into the picture again — after he was picked up by the Border Patrol for the second straight day.

Up and down the river on that morning of May 20, other thousands of Mexicans were making that same illegal trip across the river — to regular jobs in the border cities, to temporary jobs on the thousands of farms along the border, to look for jobs at whatever wage they could get, generally from 20 to 30 cents an hour, or to try to work their way inland where the Border Patrol would be less apt to find them.

These are the wetbacks — carrying all their possessions on their backs, ready to bed down at night in whatever shelter comes to hand — or without shelter; able to exist on a few beans and a little flour for tortillas; spending only the few cents a day such meager fare requires; and saving the rest of their earnings for their return to Mexico.

These are the wetbacks — forced by circumstances and the avarice of employers to use a hole in a canal bank as "home," and to sleep amidst a swarm of flies which alternate between the nearby filth and the napping children.

These are the wetbacks — illegally in this country and thus at the mercy of employers who can — and will — turn them over to the Border Patrol if they complain about working conditions or wages, living under the constant threat of apprehension and deportation, yet knowing that, even if deported, they will undoubtedly make the return trip across the river the next day or the day after.

These are the wetbacks — unfortunate human beings whose ignorance, poverty, illegal status, and willingness to accept indescribable hardships places them at the mercy of unscrupulous employers.

These are the wetbacks — hundreds of thousands of them pushing across the Rio Grande day after day, pushing their blood brothers, American citizens of Mexican descent, out of jobs in the border country and into competition farther north, pushing wages down, down, down.

These are the wetbacks — sad-eyed and sick, desperate beings unaware that their illegal entry and existence bring with them to the areas they infest soaring statistics on syphilis, tuberculosis, infantile diarrhea and other diseases, along with a host of crime and other socio-economic problems.

These are the wetbacks — forced by circumstance to willing adaptation to exploitation, never gaining the fabulous fortune in greenbacks that lures them as a pot of gold across the Rio Grande, but always managing to give a relatively few fortunate employers far above normal profits through a subsidy of sweat, blood, and even the lives, of men, women and children.

Yes, these are the *wetbacks* — as we pity them, as we see them, as we know them, and, as we fear them from the standpoint of health, national security, welfare and economy. These are *espaldas mojadas* (wetbacks), usually condensed to plain *mojados* when speaking in Spanish and "wetbacks" when speaking in English.

The vast majority of wetbacks are plain agricultural workers, including women and children, mostly from the peasant class in Mexico. They are humble, amenable, easily dominated and controlled, and accept exploitation with the fatalism characteristic of their class. A common term applied to them is Guanajuato Joe, for the Mexican State of Guanajuato which supplies a large percentage of wetbacks apprehended in farm work. This type of wetback wants only to find work on a farm, mind his own business and be left alone by the Border Patrol. He accepts good or bad treatment, starvation wages, diarrhea and other sickness for his children from contaminated drinking water and unsanitary living conditions — all this he accepts stolidly and philosophically. He does not think in terms of native labor displacement, lowering of economic standards and the socio-economic effects of his presence in the U. S. Ideologies are beyond his comprehension. He understands only his way of life: to work, to suffer, and to pray to the *Virgen de Guadalupe* for a better life in the hereafter.

Another distinct type involves the so-called *Pachucos*, to be differentiated from residents of the United States who during wartime were given the same descriptive term because of their zoot-suit wearing apparel. The wetback *Pachucos* sub-divide roughly into two classes. In one are found the criminals, the marijuana peddlers and users, the falsifiers of identity documents, the smugglers, the prostitutes and the homo-sexuals. The other class takes in those of higher intelligence with trade or partial professional backgrounds who are not interested in agricultural work and will not accept parole to such work when apprehended, usually in the act of being smuggled to the northern industrial centers. This class is motivated by the desire to get to the urban and industrial areas of the northern, north-central and western areas of the country where the possibility of detection and apprehension by immigration authorities is slim and where earnings are larger. Both these classes of *Pachucos* display a remarkably sound knowledge of the limitations of the immigration laws and of the Border Patrol. They know full well that a patrolman cannot use his pistol except in extreme emergencies, and they know it is against the policy of the Border Patrol to physically abuse a wetback in any manner. They know the limitations of investigative personnel and facilities and that false papers are almost certain insurance against apprehension.

Along the Mexican border in Texas, the wetback problem ranges from "under fair control" in far West Texas around El Paso to "completely out of control" in the Lower Rio Grande Valley despite daily round-ups of thousands of wetbacks. The thousands are merely the maximum numbers the understaffed Border Patrol can pick up and process in a single day.

The Border Patrol has 491 officers in the entire Texas border country, extending 900 miles from Brownsville to El Paso and covering an area several hundred miles into the interior. From El Paso to the Pacific Ocean, an area not covered by this survey but in which similar conditions exist to a greater or lesser extent, is another 700 miles of border.

There are sections of that border where, because of the terrain, wetbacks are not, and never will be, a major problem. The hungry Mexican citizen seeking work is not going to travel the many miles through the mountains along parts of the border in order to find the centers where work is available. So the wetback becomes a major problem only in those areas where agricultural work is available near the border. Not that he sticks to agriculture. Immigration Service records in El Paso, for example, show that during the fiscal year of 1952-53, a total of 12,101 aliens were apprehended in agricultural work in the El Paso area, while 692 were apprehended in domestic work and 1,023 in industrial and other jobs. But it is the availability of farm

WETBACKS UNDISTURBED by lone patrolman's advance on Kenmueller Farm.

CAMPING OUT IN BRUSH is life of this wetback in Lower Rio Grande Valley.

WETBACKS IN TENT they called "home" on McAllen Fruit & Vegetable Farm in Hidalgo County.

PICKED UP IN ROAD BLOCK, these wetback children were on way to work at 5 a.m.

employment which is the big attraction for most of the thousands who pour into Texas, coming all the way from Central Mexico, Southern Mexico and even countries to the south of Mexico, such as Communist-dominated Guatemala.

On the other hand, the mere existence of an extensive agricultural area along the border does not necessarily mean a coincidental wetback problem. Enforcement of immigration laws with cooperation of farmers, businessmen and workers are vital factors. At the time of this survey, in the El Paso area it was found that some understanding of these factors had been reached. The El Paso Cotton Growers Association, prime contractor for the area, and its members were cooperating wholeheartedly with the international Bracero Program and policing association membership in an effort to help the Immigration Service keep the wetback out of the area. (We regret that this cooperation has since suffered a setback.)

While the problem was far from licked, consider the following statistics: In the last five years, the number of wetbacks apprehended in the San Antonio District of the U. S. Border Patrol which takes in the eastern half of Texas jumped from 168,351 in the fiscal year 1948-49 to 362,403 in 1952-53. At the same time in the El Paso District, covering the western part of Texas, all of New Mexico and part of Arizona, the number of aliens apprehended has held fairly steady — in fact has actually been lower in the years since 1948-49 (36,150 1948-49 compared with 34,508 in 1952-53.) The contrast, in part, is explained by the relative geographic isolation of the area, mountain barriers in Mexico being a great discouraging factor in keeping prospective wetbacks from going into the area.

On the other side of Texas, in the Lower Rio Grande Valley, the problem has become more acute every year (as evidenced by the above figures for the San Antonio District of which the Lower Valley is a part). Today it threatens the entire economy, endangers the health of every citizen, damages the livelihood of the entire population (except, perhaps, the wetback-employing farmers who profit beyond measure by paying starvation wages). The Bracero Program in the Lower Valley is practically non-existent; U. S. citizen labor is offered only the low wetback wage.

Through their spokesmen in the Halls of Congress, in newspaper interviews, in speeches and in statements, employers of wetback labor and their representatives invariably try to belittle the dangers posed by the wetback problem. Their arguments seemingly are that outside agitators are making a mountain out of a molehill, misrepresenting the facts, and slandering the State of Texas, in general, and the Lower Rio Grande Valley, in particular.

When Congressman John Rooney of New York in June, 1952, cited to the Congress from the floor of the House the names of numerous persons of prominence on whose farms and other property wetbacks had been apprehended time and time again, his allegations were written off by at least one of those mentioned as part of a "Washington smear campaign." This despite the fact that in his brief visit to the Lower Valley prior to his disclosures, Congressman Rooney was able to visit in person some of the farms in question and to check Immigration Service records of apprehensions in the others.

As a result of the public controversy that ensued, the Temple (Tex.) Daily Telegram said in an editorial on June 7, 1952:

"If these charges are part of a smear campaign, the (person involved) deserves to have that proved in simple fairness. If the charges are factual, the people of Texas deserve to know it. They may not be too much concerned about the presence of wetback labor, but they

would be concerned about profits being made through exploitation of these poor laborers.

"Let the facts be established. The People of Texas will be able to judge for themselves."

It is to prove these facts that this report contains interviews, supported by pictorial documentation, of wetbacks interviewed while at work or otherwise engaged on the very farms where revelation of their presence and responsibility for their employment were written off as a "smear campaign" some 18 months ago. It must be remembered that these interviews and pictures were taken by Texans and not by outsiders—one being born and reared on the border, the third generation of his family to do so; the other being a long-time resident and businessman of the area who is in daily contact with the situation documented herein. Both know the country and the people intimately and speak and write Spanish fluently.

Let us take a look at some facts on several Sharyland Farms in Hidalgo County in the Lower Rio Grande Valley visited by the survey team one year after charges of wetback employment and the responsibility for such employment on those farms were written off contemptuously as a "Washington smear campaign." On June 10 and 11, 1953, the survey team visited three Sharyland Farms in the Lower Rio Grande Valley.

At the first farm, located about seven and one-half miles north and one-half mile west of Mission, three wetback children were found in a screenless hut. Their parents were out in the fields and had left them alone for the day. The only adult in the entire camp at the time was asleep in another hut down the way. He was Adan Garza, a wetback from Monterrey, who had been on the Sharyland farm for two months and who knew full well his employer was of high prominence in Texas political life. Garza was being paid $1.50 per 100 pounds of cotton picked. Day labor on the farm, he declared, was getting $2.50 for a 10-hour day. Adolfo Resendes, a tractor driver living with him and who was driving a tractor on the far side of an adjacent field, was earning $4.00 for a 10-hour day, Garza said.

Where did they get their drinking water? Garza pointed to a nearby concrete cistern into which canal water was dumped. The cistern was 21 feet from a nearby outhouse.

On the second Sharyland Farm, near Five-mile Road north of Mission, the interviewers talked with Cruz Perez of China, Nuevo Leon, who had been on the farm two days, and Vicente Martinez of San Francisco del Rincon,

SHARYLAND SCENES: Houses in which wetbacks live on one Sharyland Farm; wetback children outside their screenless house on Sharyland Farm waiting for return of parents from fields; house in which the children were living; Ed Idar stands beside wetback water supply cistern only a short distance from outhouse.

Guanajuato, two months on the farm. Both were being paid $2.50 for a 10-hour day. With them were Maximo Moreno and Thomas Cortez, both of China, Nuevo Leon. These wetbacks said they sent from $8 to $10 home to Mexico every two weeks, the foreman getting their money orders for them.

As the third Sharyland farm was approached by the Military Highway, a stop was made beside a field where a laborer, obviously a wetback, was tending an irrigation canal. The approach of the Border Patrol car sent him flying across the field never looking back. He disappeared in the brush along-side the canal a half-mile away. Checking back an hour later, the irrigation water was found to have burst through the earth bank of the canal at one point and to be spilling along the edge of the field—a needless waste of precious water at the height of the Valley drought, waste which could have been prevented by the simple expedient of hiring citizen labor who would not have fled at the sight of a Border Patrol car.

At the farm house, located two miles east of Madero, were found:

Eulalio Luna of Rio Verde, San Luis Potosi, a 14-year-old who said he was paid $1.00 a day for a 10-hour day. Eulalio said he was "in charge of the horses and cows," had been on the farm two weeks, and had been hired by Ed Meyers, Sharyland foreman.

Ignacio Ramon of Durango, who testified that he had been on the farm eight days, earning $2.00 per day.

Gabriel de Lira of Aguascalientes, who said he had been on the farm for seven years, having been deported six times but always returning to the Sharyland farm. On further questioning, he named the prominent individual whom he considered responsible for management of the farm, saying that he had seen this individual on the farm on several occasions and had exchanged greetings with him. To the question if this individual knew de Lira and other workers to be *mojados*, he replied with a grin, "*Pos como no, senor!*" ("But how not?")

On the same farm were two brothers, Noe Hernandez, 19, and Luciano Hernandez, 15, both American citizens from Edinburg. Noe reported he earned $3.50 per 10-hour day, while Luciano earned $3.00. They had been on the

SHARYLAND WORKERS: Four wetbacks who said they were earning $2.50 per 10-hour day on Sharyland Farm—Maximo Moreno, Tomas Cortez and Cruz Perez, all of China, Nuevo Leon, and Vicente Martinez, San Francisco del Rincon, Guanajuato; wetback irrigator flees at approach of Border Patrol car; Idar interviews Eulalio Luna, Rio Verde, San Luis Potosi, 14 years old, earning $1.00 per day; Gabriel de Lira, Aguascalientes, who said he had been working on Shary Farms for seven years, had been deported six times.

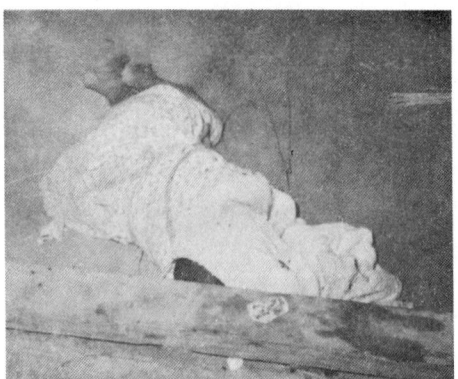

FLIES SWARM around little Juanita Hernandez while she sleeps on Texan Care Farm.

farm four months. Noe supports his father and two sisters, one 17 years old and the other 13, the youngest one going to school while the other keeps house.

Another farm visited on June 10, 1953, is operated by Texan Care Co. It is located some seven miles north and five miles west of Mission. As the Border Patrol car neared the spot on this farm where a crew of men were baling broom corn, several of the workers took off into the brush along the nearby canal bank, but most remained on the job. Sotero Quilantal of Monterrey told the interviewers that he was in charge of the crew while the foreman was elsewhere and was being paid 50 cents an hour. The others, all wetbacks, were being paid 25 cents an hour, he declared. All had been hired by Eusebio Rodriguez, the foreman, he explained.

Only a stone's throw from the baling work was the wetback camp of the workers. The families—women and children—were in the houses provided for the illegal workers. Sleeping in the dirt behind one dilapidated hutment was three-year-old Juanita Hernandez, ill with diarrhea, her body covered with flies. A short distance behind the hut was the canal, lined with trees and brush, which was being used as an open latrine by the transient workers. Flies buzzed around the excrement. Flies also buzzed around little Juanita and around the food supply in the screenless huts. No doubt flies also buzzed in the homes of nearby Valley residents and in downtown cafes and other eating places.

During the Rooney controversy, referred to earlier, Texas Congressmen from South Texas and elsewhere were notoriously active in attempts to scuttle appropriations considered essential by Immigration Service authorities for adequate enforcement of the laws placed in their jurisdiction. These same Congressmen battled, this time unsuccessfully, to prevent inclusion of a provision in the McCarran-Walters Immigration Act that gave the Border Patrol authority to search private lands, but not dwellings, without a search warrant within a twenty-five mile zone of the border.

One of these Congressmen took Congressman Rooney to task for diclosing that he had seen wetbacks paid in his presence as little as $5.00 for a week's work. The Valley Congressman was quoted in a Washington dispatch to the *San Antonio Light* as saying: "The idea of taking one little incident like a fellow paying a Mexican $5.00 for a week's work and saying that was generally applicable to the Valley farmers." In the Valley itself, Hidalgo County Judge Milton D. Richardson was quoted by the Associated Press as saying: "This fellow Rooney—whatever his name is— is all wrong when he says we pay them $5.00 a week. Down here we pay them more than $5.00 a day."

In their report on wetbacks, published in July, 1951, by the University of Texas Press, Olen E. Leonard and Lyle Saunders* on Page 69 of that report quote a synopsis of an interview with a Valley farmer whom they describe as a man owning a large acreage west of Mission. In question and answer form, they report the interview as follows:

Q. Why is it, we asked (the farmer) that all the people we see doing hard work in the Valley are Mexicans (meaning Mexican-Americans)?
A. That's town work, the (farmer) said, yard work, filling station work, construction work and stuff like that.
Q. But hard work, we asked, it is hard work, isn't it?
A. Yes, but for that they get six or eight dollars a day.
Q. Would they work in agriculture for six or eight dollars a day?
A. They might.

*The wetback in the Lower Rio Grande Valley of Texas by Lyle Saunders and Olen Leonard, University of Texas, 1951.

$3 FOR 12-HOUR DAY: On Ritchie Bros. Farm, Jesus Betancourt, Juan Betancourt, Carlos Villareal, Rosendo Sanches, all from Coahuila.

Q. What *would* they work for in agriculture?
A. I don't think they'd work at any wage.
Q. Would they work, for say, $15.00 a day?
A. Yes.
Q. Ten dollars a day?
A. Yes.
Q. Eight dollars a day?
A. Yes, they would.
Q. Five dollars a day?
A. No.

The President's Commission on Migratory Labor* in its report, pages 78 and 79, has other illuminating comments on wage rates in the Lower Rio Grande Valley. After holding hearings in the Valley, the Commission reports its conclusion, based on its findings, that Valley growers in 1950 had their cotton picked for an average of $1.25 per hundredweight. It points out the statewide average 1950 rate for Texas cotton picking was reported officially by the United States Department of Agriculture to have been $2.45 per hundredweight. "Thus, the Lower Rio Grande Valley cotton growers get their cotton picked for apparently one-half the wages paid by the average cotton grower of Texas," the Commission concluded.

To support the Saunders-Leonard findings and those of the President's Commission and to show that the wage picture had hardly changed during the summer of 1953, here are results of additional interviews conducted by the survey team.

Leonardo Moreno of Monclova, Coahuila, on the Ritchie Brothers Farm near Eagle Pass, May 20, 1953, was earning $3.00 for a 10-hour day. He was picked up by the Border Patrol for deportation.

Migratory Labor in American Agriculture, U. S. Government Printing Office, 1951.

WORK PROMISED on Thompson Bros. Farm north of Mission at $1.50 per 100 pounds of cotton picked holds these wetbacks—Angel Paramo, Irapuato; Aurelio Rodriguez, San Luis Potosi; Alfredo Ortiz, Michoacan, and Adolfo Ramirez, Guanajuato.

WETBACK BRICK-MAKERS: Idar interviews wetbacks at Anderson Brick Plant in Lower Rio Grande Valley. Diego Reynosos, Torreon, Coahuila, third from left, said he had been there two months, that he and family made 1000 bricks a day for $4.00, had been deported five or six times, never separated from family.

Baltazar Martinez of Zacatecas, on the same farm, also was getting 30 cents an hour. Picked up by Border Patrol.

Carlos Villarreal Flores of Piedras Negras had been working on the Ritchie Brothers Farm near Eagle Pass, 15 days at $3.00 per 12-hour day when he was picked up by the Border patrol on May 20.

Humberto Hernandez of Piedras Negras was interviewed at Border Patrol headquarters in Eagle Pass after being apprehended. He told the interviewers that he had come to the U. S. on May 15, that he was 13 years old, and that he had been working in the T. G. Barrientos Grocery Store from 6:00 a.m. to 9:00 p.m. daily, getting only enough time off to grab a bite to eat at noon and in the evening. He said he had worked six days and was paid $4.50 at the end of that time. He slept in a warehouse by the store on a canvas cot.

On May 21, in Border Patrol headquarters at Eagle Pass, Jose Hernandez Ramirez of Guanajuato, 10 years old, reported he had worked from 9:00 a.m. to 5:30 p.m. the day before, being paid $1.40 at the rate of 10 cents per sack of onions sacked.

Guadalupe Martinez of Guanajuato, 11 years old and in the first grade at school, had come over the morning of May 21—his birthday—and had managed to pick one sack of onions before being apprehended. He was paid 12 cents at Border Patrol headquarters in the presence of the survey team.

Adan Rios Zapata of Piedras Negras, 15 years old and in the fourth grade, said he had been to the U. S. six or seven times. He had picked two sacks of onions before apprehension and was paid 24 cents at Border Patrol headquarters.

Santos Pardo Martinez of Piedras Negras came over

on May 20 and was apprehended on May 21. He picked 15 sacks of onion on May 20 and one sack on May 21 before being apprehended. He received $1.92 for his work from 8 a.m. to 5 p.m. the day before plus the work on May 21.

On the farm operated by Texan Care Co. near Mission, the 17 wetback workers were being paid 25 cents per hour.

On the first Sharyland Farm visited June 10, day labor was being paid $2.50 for a 10-hour day.

On the second Sharyland Farm visited June 10, Cruz Perez of Nuevo Leon and Vicente Martinez of San Francisco del Rincon, Guanajuato, said they were paid $2.50 per 10-hour day.

On the third Sharyland Farm, visited June 11, 14-year-old Eulalio Luna of Rio Verde, San Luis Potosi, said he was being paid $1.00 per day, while Ignacio Gamon of Durango said he was earning $2.00 per day and Gabriel de Lira of Aguascaliente said he was earning $2.50 per day.

On the Kenmueller Brothers Farm in Hidalgo County, Macaria Bonilla de Marus said that her husband was paid $3.00 per day.

On the Carl Schuster Farm, the Border Patrol picked up Rafael Barva of Jalisco on June 13. He said he had been working seven days a week for $15 per week and had been working for Schuster for two months.

(Schuster is the same man, who, in press reports of September 14, 1953, was mentioned by John W. Holland, director of the San Antonio District of the U. S. Immigration Service, as being the individual, together with his brother, Frank, in whose employment the Border Patrol had apprehended more than 5,346 wetbacks from July 1 to September 4, 1953.)

At the McAllen Detention Center, the survey investigators interviewed a number of wetbacks who had been apprehended and were awaiting their return to Mexico. A sample of the interviews:

Rosa Cano Banda of San Miguel de Camargo, Tamaulipas, had no money on her when she was picked up, although she said she had been paid $10 (plus food) for about two weeks of cotton-picking work at the rate of $1.50 per 100 pounds. She had crossed the Rio Grande at Reynosa with her father, a sister and an uncle. In Mexico she had worked as a house-maid.

WETBACK WAGES: Adan Garza, top, Monterrey, said he was earning $1.50 per 100 pounds of cotton picked on Sharyland Farm; middle, Guadalupe Martinez, Guanajuato, apprehended on his 11th birthday, was paid 12 cents at Border Patrol headquarters for his work prior to apprehension; Adan Rios Zapata, Piedras Negras, 15 years old, was paid 24 cents for his work prior to apprehension (for the sixth or seventh time).

Two days work during his week in the U. S. was all Guadalupe Zepedo of Linares, Tamaulipas, had been able to find. In the two days, the 14-year-old boy had picked 200 pounds of cotton at $1.50 per 100 pounds before being picked up. He claimed to have come to the U. S. every year for the past seven years.

Cristobal Desiga of Guanajuato, a 38-year-old widower with eight children, declared that he had worked two and one-half days picking cotton at $1.50 per 100. Since he had to pay for his cotton sack, he wound up with 75 cents and his sack.

Maria Isabel Gonzales de Nevarez of Aguascalientes, 23-year-old mother of four children, had $2.00 cash on hand when apprehended and had managed to send $16 to her mother in Mexico—or, at least, she hoped the money had reached her mother. In her many times of crossing the river to work in Texas, she had been apprehended and returned to Mexico only three times.

The usual wage for the wetback laborers in agriculture in the Lower Rio Grande Valley is 20 to 30 cents an hour. The 30 cents, in fact, practically amounts to the maximum paid, with some exceptions. The working day generally is 10 hours but frequently runs 11 or 12 hours, or from sunrise to sunset.

Actually, the continued use of wetback labor in certain areas of the border country, particularly in the Lower Rio Grande Valley, amounts to nothing more than a subsidy to Lower Valley farmers. They raise the same crops and sell on the same markets at the same prices as do the farmers in other areas who are paying more nearly adequate wages. Yet, they are paying much lower wages for the labor of producing these crops than are the farmers in other areas of Texas and the United States. The cotton farmer in the Lower Valley who pays $1.25 to $1.50 for picking 100 pounds of cotton thus enjoys a direct subsidy of at least $1.50 per 100 pounds compared with the farmers in Arkansas or Mississippi or the Texas South Plains who pay $3.00 or more per 100 pounds.

This poses the question of why and how long are the great majority of farmers of the United States going to allow this unfair competition to exist?

How can a national farm organization, such as the American Farm Bureau Federation, which purports to represent

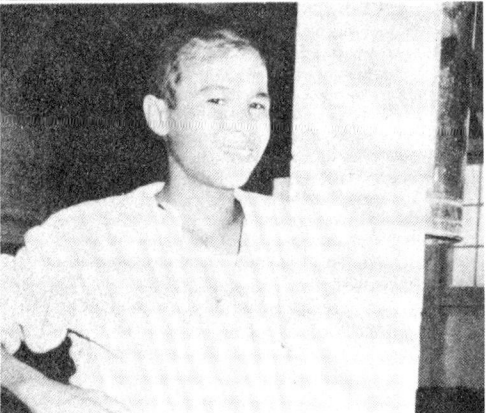

THREE WETBACKS: Top, no other clothes in his possession when apprehended; middle, Alfredo Hernandez, of Michoacan, working on Salado Farm near LaGrulla in Starr County, contracted by a trucker out of Donna; bottom, Santos Pardo, of Piedras Negres, whose haircut indicated he had just gotten out of jail, a fact he admitted.

the interests of all its members throughout the nation, oppose measures to stop the wetback tide merely because a small segment of the organization wants to hold on to its competitive advantage by paying wetback wages?

Are the few County Farm Bureaus in the Lower Rio Grande Valley the tail wagging the American Farm Bureau Federation dog?

Does the Texas Farm Bureau Federation represent its farmer members from one end of Texas to the other—or just its farmer members in the Lower Rio Grande Valley?

Members of the AFBF and the TFBF who are paying a living wage to their farm workers might well wonder about their leaders joining the LRGV Farm Bureau Federation in asking for loosening of immigration restrictions by adoption of a "crossing card system." According to a United Press dispatch from Washington, a delegation urging such action called on Assistant U. S. Attorney General J. Lee Rankin immediately after Attorney General Brownell's pledge to stop the wetback tide. The delegation included John C. Lynn of the American Farm Bureau Federation, J. Banks Young of the National Cotton Council, and C. H. Devaney of the Texas Farm Bureau Federation.

In the El Paso Valley area, where conditions at the time of the survey were fairly good and indications were that the area farmers were gradually accepting more and more the international Bracero Program as an adequate substitute for wetback labor, leaders of the El Paso Valley Cotton Growers Association frankly admitted in a luncheon conference with the survey investigative team that they had no desire to return to wetback labor. Yet, on being queried as to why their association did not lend support to legislation and other measures to control the wetback problem, they admitted cold-bloodedly that, with the border closed and the wetback eliminated from the picture, the agricultural interests they represented would lose a great amount of bargaining power when new negotiations on the Bracero Program were undertaken between Mexico and the United States. In news reports following the Lower Valley delegation's interview with Assistant Attorney General Rankin, the El Paso Valley Association's leaders were quoted as seconding the Lower Valley's efforts at implementation of the "white card crossing" system.

Attorney General Brownell's proposal—and President Eisenhower's public announcement that Brownell had been given authority to "use all the resources at his command" to stop the wetback flow—brought on a storm of protest from along the border. The *El Paso Times*, for example, double-talked around the problem by demanding "full-fledged warfare against aliens illegally in other parts of the country." The *Times* editorial writer assumed that, like the wetbacks, all other foreigners are in the country illegally.

In other parts of the country, the Brownell announcement aroused some realization that the problem must truly be a real one. For example, the *Dallas Morning News* minced no words, pointing out: "Drastic steps should be taken to stop illegal entry. It can be controlled if the government puts sufficient force along the border to do so."

And in El Paso, Federal Judge R. E. Thomason, who finds his court loaded down with immigration cases, declared on the occasion of his sentencing of 255 wetbacks (with suspended sentences, as is the custom for first offenders) that in the wake of the rising tide of wetbacks there were doubtless Communist agents and narcotics peddlers.

"The most practical way to halt this illegal influx of aliens, and possibly what would prove to be the real solution of the problem, would be to expand the Immigration Border Patrol," he said in court, according to the *El Paso Times*. "We have a fine Immigration Service and an excellent Border Patrol, but the trouble is there aren't enough border patrolmen to cope with a situation that is constantly assuming larger and more serious proportions.

"More border patrolmen and not soldiers is the only possible answer. The patrolmen are acquainted with this border and the wetback problem. They know how to handle it," the judge said.

Judge Thomason's suggestion that more border patrolmen be used is a sound one—except for the apparent power of the Lower Rio Grande Valley Farm Bureau and similar organizations. These groups have consistently—and successfully—opposed every effort to increase the strength of the Border Patrol. The Border Patrol has been subjected to a continual harassment campaign. Demagogic opponents of immigration law enforcement can almost always get a response by denouncing the Border Patrol as a "Gestapo" or as "pistol-packing border patrolmen," despite the fact that the patrolmen's pistols are the most unused equipment they possess. Some big farmers in the Lower Valley have two-way radio systems with which to warn their foreman and workers of the approach of the Border Patrol. Gates are locked against the Border Patrol's entry. On occasion patrolmen have been threatened with bodily injury when attempting to enter a farm in the plain performance of their duty and with congressional and executive authority to do so. Wetbacks are aided in hiding from them. Warning systems of all kinds are set up. Ordinarily law-abiding citizens adopt the attitude that anything they do to thwart the enforcement of immigration laws is an honorable step.

'TASK FORCE' STILL BUSY
Patrol Raids Net 2,000 Wetbacks

Express Valley Bureau
McALLEN. — The U. S. Border Patrol, using a "task force" of about 50 men, rounded up an estimated 2,000 illegal aliens day morning in the area McAllen to Weslaco and so the river, Patrol Chief Fl L. Rawls of McAllen rep reon. Most of the others wer Progreso area and were c trated near there, then tak the patrol's detention cent Hidalgo and to border poin voluntary departure to M The roundup started about 5 Rawls said, and went off w incident.

About 1,000 were held a Hidalgo center, to leave Re Monday night by train for across at Brownsville.

The number of apprehensions Monday was about one-third less than those in similar roundups by about 75 patrolmen last week, when about 3,000 aliens were taken

ing July were apprehended by the U. S. Border Patrol and returned to Mexico at Hidalgo, Brownsville

Crossing Card System To Be Aired At Meeting

HARLINGEN — The proposed crossing card system for Mexican farm workers, the increase re- quested in telephone long distance charges, and the controversy be- tween Texas Agriculture Commis- sioner John C. White and the U. S. Department of Agriculture over the fruit and vegetable inspection service are three "hot" subjects due to be aired at the annual con-

The Growers and Shippers protested the telephone com- panies' request to the Federal Communications commission for permission to increase charges ef- fective Oct. 1, Anson said.

The association has requested that a hearing be given the fruit and vegetable industry because

vention of the Texas Citrus and Vegetable Growers and Shippers Association in Houston Nov. 5, 6 and 7.

John B. Hardwicke of Odem and Corpus Christi, president of the Inspection Association, Inc., re- cently organized by growers and shippers to contract with the fed- eral department of agriculture for its services when White declined to renew the state department's contract, will make a full report on the work of the new association. He will be assisted by Roy Gra- ham, vice-president of the Inspec- tion Association and secretary of the Texas Peanut Growers Asso- ciation, representing some 5,000 growers.

Austin Anson, Growers and

Mexico Says Flow Of Wetbacks Encouraged

By Chicago Tribune

Mexico City — The Mexican government has charged that the wave of illegal Mexican workers in the United Sta...

1952, both Texas senators, when Johnson and Connally, as well as Senator McFarland, Democrat, Arizona, voiced against a measure to grant more funds to the Mexi- can border patrol so that its bor- der guard might be improved.

Apparently influential Texas ranchers had brought pressure to keep a weak patrol on the Mexi- can border, it is alleged. Mexi- cans point out that it is much more difficult to keep workers from departing, as they commit no offense until they are halfway across the Rio Grande.

The wetbacks, so called because they swim or wade across the Rio Grande, actually are working in all part of the country and not just in Texas, although Texas are show they are working in Colorado beet fields, in Iowa corn and in Minnesota mines as ll as in scores of other places. One of these workers intend to come, but it is believed the ma- ny never will. Only 250,000

Detention Facilities Lag For Nabbed Wetbacks

Present detention facilities for illegal entrants in the Rio Grande Valley will accommodate only 600 persons but the U. S. Immigration Service is catching an average of 800 a day.

H. P. Brady, U.S. Border Patrol chief in the San Antonio also said Thursday tha 22,861, of which 21,639 McAllen sector.

His records show th to prevent illegal entr Compelling econom behind the apparently able movement of 3 d borers northward and perts point out. Mr workers get from 55 cents a day in the M. By crossing the bo assured of $4 or $5.

However, actually ployes, payments for postal em return home with lit widows.

$20 in their pocket mailed money hom Mexico creating $29,000,000 a year sent by workers States to their fa wetback labor in Grande

Bentsen Tells Cause of Loss

Special to the Light WASHINGTON, June 6 — Two Texas congressmen said here to- day a house vote on cutting immigra- tion funds for the border patrol had not als bill had not be of declared the bot salary C. Fisher, Rep charges by Rep. Rooney, Democrat Brooklyn general wetback labor in employmen

month period ending May 31 080 aliens have been appreh compared with the 1951 fisca when 191,583 were caught.

He cited higher-wage in ments in this country, and r methods of operation utilizin ery officer to his fullest exte chief reasons for the increa

HERE THEY COME, wetbacks illegally in the United States, fugitives from the moment they arrive.

NO 'SUDDEN SURGE' NOTED
Number of Wetbacks Entering Border Counties on Increase

Caller-Times News Service
BROWNSVILLE — Crops may come and crops may go, but wet- backs go on forever.

The number of aliens illegally entering this country from Mex- ico who are caught and pushed back across the border is increas- ing steadily in the area covered by the Brownsville office of the Immigration and Naturalization Service. This area includes Cam- eron and Willacy Counties.

A recent report in the Los Angeles of a "sudden surge" of illegal crossings along the whole inter- national border stretching 1,600 miles from California to Browns- ville pictured federal officials as "mystified" as to the cause.

Federal officials at the Browns- ville office don't appear to be "mystified," however, nor is there any "sudden surge," unless a steady and sizeable increase over the last several years can be cal- led a surge.

There are simply more Mexican workers crossing the border, most of them are field hands, follow- ing the crop seasons, which means

office.

Back in 1947, there were 838 aliens deported and 20,294 making voluntary returns. Those deported go through formal court proceed- ings and are subject to legal pen- alties. If all the wetbacks were given this full treatment, the courts would be clogged for gen-

Open Border Declared Dangerous for Nation

BELLFLOWER, Calif., Sept. 18 — UP-State Attorney General Ed- mund G. Brown has charged the lightly guarded Mexican border is an invitation for "thousands of saboteurs to enter our land."

In an address before the Bell- flower Rotary Club Thursday night, Brown said the ease with which "wetbacks" crossed the border into California this year clearly in- dicated that "representatives of un- ...

Whether or not the heavy an- nual increases continue, local im- migration officials will take it in their stride. The amount of law enforcement they can give depends a good deal on the amount of money Washington puts down for

can border jumpers) to enter our state in one year could easily be the freeway for hundreds or thou- sands of saboteurs to enter for our destruction."

Brown called for "realistic con- trol of those entering this coun- try" and warned there must be federal recognition of this has

"We do not propose an Iron Cur- tain between Mexico and the United States," the state legal officer said. But, he added, "it is certainly unrealistic that we maintain strin-

Wetback Charge Distorted, Says Valley Farmer

WESLACO, June 8 — Rep. J. Rooney's statement in Congress on employment of "wetbacks" by prominent Rio Grande valley grow- ers was "distorted."

Ogle, president of the Rio Grande Valley Chambe said in a telegra legraphed Sons. and Tom Conna charged that Ro xpert on border ding 25 hours l weeks ago or sponsored trip t

Wetback Surge Seen as Patrol Moved Back

SAN ANTONIO, July 3 — Announcement that most U. S. border patrolmen will be with- drawn from the lower Rio Grande Valley brought protests Tuesday that "hordes of wetbacks" will invade the U. S. labor market.

Jacob I. Rodriguez of San An- tonio, district governor of the League of United Latin Amer- ican Citizens (LULAC) charged it means "abandoning a vast area to hordes of wetbacks at the ex- pense of citizen laborers."

Rodriguez announced he is fil- ing a formal protest with John

Wetbacks Push Patrol From Valley

SAN ANTONIO, July trict Immigration chief Holland, San Antonio the patrolmen back 80 mi the border to the U. caught of the face of an illegal migration from Mexico.

The move was described as strategic withdrawal from the Rio Grande Valley where the tide Mexicans invading the country has passed the 800

land said a shortage of man- forced him to redeploy his patrolmen along a line Brownsville, east to Fal Riviera, south to King- and said the withdrawal will legal entrants from spreading other parts of the ....

ley will not be over- land continued. thousands of Mexicans the region, in the next stopped." He said as many as from

WETBACKS INCREASING

Mexico Says Texans Blocking Effective Patrol of Border

Copyright, 1953, Chicago Tribune
MEXICO CITY, Aug. 23. — The Mexican government has charged that the wave of illegal Mexican workers in the United States, reported to be 1,750,000, is due to pressure by Texas and Illinois farmers to maintain an ineffective United States Border Patrol Service.

The Mexican secretary of foreign relations, Luis Padilla Nervo, is being quoted in the Mexican press as saying that the increasing number of illegal entries from Mexico into the United States has been encouraged because American ranchers and farmers prefer to use illegal entrants, as they can pay them lower salaries and are not forced to offer any guarantees such as are extended legal migratory labor. Legal entrants are guaranteed minimum wages and living conditions as well as transportation.

While the Mexican officials have not made any public statements, they let it be known that they are aware that on June 26, 1952, both Texas senators, then Johnson and Connally, as well as Sen. McFarland (D-Ariz.) voted against a measure to grant more funds...

shortage of male help. These officials say they will welcome a proposed measure to have U. S. troops guard the Mexican border to prevent illegal entries.

Mexico has said it will cooperate in the effort to pick up as many of the illegal Mexican workers in the United States as possible. But experts realize it is a hopeless task.

Compelling economic reasons behind the apparently uncontrollable movement of Mexican laborers northward are plain, experts point out. Mexican farm workers get from 55 cents to 90 cents a day in the Mexican fields. By crossing the border they are assured of $4 or $5.

However, actually most of them return home with less than $10 or $20 in their pockets. Some have...

mailed the money home, the Bank of Mexico crediting dollar income of $29 million a year to postal orders sent by workers in United States to their families in Mexico. But most of them find they charged for bed and board by farmers, can't resist having iron clothing, which is cheaper better than Mexican cloth visit the innumerable cheap spots which do a big business visitors.

Studies have shown that Mexican wetbacks actually small plots of land in which they leave to their farm while they go to earn money for a help But scores lose their lives ing the Rio Grande in which ually a dangerous attempt ter themselves.

Immigration Of Wetbacks On Increase

New York Times News Service
LOS ANGELES, May 9—Illegal immigration from Mexico into the Southwestern United States, on the increase since World War II, has reached such overwhelming proportions that officers of the United States Immigration Service admit candidly, if unofficially, that there is nothing to stop the whole nation of Mexico moving into the United States if it wants to.

The numerical equivalent of more than 10 percent of the population of Mexico has come in already.

A record total of 87,416 border jumpers was caught last...

Valley Raids Net 2,500 Wetbacks

EXPRESS VALLEY BUREAU
RUSSELLTOWN—A "task force" of 75 border patrolmen, directed by plane-to-ear radio, apprehended an estimated 2,500 illegal aliens in this area Wednesday in a five-hour period, the largest one-day haul of the season in the Valley, John W. Holland of San Antonio, district director of immigration and naturalization, said the patrolmen covered some 30 or 40 square miles, starting about 4:30 a.m. and taking most of the aliens into custody by 10:30 a.m.

Asst. U. S. Com. of Immigration Willard S. Kelley of Washington, D. C., came to the Rio Grande Valley personally to direct the huge roundup.

The aliens were collected at his small settlement midway between Brownsville and San Benito for voluntary departure to Mexico. Holland said about 1,000 were taken to the detention center at Hidalgo to leave by Reynosa on the Wednesday night train to Torreon. Nearly all the rest were sent directly to Matamoros or Reynosa. Some were held for questioning, Holland added, including several

workers before they were returned to Mexico.

The aliens included men, women, children and babes in arms. Most of them appeared to be fairly recent arrivals, Holland said, and most of them were employed as cotton pickers.

Some, he added, were living in shacks, some in tents, some under trees or tarpaulins and some of the men were sleeping in cotton rows, using partly-filled cotton sacks as mattresses. Many were women and children, he said, and their living conditions were not conducive either to their own health or that of the community where they were found.

Patrolmen questioned other workers in the area, Holland

CROSSING THE RIO GRANDE when it is low is easy, even within sight of bridge where law enforcement officers work.

Quick Hiring on Farms Cause of Wetback Rise

BY ASSOCIATED PRESS
MEXICO CITY, Aug. 20.—The foreign ministry said Thursday the basic reason for illegal migration to the United States is the willingness of U.S. farmers to employ wetbacks.

Jose Gorostiza, vice-minister of foreign affairs, said the only sure way of halting the movement of the illegal aliens would be a United States law making a crime to hire them. His statement came on the heels of a talk with Manuel Tello, the Mexican ambassador in Washington, on plans to reduce the flow of the migrants.

The Truman administration presented a law providing penalties for employment of illegal migrants. It was defeated in Congress.

Gorostiza said the movement of wetbacks recently has been no greater than usual. However, he said the lack of farm work in the United States, due to drought, has increased farm unemployment. This, in turn, has left wetbacks without jobs so their presence is more apparent.

He added that farmers prefer the illegal migrants to legally contracted workers because they can pay them less and do not have to meet minimum housing requirements which Mexico demands for...

Valley Reaps Rich Harvest

McALLEN, June 18. — Lower Rio Grande valley farmers and produce men harvested a nice harvest on cantaloupes and tomatoes this spring.

The biggest known shipment was $300,000 from 300 acres of cantaloupes in a field about 9 miles west of McAllen.

The highest authenticated return on an 80-acre field. A tomato grower, T. B. W., former McAllen mayor, expects to harvest $1000 worth of tomatoes per acre field. In one week he had $400 worth of tomatoes per acre. He had made more than the highest previous before that, was still receiving.

It brought the total of apprehensions for this year to 292,183, and was receiving increase over the corresponding 16 cents per pound period last year of 164,773, or 77 percent.

$1500 AN

Shig Narhara of loupes at the rate acre. A produce the sale of $60,00 taloupes from 8 Wilfred Dev...

WETBACKS

Column 2, back page, this section

hensions exceeded by 1,553 the previous monthly record of 85,863, registered in August 1952. More actormal harvest season peak of illegal immigration in the fall, provided convincing evidence that apprehensions in the previous months of this year reflected a trend to new levels.

The April total was 12,721 above the previous month; 41,755 more than in April last year, and 13,465 more than the highest previous April, in 1951.

It brought the total of apprehensions for this year to 292,183, an increase over the corresponding period last year of 164,773, or 77 percent.

On the basis of the first four months, this year's apprehensions would total more than 876,000, as compared with 316,000 last...

Agricultural Council Head Raps Deportation Policies

McALLEN, Oct. 28. (AP)—Jim, president of the American Agricultural Council, charged day that hearings on the legitimate requests of Mexican aliens main in the United States certain conditions are...

said that the results of such policy are concluded by policy as the Rio Grande. of the commissioner nation and naturalization. blames the "policy making Washington for the situation, He claims the results of deportation of 500 U. S. Mexican-U. S. day along the said an amendment to migration law makes it possible to suspend deportation until it would work a hardship to citizens of the

Griffin (district immigration service chief at San Antonio that the law enforcement...

signal action as is provided by Council was organized by a group of farmers to work together on problems involving Use of Mexican labor.

"The American farmer doesn't want to work with difficulty...

offense until they are a citizen of the wetbacks, so called because they swim or wade across the Grande, actually are working in all parts of the country and not just in Texas, although Texas farmers are more dependent upon them than any others. Studies here show they are working in Colorado beet fields, in Iowa cornfields, and in Minnesota mines as well as in scores of other places. Some of these workers intend to return, but it is believed the majority never will. Only 250,000 legal migratory workers went north this year and practically all will return as bonds are posted compelling it.

Mexican government has...

HEALTH AND SANITATION
"TAMPIQUITO"

They call it *Tampiquito* (or little Tampico) but why, nobody knows. It is a wetback camp lying just off the Military Highway almost due south of Donna, Texas, in the Lower Rio Grande Valley. *Tampiquito* grows haphazardly out of the north bank of the Rio Grande.

If the wind is from the south or the southeast, it is difficult to enter the camp from the Military Highway . . . the stench is sickening, and more than one visiting reporter or investigator has emptied the contents of his stomach after or during a brief visit to the camp. Seasoned veteran Karl Detzer, roving correspondent for the *Readers Digest*, became violently ill during a visit to the camp several weeks before the survey team was there. Father Matthew H. Kelly, executive director of the Bishops' Committee for the Spanish-Speaking, stated that he had never seen so much misery and filth concentrated in such a small area.

Garbage, filth, excrement (human and animal) are scattered everywhere, with children running and playing in the unwholesome atmosphere. Hordes of flies blanket the foul-smelling debris and then disperse to contaminate the food of the camp's occupants and bring disease and possible death to all—particularly the innocent, helpless children.

This is *Tampiquito*—one of hundreds of wetback camps along the Rio Grande, filled almost as soon as it is emptied by a Border Patrol raid, passed daily by hundreds of U. S. citizens and tourists who are unaware of its existence—and who never realize that this breeding ground for disease and death lies only a few hundred yards from the well-travelled Military Highway. Little do they realize the squalor hidden behind the artificial facade of the famous "Magic Valley."

A dirt road leads to the river bank and the camp. Between the road and the camp runs a deep ditch, through which, during the wetter seasons, runs seepage water carrying with it sewage and other filth—the only source of drinking and bathing water for the unfortunate wetback inhabitants of the camp. There is no design or pattern to the camp; lean-tos and shacks, carelessly thrown together, stand or lean wherever there is a little shade cast by a tree. Canvas, stretched between the trees serves as a roof, stacked fruit boxes serve as beds, and mother earth is the only floor. The camp covers almost half an acre and undoubtedly accomodates, at full capacity, more than five hundred men, women and children.

For lack of adequate facilities, no doubt "too expensive" for the camp operator to provide, the daily necessities of the inhabitants, according to all visible evidence, are performed anywhere and everywhere. These reporters saw drinking water being drawn from the canals running alongside the camp—which were carrying seepage being pumped up from the relatively dry river bottom. Innocent children were bathing in the same "*Charcos*" or water holes—without soap.

Two visits to the camp were made by the reporters of this survey. The first, during the afternoon of June 12, was made in the company of Senior Patrolman Sam Mc-Cone of the McAllen Border Patrol Unit in one car. The wetbacks, seeing only one car with three occupants, remained indifferent. Past experience told them this was not a raid and that it would be impossible to apprehend and haul away any of them from the camp. Their indifference and disdain for one Border Patrolman and two reporters were all too evident. Curious ones blocked the paths, wait-

WETBACKS ESCAPE from Tampiquito across the Rio Grande to Mexico.

ing until one of the party asked permission to pass before moving aside. Not one of them showed the least inclination to head for the brush or the river bottom lying just a few hundred feet away. The women went about their business. Some of the young men continued with their crap shooting, and the visiting party was almost totally ignored except for the children who were fascinated with the camera and flash bulbs.

One young man was courteous enough to point out the cemetery with the little wooden crosses showing where a number of wetback children had been buried. A woman pointed out a dilapidated lean-to where five expectant mothers were congregated awaiting the birth of their children. All of them showed signs of nutritional deficiencies and had unhealthy pallors. Two had skin sores, indicating that the unborn children had two strikes against them before birth. Three of the prospective mothers were common-law wives, stating that they had been married without benefit of any ceremony, church or civil.

In almost every lean-to or shack were children obviously suffering from nutritional deficiencies and the consequent anemia and rickets. Their little spindly legs and arms and their grossly distended bellies were reminiscent of concentration camp pictures of Nazi Germany—the facial bone structure clearly etched by the tightly drawn translucent skin; deathly pale, large, innocent, pitiful eyes, staring, as if in wonderment, and set back deep in the eye sockets. It was easy to understand the reason for the cemetery and the little wooden crosses, but difficult to understand why such conditions were allowed to exist in the Lower Rio Grande Valley, the so-called "Magic Valley."

On the river bank, a few feet away from the camp, a pumping site was being used that day as a laundry. Only one woman, surrounded by a gang of children, was washing clothes. A large group of young men lolled nearby, watching the operation with critical eye. The visiting reporters were ignored until the first camera flash-bulb was used, after which resentment was shown with black looks directed at the cameraman and with cracks about the Border Patrol.

A group of women, better dressed and groomed than the average, were interviewed. Acording to all of them, they were "laundresses" doing the laundry for the young men in camp who had no womenfolk of their own. However, in a later interview with another woman living with her husband and family in a nearby hutment, it was claimed that the "laundresses" were the camp prostitutes and

TAMPIQUITO: Wetback hut at camp known as Tampiquito; lone patrolman, left foreground, doesn't disturb wetbacks who know it takes more than one to gather them in; canal provides water for all purposes, including washing of clothes.

rarely did their own personal laundry, let alone that of anyone else.

The second visit to *Tampiquito* was made the following morning shortly after dawn, this time with what is known as a Border Patrol Task Force. The Task Force consisted of eight patrolmen, a truck, a passenger bus and two cars, with all vehicles controlled and directed by a two-way radio system under the orders of Senior Patrolman Sam McCone. The camp was approached from the north, the east and west; there was no way of approaching from the river bottom lying to the south. All three sides covered were approached simultaneously, but as the first clouds of dust rose from the roads, signalling the movement of the vehicles, the camp inhabitants scattered like quail into the brush and across the dry river bottom to the Mexican side where they stopped in plain view of the frustrated Border Patrolmen. By the time the members of the Task Force reached the camp, a matter of seconds, the able-bodied and speedy of both sexes had already "flown the coop." Those left in camp were only the children, the sick, the old and the feeble, and the few citizens supervisors. Out of an estimated 500 wetbacks, only a little over 100 were apprehended. This in a matter of a few minutes.

Meantime, those who had scattered across the dry riverbed to the Mexican side sat there in full view of the patrolmen, laughing, joking and gesticulating at the discomfiture of the practically empty-handed officers. Some climbed trees on the high Mexican bank, scouting the situation and preparing to give a signal on the departure of the patrolmen.

The abandoned children, many of whom were already tackling the duties of the mother, keeping the charcoal brazier going and palming out the tortillas, showed no fear of the Border Patrol and stated that their parents would be back just as soon as the Task Force left. They knew from experience that the Border Patrol was powerless to move them from camp without their parents.

Senior Patrolman McCone, disturbed by the meagerness of the apprehensions, stated that the camp was raided frequently, or as frequently as personnel and facilities permitted, but no matter how fast the Border Patrol emptied the camp, it was just a matter of hours before it was filled to capacity again. Asked if the operator of the land on which *Tampiquito* was located was big enough to use such a large wetback laboring force, McCone was of the opinion that a number of wetbacks were living in the camp but working on neighboring farms. Had the operator ever used *braceros?* Not to McCone's knowledge. But, of course, the answer to the Bracero Program and the International Labor Treaty lay there, before the eyes of anyone who cared to look . . . . . . *Tampiquito!*

TAMPIQUITO HOUSING: Huts and tents share the crowded area known as Tampiquito.

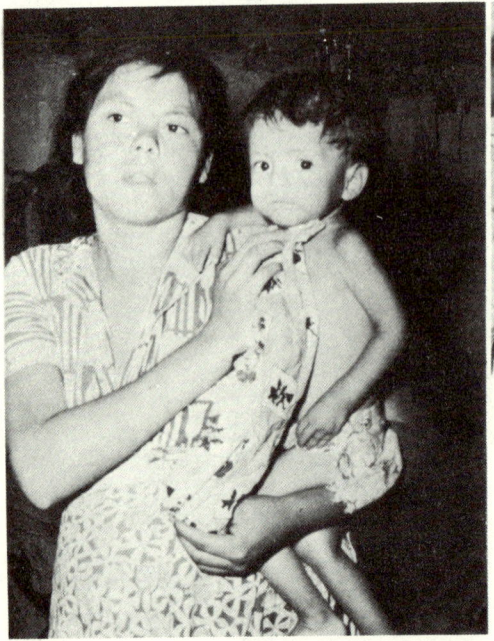

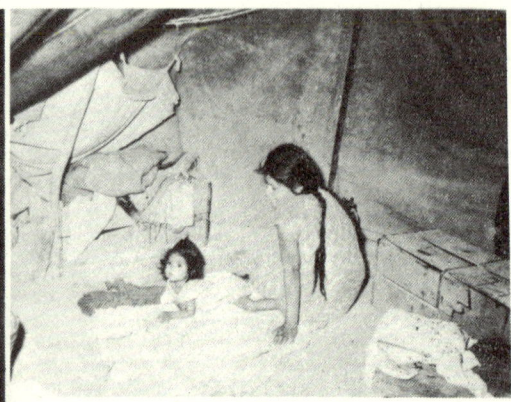

NO DOCTOR: Mother and child at Tampiquito, both ill, but unable to have a doctor.

WETBACK CHILD: Maria Emeteria Moreno holds Jose Moreno, 14 months, in their Tampiquito home.

TAMPIQUITO CHILDREN: These five abandoned children at Tampiquito, whose parents fled across the Rio Grande when the Border Patrol raided the area, were certain their parents would return as soon as the Patrol departed.

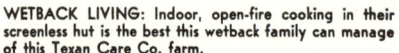

WETBACK LIVING: Indoor, open-fire cooking in their screenless hut is the best this wetback family can manage of this Texan Care Co. farm.

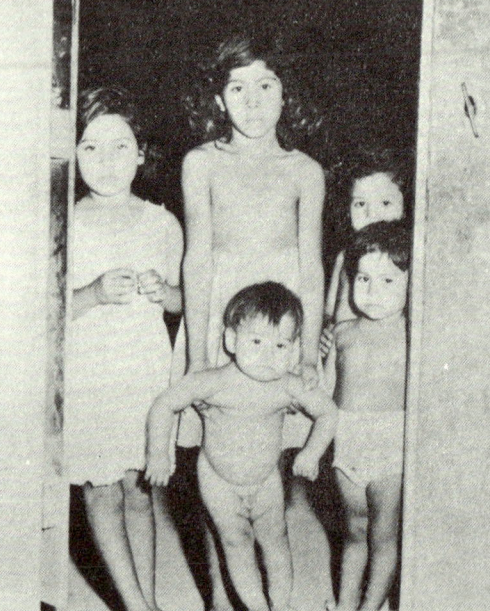

WHAT PRICE WETBACKS — *in Disease?*

DISEASE RATES: 1952

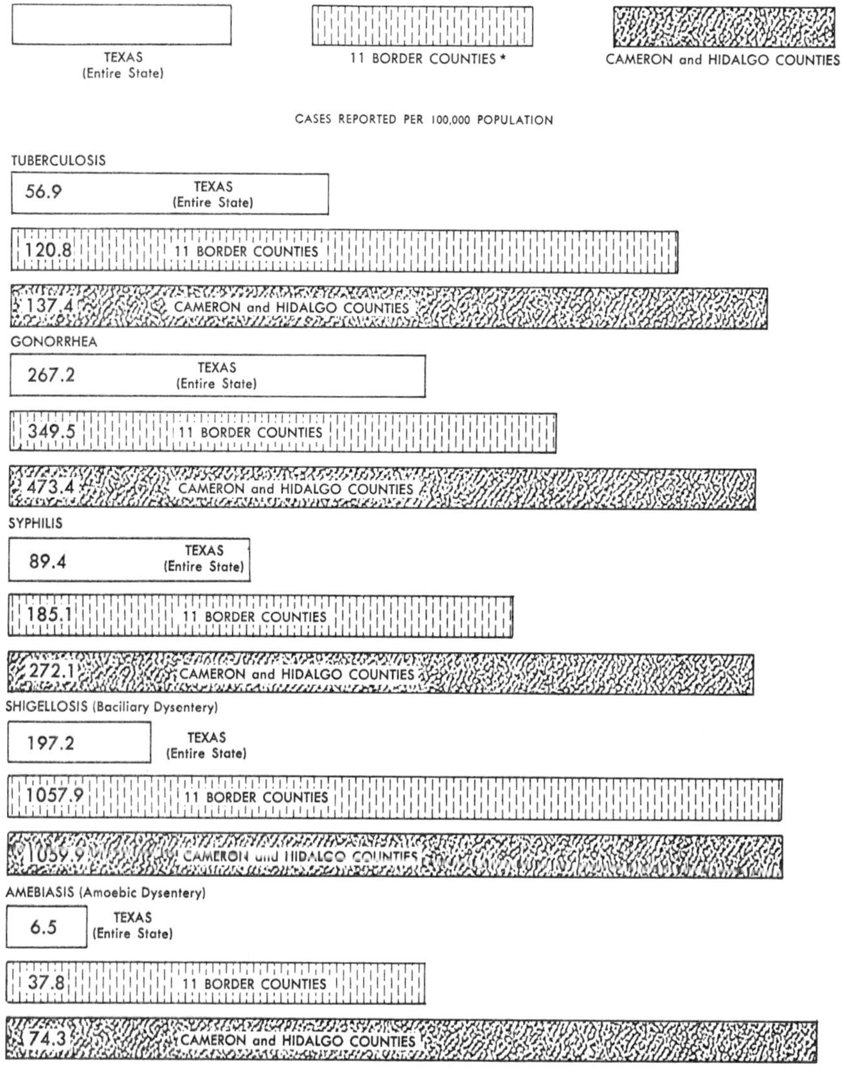

| TEXAS (Entire State) | 11 BORDER COUNTIES * | CAMERON and HIDALGO COUNTIES |

CASES REPORTED PER 100,000 POPULATION

TUBERCULOSIS
- 56.9 — TEXAS (Entire State)
- 120.8 — 11 BORDER COUNTIES
- 137.4 — CAMERON and HIDALGO COUNTIES

GONORRHEA
- 267.2 — TEXAS (Entire State)
- 349.5 — 11 BORDER COUNTIES
- 473.4 — CAMERON and HIDALGO COUNTIES

SYPHILIS
- 89.4 — TEXAS (Entire State)
- 185.1 — 11 BORDER COUNTIES
- 272.1 — CAMERON and HIDALGO COUNTIES

SHIGELLOSIS (Baciliary Dysentery)
- 197.2 — TEXAS (Entire State)
- 1057.9 — 11 BORDER COUNTIES
- 1059.9 — CAMERON and HIDALGO COUNTIES

AMEBIASIS (Amoebic Dysentery)
- 6.5 — TEXAS (Entire State)
- 37.8 — 11 BORDER COUNTIES
- 74.3 — CAMERON and HIDALGO COUNTIES

SOURCE: TEXAS STATE HEALTH DEPARTMENT

*BREWSTER   CAMERON   DIMMIT   EL PASO
HIDALGO   HUDSPETH   MAVERICK   STARR
TERRELL   VAL VERDE   WEBB

SANITARY LIVING: This German "wetback", who jumped his ship in Mexico and crossed the Rio Grande into Texas, was working in a municipally-owned but privately-operated slaughterhouse in McAllen, sleeping on this fly-infested cot alongside the fly-covered animal waste, below.

WETBACK BABY: At Tampiquito, Marina Rodriguez, age 9, holds 7-month-old Moleno Morales, whose distended belly and pus pockets in eyes show the urgent need for medical care.

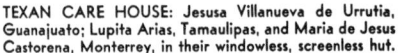

TEXAN CARE HOUSE: Jesusa Villanueva de Urrutia, Guanajuato; Lupita Arias, Tamaulipas, and Maria de Jesus Castorena, Monterrey, in their windowless, screenless hut.

DISEASE

Disease observes no racial or nationality lines. Germ-carrying flies and other insects find the short distances from the open privies of the wetback camps to the fine homes of wetback-employers and other border residents no insurmountable difficulty. Disease and infant death rates in the border country show that the unfortunate and poverty-stricken wetbacks are a constant danger to the health and lives of all border residents, particularly those of Mexican descent who are already suffering a tremendous toll of disease and mortality rates.

These high disease and death rates are not the fault of the people who suffer from them. They don't approve of dirt and disease and death any more than do other more fortunate people. They are living the only way it is possible to live under an employment system which sets wages of 25 or 30 cents an hour—or less. They know nothing about modern sanitation methods or disease control—and couldn't afford them if they did. They know about doctors, but they also know that they can't afford to pay them.

The two Lower Rio Grande Valley counties of Cameron and Hidalgo provide the most striking illustration of what the wetback invasion does to the health of an area. Can the people of these two Lower Valley counties be proud of the fact that in 1952 they had more reported cases of syphilis than Dallas County had—although Dallas has four times as much population? Or are they happy in the thought that their two counties had more than half as much gonorrhea reported as did Dallas?

Do the people in the two Lower Valley counties of Cameron and Hidalgo ever wonder why their two counties, with only 3.6 percent of the population of Texas, in 1952 reported 42 percent of the amoebic dysentery in the state, 6 percent of the gonorrhea, 11 percent of the syphilis and 9 percent of the tuberculosis?

Every citizen of the border country should understand what the wetback tide means to the health of himself, his family, and his neighbors. And every citizen, however far removed from the border, should realize that the spread of the wetback invasion brings these same dangers ever closer to them. Consider these reports, for example:

In 1952, reports from eleven counties* along the U. S.-Mexico border reporting incidence of communicable diseases to the Texas State Department of Health, showed:

2,115 cases of gonorrhea, a rate of 349.5 per 100,000 population compared with a rate of 287.1 for the entire state (the combined rate for Cameron and Hidalgo Counties in the Lower Rio Grande Valley was 475.1).

6,383 cases of shigellosis (bacillary dysentery) a rate of 1054.9 per 100,000 population compared with the state

*Brewster, Cameron, Dimmit, El Paso, Hidalgo, Hudspeth, Maverick, Starr, Terrell, Val Verde, Webb.

rate of 352.7 (and 1063.6 for Cameron and Hidalgo Counties).

1,120 cases of syphilis, a rate of 185.1 per 100,000 compared with 101.9 for the state (and 273.0 for Cameron and Hidalgo Counties);

731 cases of tuberculosis, a rate of 120.8 per 100,000 compared with 57.2 for the state (and 137.9 for Cameron and Hidalgo Counties).

The Report of the President's Commission on Migratory Labor declared: "One of the most sensitive indicators of the state of public health in any population is the rate of infant mortality. This is defined as the number of deaths under 1 year of age per 1,000 live births. For the United States at large, this rate in 1948 was 32. The statewide rate for Texas was 46.2 per 1,000 live births; for the 28 counties of Texas on or immediately adjacent to the border, the rate was 79.5. In the three counties common-

SANITARY DRINKING: Wetback Salvador Padillo, of Valadez, drinks from canal on Salado Farm, Starr County.

ly regarded as constituting the Lower Rio Grande Valley, the infant mortality rates were as follows: Cameron 82.5; Hidalgo, 107.2; Willacy, 127.6."

Records in the State Department of Health show that these infant mortality death rates had dropped in 1952, but the three Valley counties mentioned still had rates far above the Texas rate of 34.2 and the U. S. rate (provisional) of 28.5: Cameron, 52.4; Hidalgo, 60.2; Willacy, 55.1.

The Department of Health and President's Commission findings on infantile mortality are shockingly corroborated by the findings of the Saunders-Leonard report on wetbacks, by a medical treatise published by the School of Medicine of the University of Texas, and by a spot check of inquest records in one typical Lower Valley Justice of the Peace precinct made by the investigative team.

On Page 25 of the Saunders-Leonard report is a table, based on mortality records, on the death by age at death for the English-speaking and the Spanish-speaking populations of Hidalgo County in 1949.

The table shows that among the English-speaking population a total of 366 persons died during 1949 in Hidalgo County. Of these, 11.5 percent died between the ages of birth and 4 years and 10.7 percent died between the ages of birth and one year. At the other end of the scale, the table shows that among the English-speaking population 53.2 percent died at age 65 and over.

For the Spanish-speaking population, the table shows that 48 percent of the 1,378 deaths occurred between the ages of birth and one year and 59.5 percent of the deaths occurred between the ages of birth and four years. At the other end of the scale, only 12 percent of the Spanish-speaking deaths occurred at age 65 or over.

Even allowing for the fact that the Spanish-speaking population out-numbers the English-speaking population at the rate of three to one in Hidalgo County, there is only one explanation for the unequal distribution of the deaths by age among both groups—the poverty, squalor, and disease which the wetback suffers and which he spreads to the American citizens of Mexican descent, in whose midst he lives, by pulling their standard of living down to his own level.

The University of Texas School of Medicine in its quarterly publication, *Texas Reports on Biology and Medicine*, Volume 10, No. 3, Fall of 1952, publishes a medical treatise entitled *Infantile Diarrhea in Texas*. In the first section summarizing the magnitude of the problem, the authors explain that: "Texas comprises about 5 percent of the population of the United States. In 1941, about 10 percent of the diarrhea deaths in the country occurred in Texas infants; whereas, in 1948, 25 percent of the diarrhea deaths in this age group were in Texas children."

Relating the Texas situation to that of New York State, the treatise points out that: "The number of deaths each year in these two states is in the same order of magnitude, yet New York has approximately twice the population as Texas." The treatise further explains that in Texas "the deaths from diarrhea are greatest in the counties of the state with admittedly high Latin-American populations," this finding being based on statistical information from the Texas State Department of Health.

It is noteworthy to observe that the period of 1941 to 1948 during which Texas gained the dubious honor of raising its contribution to national infantile mortality from 10 to 25 percent is the identical period during which the wetback problem has grown from insignificant to major proportions.

The spot check in the Valley Justice of the Peace precinct conducted by the survey investigative team showed that the inquest records for the period May 5, 1951, to December 2, 1952, had a total of 81 deaths listed. Of these, 40 were among children less than four years old. Another check for the period January 1, 1953, to June 8, 1953, showed that of 26 deaths recorded, 10 were among children less than four years old. Although the inquest records did not show the citizenship of the dead persons, the vast majority of the child deaths were classified as Latin-American babies and the Justice stated that from his personal observation most of the babies were wetback babies. The crosses at the *Tampiquito* graveyard take on added significance in the light of this data.

The wetback is a creature of circumstance—circumstance not necessarily of his own choosing or creating but circumstance nevertheless—but there is no justification for an agency of the U. S. government needlessly contributing to those circumstances.

Article 5 of the International Labor Agreement deals in part with the participation of the U. S. Public Health Service in the program. The *bracero* (the legally-contracted Mexican farm laborer) at the recruiting centers in Mexico is first given medical clearance by the Mexican Public Health Service, then given another by the U. S. Public Health Service. However, the U. S. Public Health Service has the right to give additional health checks in the contracting stations on the U. S. side of the border. The most important diseases being sought out are the social diseases and contagious diseases such as tuberculois and silicosis, two diseases which can be found only by x-ray. The U. S. Public Health Service maintains neither x-ray equipment nor technicians in any of the recruiting stations in Mexico, insisting that the *bracero* must travel all the way to the border before being x-rayed, the survey team was informed.

The *bracero* makes considerable personal sacrifice to raise enough money to reach the U. S. border. In addition to the many *"mordidas"* (tips or bribes) to the various officials involved in the procurement of a work contract, there are the incidental expenses incurred in waiting, travelling and arriving at the border with enough work clothes. Most of the *braceros* interviewed admitted that they had arrived at the contracting stations in the United States with but a few cents left.

This is true likewise of the *braceros* who are screened out for health reasons at the U. S. contracting centers. According to figures submitted to this survey by the U. S. Department of Labor, of the bracero aspirants sent to the border in 1952, 844 were screened out for health reasons, 65 percent for tuberculosis.

What happened to these tuberculars who were screened out by the U. S. Public Health Service? Is it logical to assume that, after making the many personal sacrifices to reach the border, the rejected *bracero* will return to his place of origin, hundreds of miles to the south? Many of these *braceros* are heads of families with dependents; many of the single men have depended on the sacrifices of all the members of their families. These screened-out *braceros* arrive on the border without money, and there are no facilities to see that they are returned to their place of origin or to compensate them for the expenses incurred.

So, they do what you would expect: Many return to the Mexican side of the border, wait until nightfall, and cross into the U. S. through an open border as wetbacks, bringing their contagious diseases with them.

"RELAMPAGO"

South of Mercedes, and well below the Military Highway, lying immediately above one of the larger *resacas* of the Rio Grande, stands the Anderson Brick Plant where the Aztec bricks are made. The place is named *"Relampago"* meaning "lightning." Bricks manufactured in this plant are sold throughout the United States, no doubt because of their unusual size and their relatively low price. The bricks are made by hand—and the sweat of wetbacks who are required to make, according to their own statements, 1000 bricks for $4.00 (a good day's work for a man and his family—if the family is big enough). The only piece of mechanical equipment seen on the place was a small power-driven circular saw being used to trim and square broken bricks. All the rest of the work is done with hands and feet, with the clay used in making the bricks being mixed in huge flat troughs by the feet of the wetbacks, using leg power.

Most of the shacks were built of loose bricks, piled one on top of the other to form the walls. The door was made by leaving out one wall. The roof was a canvas stretched over the structure—or a number of loose boards laid across the walls. The good solid earth was the only flooring—and, in many instances, the only bedding. Water for bathing, drinking and cooking was being drawn in huge cans from the *resaca* where it had been stagnating for months during the long drought. The stench was present—but not as strong as it had been at *Tampiquito*.

Most of the inhabitants of *Relampago* were from the State of Guanajuato. A number of them admitted frankly that conditions were bad in Guanajuato—but worse in *Relampago* and that, for the children's sake, they wished they were back in Mexico, but 900 long miles stretched between them and home. As at *Tampiquito*, most of the younger children were ill, running high temperatures from diarrhea and malnutrition. The older inhabitants at *Relampago* couldn't remember how many children had died there, but it was *"en cantidad,"* a considerable number.

RELAMPAGO: This wetback family, top, said they had been trying unsuccessfully to save enough money to get back to Guanajuato, had been in U.S. two years without ever being picked up, wound up each week with two or three dollars after commissary deductions and without any money for medicine for the sick baby; Simon George Herrera, wetback, displays social security card No. SSC 395-26-4892, obtained while working for Central Wisconsin Canneries at Rosedale, Wisconsin; interior of living quarters at brick plant.

HOUSING

In their 1951 report on "The Wetback in the Lower Rio Grande Valley of Texas," Lyle Saunders and Olen E. Leonard declared "without exaggeration that almost all (shelters provided for wetbacks) are small, bare, dark, untidy, under-furnished and overcrowded."*

Saunders and Leonard made on-the-spot investigations of wetback "housing" in the course of preparing their report. Wetback shelters today are the same, if not worse. In many of the wetback camps visited by the GI Forum-Federation investigators, the same huts visited by Saunders and Leonard are being used today—dirtier, more rundown, more dilapidated. Their general description of wetback housing still holds true today:

"Shelters vary in quality from one farm to another, but generally provide nothing beyond the bare minimum. The most common type is a single room shack, seldom larger than 8'x10' or 10'x12'. The better ones are constructed of eight or ten planks nailed on a 2x4 frame. The rare new or nearly new ones may be painted. Most are old, weather-beaten, dark, and draughty. There may or may not be a plank floor; in most cases there is not. Many of the shacks are built of palm fronds; others are thrown together from parts of old packing cases, scraps of tin or galvanized roofing, pieces of brush, or whatever else may be handy. Some few growers supply tents during the harvest seasons. A few provide large open sheds which serve as dormitories. Most of the shacks have a single door and a single window, both unscreened. Some have no windows. There is rarely much furniture. Cooking is done over an open fire kindled in a tub, bucket, or pan which has been filled with ashes. Clothes are hung on nails driven into the walls. The floor serves as chair, table and bed. Some of the larger growers who use wetbacks the entire year provide somewhat better living quarters, but even the 'better' furnishings seldom include more than a small, portable kerosene stove; a few orange crates nailed to the wall to serve as shelves; a table; a chair or two; and, perhaps, a battered iron cot, without mattress.

"The density of wetbacks per room is generally high. It is seldom less than three per room and may be many more. Sometimes individual families are given shacks, sometimes not. One shack on a farm visited by the authors held two women and five men; another one woman and four men. In another lived a woman and five children. One of the children, a daughter of 13, spoke good English and had just finished the sixth grade in the local school. On another farm we saw a one-room shelter containing two beds. In this room lived three women and eight men. These observations could easily be duplicated in almost any part of the Valley."*

We already have seen some examples of wetback housing in this report. A few more pictures should suffice to bear out the truth of the statements made, and the fact that the Saunders and Leonard description of 1951 is just as accurate in 1953.

*Saunders-Leonard Report on Wetbacks.

HOME IS A HOLE: Apprehended wetback emerges from a hole in the ground which had been serving as his home.

HOME IS A CAVE: Wetback homes are dug wherever there is a bit of space available, just so they can have some sort of roof over their heads.

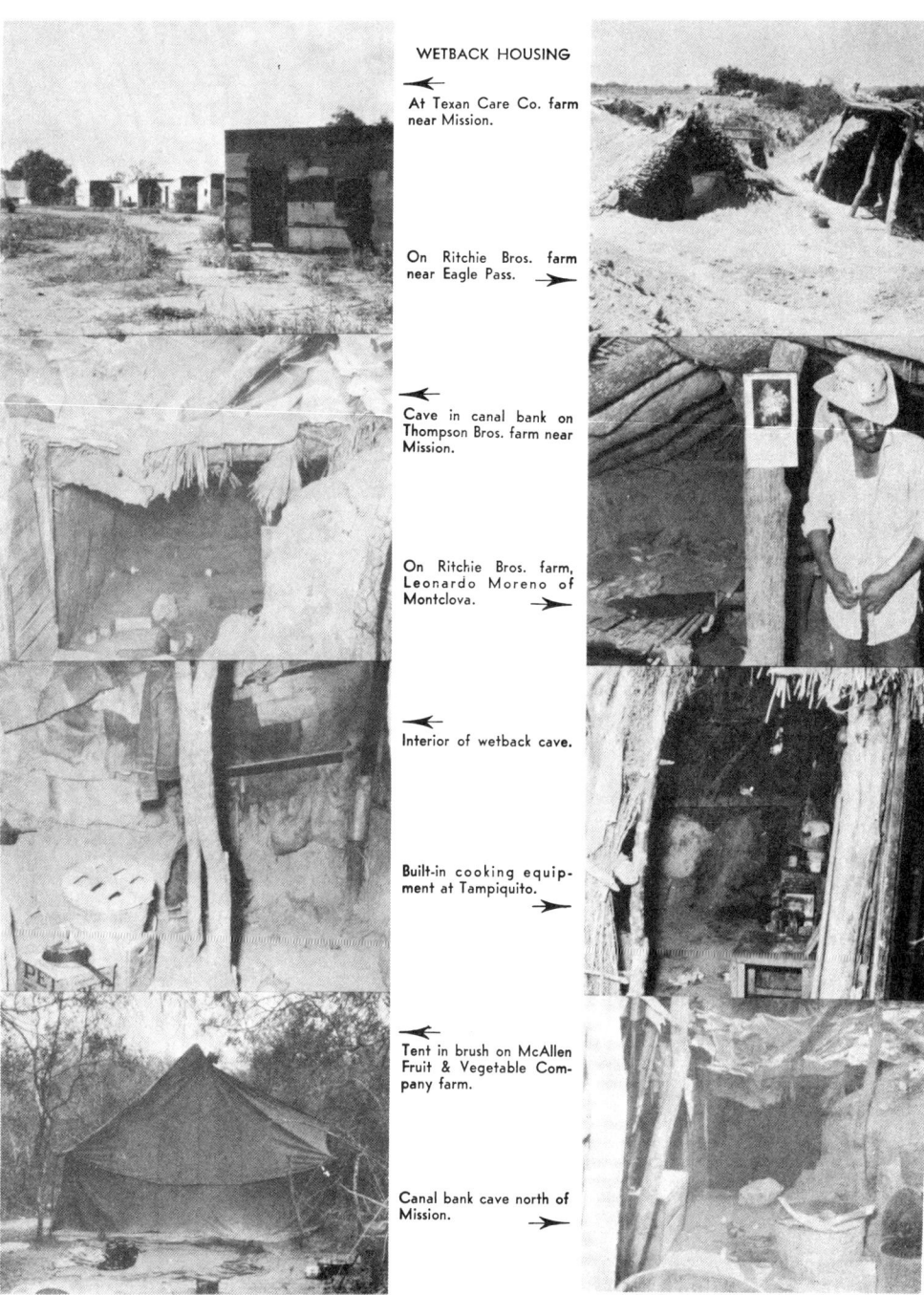

WETBACK HOUSING

At Texan Care Co. farm near Mission.

On Ritchie Bros. farm near Eagle Pass.

Cave in canal bank on Thompson Bros. farm near Mission.

On Ritchie Bros. farm, Leonardo Moreno of Montclova.

Interior of wetback cave.

Built-in cooking equipment at Tampiquito.

Tent in brush on McAllen Fruit & Vegetable Company farm.

Canal bank cave north of Mission.

WETBACKS AND CRIME

Accurate figures on the extent of criminal activities by aliens along the U. S.-Mexican border are impossible to obtain because in so many cases it is never determined for certain whether the criminal concerned is a wetback. But law enforcement officials along the border who dare to speak their minds have no doubt about the contribution wetbacks make to their problems.

In its July 15, 1953 issue, the *San Antonio Light* published the fourth in an excellent series of articles by Ed Castillo, who had toured the Lower Rio Grande Valley investigating wetback conditions. Headlines on the article read: "Migrants Roaming Valley Commit High Percentage of Felonies, Burglaries, Murders; Sick Crowd Hospitals — Wave of Crime, Health Problems Follow Tide of Illegal Aliens into U.S."

The article quoted J. R. Alamia, district attorney in Hidalgo County: "Present figures show 75% of the felonies committed in our country are by aliens. At least 95% of our burglaries are committed by illegal entrants and 50% of our murder cases are those of aliens." (Alamia has since stated that 85 percent is a more accurate estimate of the felonies committed by aliens.)

Alamia further expressed the opinion that many of the unsolved crimes were committed by aliens who then returned across the border to the sanctuary of their native land.

Chief of Police C. D. Mussey of McAllen in Hidalgo County expressed his opinion of the prevalence of wetback crime in a letter to one of the GI Forum-Federation investigators:

"The presence of illegally entered aliens in this city certainly increases by many times the work of the local law enforcement officers.

"1. They are responsible for a large percentage of our major crimes.

"2. We have to spend much of our patrol time checking, arresting and transferring this type of alien to the Border Patrol.

"3. We have arrested the same alien several times on numerous occasions.

"4. We have to be constantly alert and continuously checking and picking them up or our crime rate would be higher.

"5. We catch many of them before they commit a crime.

"6. The alien prostitutes will increase overnight if given a chance.

"7. The alien juvenile is our largest problem. The State of Texas and the Federal Government will not handle the alien juvenile criminal. As a result, we repeatedly arrest and deport this type of thief or burglar,

Illegal Aliens Blamed For Crime in Hidalgo

By ELEANOR MORTENSEN
Caller-Times Staff Writer

EDINBURG — Illegally-entered aliens or wetbacks are responsible for approximately 75 percent of all crimes committed in Hidalgo County, Dist. Atty. Joe Alamia reported.

Sheriff Vickers Blames Drouth For Burglaries

EDINBURG, June 15 — At least seven [hand] burglaries [...] place [...] office. iff R[...] were "ju[...] stre[...] wa[...] o[...]

Young Wetback Charged With Table Cloth Theft

[obscured text]

Wetback Admits Raping Child

EDCOUCH — Almost a week la[...] after to the hour, a slight 20-year-old peon laborer, Fermin Morales de la Cruz of Edcouch, admitted taking the five-year-old daughter of little Linda Crual child from her bed after his arrest and brutal assault at an Edcouch tavern at 12:50 early Sunday morning[...] Barker, [...] confessed and reenacted the crime with assault with intent to rape breakins have — [...] He was charged in Line. [...] waived examining trial before Justice of the Peace J. M. Chapa Officers said in many cases the Wingert said 7 a.m. Sunday. burglars take their loot back across the Rio Grande immediately, thus making it very difficult to catch them.

$250 in Cash Stolen

One of the latest group of burglaries involved the theft of [...] in cash, [...] usually large ha[...] The m[...] Chief De[...] and De[...] burgla[...] house [...] airy. [...]

Knife-Wielding Thieves Loot Aliens on Way Home

[obscured]

Murder of 3 Still Probed

EDINBURG — Hidalgo County authorities said today they had not yet identified the two Latin-American women whose murdered bodies were found east of Hidalgo Wednesday, but they were continuing work on several leads in the case.

Chief Deputy Sheriff Tom Wingert and Assistant District Attorney Willis Perkin directed the investigation which, they said, was far from closed.

Perkin said officers believed that the two women had at one time worked in Texas. He said it was considered likely that they had relatives who were now working in the Valley area.

Perkin said the women had parently been murdered last [...] into the residence of Fra[...] night after crossing the Cavazos Salinas. A billfold containing $53 and seven pesos Grande from Mexico. Their bodies were found [...] taken, along with the clothing. nesday by a farmhand while looking for stray cattle. Wingert said they had been raped.

There were no papers to indicate who the women were. One was about 40, the other 16 or 17.

Perkin said there was apparently no connection between the murders of the women and the killing of a Latin-American man, abo[...]

Alien Charged With Burglary at Mission

EDINBURG — A charge [...] glary has been filed agai[...] Gallegos Ramirez, a 25[...] alien, in connection with [...] of money and clothing from sion home on July 18. Ramirez was accused of [...]

Alien Held For Billfold Theft

EDINBURG — Abundio Busta[...] mante, a 21-year-old alien, was charged today with stealing billfold of Jubentino Gabriel, also an alien, while Gabriel w[...] asleep.

Authorities said both men were ed near McCook. Deputy Sheriff R. H. Gilliam and Henry Goet-rick reported Bustamante and Gabriel slept in the same room witl a number of other alien workers Officers said the wallet contair $35 and 45 pesos.

---

many of whom we have arrested several times. They will steal anything that is movable.

"Holders of local crossing cards commit a much larger percentage of our petty theft, such as shoplifting, than do the illegally entered aliens.

"Without the alien criminal, our job of policing would be considerably easier. Although we are undermanned, according to national standards, we are burdened with the additional duty of trying to keep our town clean of the alien criminals who roam over our streets at will."

Chief Mussey was quoted as saying substantially the same thing in the *Light* article by Castillo.

Just as the wetback often is the perpetrator of crime, so also is he the victim of those criminal elements within his own group. Countless cases have been recorded in the Valley and along the Rio Grande elsewhere of unfortunate wetbacks who fell victim to roving bands who lurk in the paths leading to and from the river bank, waiting to snare the unlucky wetback as he heads back to Mexico with his savings of American dollars. These criminal elements do not hesitate in taking human life, even for the few, paltry dollars in their victims' pockets or for the clothing and the other meager personal belongings that the victim may carry with him. Case after case has been recorded all along the Rio Grande of unidentified bodies of wetbacks found floating in the stagnating, murky river or along its banks.

The river affords a quick escape route both ways for criminals on both sides of it. The survey investigators were present one afternoon in mid-June when Mexican police in Reynosa alerted the U. S. Border Patrol to the escape into the American side of two criminals who had just robbed, in plain daylight, a Reynosa jewelry store of 25,000 pesos worth of watches and other items. The meager personnel of the Border Patrol on duty at the time was quickly withdrawn from other duties and assigned to patrol the area where the criminals had last been seen on the American side. Despite a two to three hour watch along the bank and side roads leading out of the area, the criminals escaped through the thick brush.

Crime, of course, is not limited to the wetback, but there can be no denying that the presence of thousands of people in bad economic circumstances with an easily-crossable river affording quick escape is certain to mean that a large percentage will have no hesitancy at breaking laws, at committing crimes. To many — particularly the *pachuco* types — laws are meant for only one purpose — to be broken, whether they be immigration laws or other laws.

Border areas such as the Lower Valley are certain to have a perpetual crime wave just as long as the border is left open for the unchecked travel of anybody south of the border who wants to come north.

Mexico Center of Red Spy Ring In Hemisphere, Newspaper Claims

FTH COLUMN SEEN

Alien Influx Perils Nation, Senate Told

WASHINGTON —(P)— Senator McCarran (D-Nev.) said today a assive, illegal infiltration of aliens into this country is "potentially ore dangerous" than an armed invasion.

This influx would provide an enemy nation "a ready-made fifth lumn," McCarran said.

The secret testimony of immigration ent, showed:
1. Aliens illegal¹¹
y are cou¹¹
id may tot¹
2. Among
ommunists,
her crimina¹
3. The imm
ade only sn
id deport th
gners becaus
ctors, includ¹
id money.
For instance,
a judiciary au
at last spring
e immigration
ork were unde
und up cases
i their own initia
aff could not ke
ne work.
McCarran's stat
anied a report to
subcommittee whi
a investigation of
vities.

Border Entrie
Another member of
ittee, Senator O'C
aid in a separate st
Vindsor, Ontario, an
ssembly points for all
legal entry into the U.
rrests for attempted
lexico total 500,000 a y
f these are "wetback
ans who cross the sh
rande River to look fo
arm hands.
O'Conor said there a
50,000 aliens from Euro
i Cuba and that "many a
iunists, with the result th
a is a hot-bed of communi
The subcommittee report
H. Pennington, chief of t
iigration service's New Yo
estigating staff, as testi
bout rich and powerful
muggling rings, well organ
nd aided by high-powered
ers skilled at finding loophole
he laws.
Some of these lawyers, Penn
on said, "appeared to have bi
acts whereby they can have bil
ntroduced in Congress as special
egislation for the benefit of
articular alien

Illegal Aliens Flood Nation

BY ASSOCIATED PRESS
WASHINGTON, Aug. 20.—
Senator McCarran (D-Nev.) sai
Monday that possibly 5,000,0
aliens have poured into t
country il
gally, creat
a situation
tentially n
danger
than an a
invasion.
Vast
bers of
tant C
nists,
banditi
othe
nal s
among the 5,000,000, M
stated.
He said they woul
an enemy nation with
made fifth column."
McCarran is chair
Senate subcommitte
nal security. He has
completed an inve
alleged subversive
the United States.
Senator said his
about illegal alier
secret testimony
tion officials.
Handicapped b
and staff, m
Service has m
to seek out un
ers and deport
said. His st
panied the st
port to the Ser

Woman's Arrest Breaks Border Smuggling Ring

BROWNSVILLE—A smuggling ring specializing in undesirable European aliens — communists, criminals and anyone else who couldn't get legal entry papers — has been broken up in Brownsville, U.S. Immigration today.

rged $2,000 a head, ice for the service in these parts. an woman has al ed and convicted in here. An Argentine picked up in Hous ted. One Puerto Ric Galveston fled when ached and another st when immigration ded they didn't have nce to make a case court.

we broke up a smug pecializing in Europ a just beginning big scale," S. L. immigration investiga As far as we know aid is the highest fe ed in this locality for ice."

who gave her name as na Sanders was co federal court here this

MUGGLING, Page 2)

Agents Enter As Diplomats

MEXICO CITY, June 4 —UP— The newspaper "Excelsior" charged Thursday Mexico is the center of a Soviet spy ring commissioned to undertake subversive campaigns in the United States and South America.

Excelsior in a front-page story aid Red agents enter Mexico freely under diplomatic passes" through direct instructions a campaign to gradually con er Mexico and the Central and th American countries."

he paper charged the Soviet bassy in Mexico City "controls Communist centers throughout ico and South America but er acts directly... everything lone through the Polish and hoslovakian legations."

e paper added, "The Kremlin he secret Russian police have al agents in the Soviet em to give instructions to fel ravelers.

e agents come to Mexico di from Russia or some other ean nation and the enter the y freely, carrying documents Russian embassy. According to their passports, they are

SUBVERSIVE WETBACKS?

Along a wide-open border, such as that of the United States and Mexico, anything can happen. While the nation spends millions of dollars each year seeking out subversives within the country, any given number of them could easily slip into the country to replace those apprehended.

Who is to say how many Communists mingle with the hordes of wetbacks wandering casually into the country across the Rio Grande?

If one out of every two wetbacks—or one out of every five—is arrested, does the same ratio hold true for subversive agents and spies? Or won't the ratio of those unapprehended be much greater, considering the intelligence and training of the subversive or the spy?

In July, 1953, the District Immigration Office at San Antonio reported that in two and one-half years, 15 aliens who had come in from Mexico had been deported under subversive charges. They were of the following nationalities: Mexico, England, Germany, the Philippines, Iraq, Palestine, Poland, Russia and Chile. How many slipped in without being apprehended? How many from communist-dominated Guatemala came over masquerading as Mexicans?

During the time that the survey investigators were up-river at Eagle Pass, news reports from the other end of the river reported that a smuggling ring headed by a Spanish-speaking Costa Rican woman had just been broken in Brownsville by Immigration Service investigators. This particular ring, the news reports stated, was

WETBACKS CITED AS AID TO MOBS AND SUBVERSION

SAN FRANCISCO, Cal., Aug. 16 —ty. Gen. Herbert Brownell, Jr. aid Sunday the "wetback invasion" from Mexico has created a major law enforcement problem in the United States, increased racketeering and heightened the danger of subversion.

The number of Mexican nationals entering the U. S. illegally "is increasing to an all-time high," Brownell said, "while tens of thousands of illegal entrants pour across the border."

Organized crime groups prey upon these wetbacks, the attorney general said, as dupes for prostitution number of murders and lots of saults and thefts have been repo ed, he said, because the wetbac are afraid to complain to author ties.

The danger of subversion has been increased considerably by the invasion, Brownell said, pointing out the ease with which spies could enter the country in the guise of a wetback seeking farm employment in the U. S.

"We haven't received any authenticated cases of subversion," he said, "but the danger certainly exists."

on American did in Guiana rece Britain did in Guiana rece and to self-determination for peoples left no doubt about whom he was talking.
IT WAS probably coincidence, but Assistant Secretary of State John Moors Cabot said in Wash ington on the same day that the government of Guatemala is "openly playing the Communist game." He pointed out that "the official Guatemalan newspaper follows the Communist line."
Guatemala, of course, denies vigorously that it is Communist even Communist inclined. Its president, Jacobo Arbenz, insists that he is not a follower of the Kremlin. Nevertheless, Mr Men doza obviously voiced the views of his government.
HE SPOKE in Spanish, but phrases translated into Eng kably like those

iously av ment of its onsidered se rather Guatemalan plantations being subjected to wage demands and taxes which it con siders excessive.
A strike of railway workers paralyzed the country's trans portation system this year, and gave the government an extra excuse to proceed with plans to take over the narrow-gauge sys tem.
THE UNITED States sent a note earlier this year in which it reminded the Guatemalan gov ernment that Washington takes a dim view of expropriation of American-owned assets an America capital but did no where. The American capital but did no deter it from seeking to co the United Fruit under a pl gram of "land reform."
Also affected by it govern becc is what had tou

Communist Tendencies In Guatemala Cause Worry

By RALPH CHAPMAN
New York Herald-Tribune News Service

UNITED NATIONS, NY—Be for and during both world wars the presence of German and Japanese agents in Mexico was a source of constant worry to the United States. It became increasingly evident here for the week that a similar cause for

tions, and the desire for free dom.
Another phrase which rang fa miliarly in the ears of UN ob servers was that the people of Guiana "have been wearing the yoke of economic exploitation." What he was supporting was an admittedly leftist group which won an election in Guiana. Its prime minister, Cheddi Ja gan, had his Cabinet were re moved from office when British accused them of pre intrigues."

Going up!

Wetbacks Apprehended, Year by Year

FISCAL YEAR BASIS, JULY 1 - JUNE 30

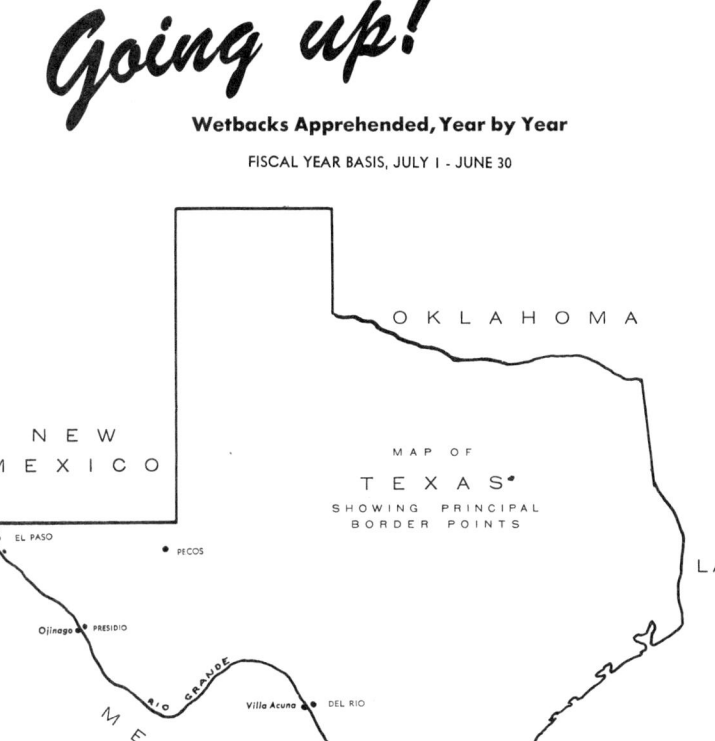

MAP OF TEXAS
SHOWING PRINCIPAL BORDER POINTS

Year	Apprehended
1934	11,200
1935	11,800
1936	12,600
1937	14,100
1938	14,000
1939	12,900
1940	11,200
1941	12,900
1942	15,400
1943	16,500
1944	34,400
1945	71,500
1946	102,200
1947	198,000
1948	197,500
1949	293,000
1950	480,000
1951	513,815
1952	543,538
1953	875,318

Source: U. S. Immigration Service

specializing in the smuggling of undesirable European aliens into the country—charging as high as $2,000 a head! Only official records, not available to these reporters because of their confidential character, can reveal the extent to which subversive elements may be using the open border to infiltrate into the country. Only the same official records can reveal how many aliens were actually smuggled in by the Brownsville ring, and, possibly, how many of these might have been subversives.

The Immigration Service is aware of this crucial phase of the problem, but its officers are the first to admit that no adequate check can be exercised with the limited personnel and investigative facilities at their disposal. In the Del Rio sector of the Border Patrol, for example, which geographically takes in more than eighty counties and extends all the way from the Rio Grande to North Texas, there were only three investigators at the time the survey team gathered its data — three investigators whose regular duties had recently been augmented with the added task of helping the Federal District Attorney prosecute his cases in court.

At the McAllen Detention Center where an average of one thousand men, women and children were being processed daily at the time the survey team visited the Center, the extent of the processing, due to the limited personnel and facilities, was simply the listing of name and address of the alien and asking him whether he was an American or not. Not even a fingerprint check was taken. It would take approximately two to three weeks to get such a check from official F.B.I. and other sources in Washington. In that period of time, the Center's population would soar to 14,000 or 21,000 persons.

This survey makes no attempt to define the extent of subversive infiltration across the Mexican Border. That is a job for the F.B.I. and other governmental agencies entrusted with this responsibility. Our duty is done by pointing out the potential that was found to exist. The American people and the legislative, judicial and executive branches of our government are the ones on whose shoulders rests the responsibility for seeing that action is taken in this regard.

AT McALLEN DETENTION CENTER, above, part of the 1000 wetbacks processed daily line up for departure and deportation.

AT ZAPATA, deported wetbacks wait on Mexican side for truck transportation to Enpalme about 32 miles away.

THE WETBACK'S DOLLAR

On March 5, 1953, *Las Ultimas Noticias*, Mexico City, D. F., carried the following news item on page 3-A:

"According to figures released by the Bank of Foreign Trade, remittances made by the *braceros* to their homes amounted to 30 million dollars last year and constituted the *third largest source* of income to Mexico, after the mining industry and tourists."

On May 1, 1953, *Excelsior*, also of Mexico City, carried a news item announcing that during the year 1952, the 204,000 *braceros* contracted to the United States had earned $67,000,000 and that the Bracero Program had become Mexico's *third largest industry*.

This realization poses three important questions for U. S. businessmen as well as U. S. workers.

How does the loss of $30,000,000 or more, exported from the U. S. by *braceros*, affect retail business in the areas where *braceros* are used extensively?

What is the effect on business of the loss of uncounted millions of dollars leaving the U. S. in the pockets of illegal aliens?

What is the effect on business of the low-wage economy under the wetback system?

The answer to the first question is simple. The $30,000,000 returned to Mexico by the *braceros* in a single year was taken out of the channels of retail trade in the areas where the *braceros* were employed. If U. S. workers had been paid that money, it would have gone immediately into the retail trade channels of those areas, ringing the cash registers of stores, restaurants, theaters, professional men, lumberyards, and other businesses, adding to the entire economy of the area and of the country. Paid to *braceros*, the $30,000,000 stayed out of those local cash registers, booming only the postal money order business of the U. S. Post Offices.

Questions numbers 2 and 3 are more difficult to answer directly. Nobody knows how much money the wetbacks carry back home with them or how much more domestic workers would be paid for the same work if the wetbacks and *braceros* were not so easily available.

In fiscal 1951-1952 (July 1, 1951 to June 30, 1952) a total of 543,538 Mexican aliens—wetbacks—were officially apprehended in the U. S. and returned to Mexico. In fiscal 1952-53 the number climbed to 875,318 apprehended and returned. Officials estimate the figure for this calendar year 1953 may well run over one million.

These figures, it should be remembered, represent only the number apprehended and returned to Mexico. Arriving at the number who have worked and are working in the United States undetected or unapprehended would be only a fantastic guess. Even though a thousand wetbacks a day were being processed at the McAllen Detention Center at the time of this survey, in a day's drive thousands more could be seen working in the fields unmolested. For lack of processing facilities, the Border Patrol in the Lower Rio Grande Valley was being forced *to limit apprehensions to one thousand a day* at the time the survey team was making its survey. The number could have been multiplied many times, depending only on the availability of manpower and facilities.

Because the wetback wage is considerably lower than that of the *bracero*, it stands to reason that the individual wetback is unable to take or send as much money home to Mexico as does the *bracero*. But conversely, since the number of wetbacks working in the U. S. undoubtedly is many times the number of *braceros*, then the total amount of money exported annually undoubtedly is more than the total exported by the *braceros*.

For example, a *bracero* working on a farm in the El Paso area—Carlos Rodriguez of Durango—reported to the GI Forum-Federation investigators that he earned about $24 a week at 50 cents an hour and sent from $18 to $20 a week to his family in Mexico. Simple arithmetic shows that it takes him only $4.00 to $6.00 a week to live. By that same sort of arithmetic, it can be seen that the wetback making $12.50 a week at 25 cents an hour for a 10-hour day would be able to send or take from $6.50 to $8.50 a week home to Mexico.

Even discounting the arithmetic and settling on a figure of, say, $5.00 per week send-home pay, 200,000 wetbacks would mean the export of $1,000,000 a week; 1,000,000 wetbacks (not a fantastic figure), $5,000,000 a week bypassing the channels of local retail trade.

The wetback, of necessity, has buying habits different from the buying habits of the *bracero* and the domestic worker. He is in constant fear of apprehension. He avoids the roads, towns and major shopping centers, at least until he has been around long enough to blend into the population picture. He does most of his shopping through his foreman or at the small rural grocery stores that most big farm operators provide for their wetbacks. He buys only the barest essentials and eats the simplest of food.

In the survey by Saunders and Leonard,* 160 wetbacks were asked the question: "If you could earn $100 or more in the United States, what would you do with it?" Only about 20 percent indicated any desire whatsoever to spend any of the money in the United States. An overwhelming majority had specific uses for the

---
*Report on Wetbacks, Saunders and Leonard, University of Texas, 1951.

money in Mexico: "buy food, clothes, etc. for family in Mexico" or "buy land in Mexico" or "set up a business in Mexico" or "send it, or part of it, to relatives in Mexico," etc.

The best example of what happens to the wetback's dollar, of course, is the Lower Rio Grande Valley of Texas. In 1949, the three Valley counties of Cameron, Hidalgo and Willacy produced 529,364 bales of cotton and paid over $10,000,000 to get it picked. How much of that money went back to Mexico in the pockets of the wetbacks who picked the bulk of that crop? How much was lost to the Valley retail business man? To the wholesalers supplying the Valley stores? To the many other Valley enterprises?

The citizen worker spends his money in the community, pays his share of the taxes and makes a contribution to society. The wetback sends as much of his earnings as possible back to Mexico, while at the same time costing the American taxpayer millions of dollars a year in law enforcement costs—his only contribution to society being in the form of a higher crime rate, a higher disease rate, and a depressed economy. The Lower Rio Grande Valley pays a high price indeed for the privilege of permitting its farmers to use dirt-cheap labor!

At the height of the cotton-picking season, an area of heavy cotton production should find its retail sales booming. The workers are earning money and they are spending it. Even the domestic migrant worker is seeing to it that his family is well-fed and that he lives relatively well during the season, although he is saving back as much of his earnings as possible for the slack seasons. For example, Lubbock County in northwest Texas was the largest cotton-producing county in Texas in 1951. Retail sales in Lubbock, the county seat, reacted as they should during the cotton-picking season, as reflected by reports to the University of Texas Bureau of Business Research. On the chart, note the harvest months of September, October and November.

Lubbock depends upon local and domestic migrant labor to pick its cotton. Wetbacks are a minor item in its economy.

In Big Spring the retail sales curve shows the same picture. Howard County, of which Big Spring is the county seat, is one of the top five cotton producing counties of Texas. It has practically no wetbacks.

For the same reason, retail sales in McAllen in the heart of the Lower Rio Grande Valley, should be booming during the cotton harvest in June, July and August. But the graph of retail sales in McAllen, as reported by the University of Texas Bureau of Business Research, shows just the reverse. Note the harvest months of June, July and August.

McAllen's retail sales dropped 13 percent in June and another 7 percent in July during the peak of the cotton harvest. Lubbock retail sales increased 22 percent in September, 17 percent in October and 2 percent in November during its harvest period.

The explanation of the difference is simple: wetback labor which was underpaid and didn't spend in the McAllen area; domestic citizen labor which was better-paid and spent in the Lubbock area. This plus the migration from the Valley of thousands of workers who spent their money in Lubbock and the other areas where they worked. The Valley farmers may reap a rich harvest and make great profits, but all of their dollars do not feed into the retail business channels as would the dollars of individual citizen workers if they were harvesting the crop.

As just one example of the effects of the wetback and the forced annual migration from their homes of American citizen workers, the owner of a drugstore in the Lower Rio Grande Valley has provided the monthly gross receipts figures for that business. In the letter transmitting the information, the owner wrote:

"With reference to our recent conversation with respect to the effect of the wetback on our local economy here, we have decided to furnish you with our gross monthly receipts for the past two years.

"You will note, in checking these figures that as the harvest season rolls around each year, and more labor is being used in the fields, that our gross receipts tend to fall off considerably. This is almost a direct contradiction of conditions, as one would naturally assume that with increased farm employment there would be a corresponding increase in retail business. This is not the case here, as all retail outlets in this area have learned, and will undoubtedly testify should they be contacted as you have contacted us.

"The situation is reflected throughout the area. Retail sales fall below normal, collections decrease and the average retailer has difficulty in retaining his sales staff. County, school, state and federal taxes must be met. Civic institutions must be maintained by frequent contributions, and the burden falls on the retailers who are being denied the opportunity to participate in the money being earned by the farm labor . . . most of it, we have learned, is being sent or taken directly into Mexico.

"The Rio Grande Valley is not geared for a $1.75 to $2.00 a day economy, in spite of some of the Valley press editorials on our economy.

"You will notice, Mr. Idar, that the downward trend starts in May and continues until August and September. These months are the busiest as far as agricultural labor is concerned, yet the poorest in point of retail sales. We believe that monthly figures from other retail outlets will reflect the same trend.

WHAT PRICE WETBACKS — in Lost Business?

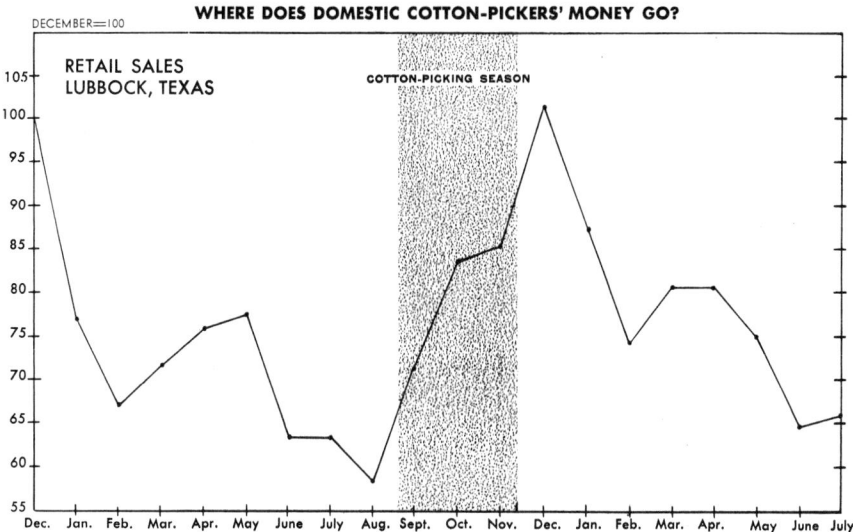

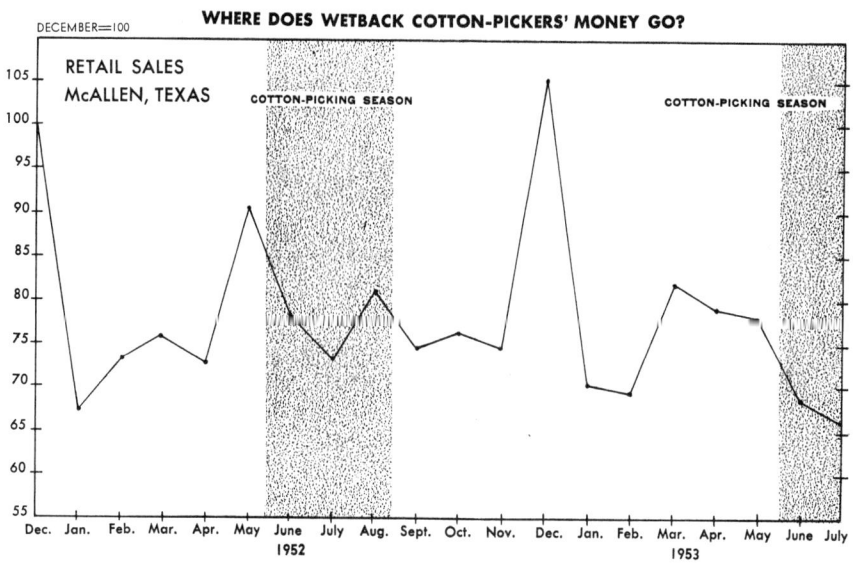

Source: University of Texas Bureau of Business Research

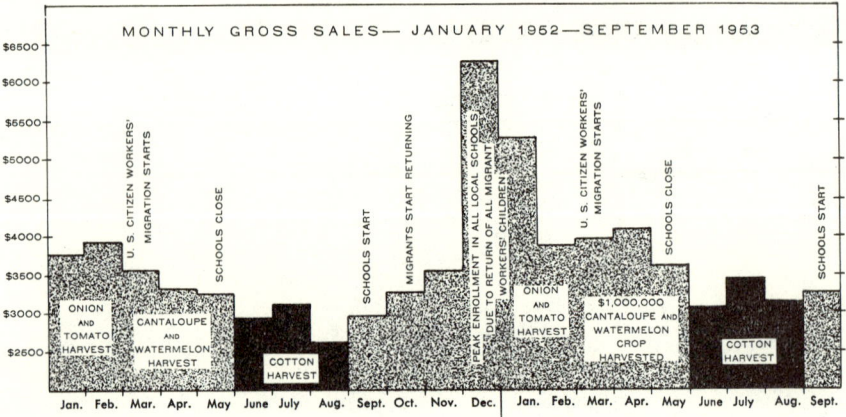

"We feel that the economic problem created by the heavy influx of wetbacks into this area has been neglected far too long. We appreciate the opportunity being given us to cooperate with the American G.I. Forum and State Federation in this economic survey. We hope that the attached information will be of some significance."

During the summer months, the citizen farm worker of the Rio Grande Valley is forced to migrate north, forced out by the invasion of wetbacks. During the winter months, he returns—minus the money he earned and spent on his unwanted travels. His return to normal living is reflected in the rise of the McAllen retail sales.

The answer to the businessmen's problem, of course, does not lie in the Bracero Program. The dollars still go out of the country—and out of the retail trade area concerned—whether the worker is wetback or *bracero*. It is the citizen worker alone who will spend his dollars with the local merchants.

In El Paso, officials of the El Paso Valley Cotton Growers Association reported that during the four months of the peak harvest season in that area, 12,000 *braceros* were contracted. The rest of the year the number ran from 3500 to 4000. These workers made a minimum of $24 a week and, during the cotton harvest, as much as $60 a week. Even calculated at the minimum, total earnings of the *braceros* in the El Paso area amount to more than $7,500,000 a year. The same officials estimated that the average *bracero* sends home to Mexico 60 percent of his earnings. Easy arithmetic again: El Paso businesses are losing on *braceros* alone, not including wetbacks, more than $4,500,000 a year in retail trade—and this from only a three-county area.

When the retail stores in McAllen or Brownsville or El Paso lose business, the loss is felt not only in those stores and those areas but also by the wholesalers, the manufacturers, the workers (and thus the retail stores) in other areas of the country. In Dallas, Chicago, New York, St. Louis, Detroit, Pittsburgh, Cleveland — throughout the country—the effects of the wetback system are felt in lower production and lower sales. What has officially become Mexico's third largest industry (and which might well be higher up the ladder if wetback send-home pay were included) is a total loss to us. The wetback's dollar (and the *bracero's* dollar, in large measure) is business that we could have and should have.

Not only do the wetbacks have an effect on business nationwide, but they themselves are moving into competition for jobs throughout the country. Despite the fact that once the wetback has cleared the immediate barriers along the border he is much more difficult to apprehend, during the fiscal year 1952-53 a total of 1700 wetbacks were apprehended in the Chicago District of the Immigration Service. At the time of apprehension, they were working in these industries: 480 in steel mills; 300 for railroads; 170 in food processing plants; 280 in other factories; 130 as general construction laborers; 80 in packing houses and 75 in grain elevators. Of the remainder, a few were unemployed, while others were engaged in miscellaneous employment, such as restaurant work, merchandising, grave-digging and hotels.

And at these jobs they are accumulating U. S. dollars preparatory to their return to Mexico.

Consider for a moment:

At the time when wetbacks were being flown back to Mexico by plane, an air-lift plane was grounded in Fort Worth with a load of fifty wetbacks apprehended in Chicago, a high wage area, where they were working in industry. Immigration Officers checking them found they had a total of $31,700 on their persons!

In April, 1952, another load of 145 wetbacks, also apprehended in the Chicago area in industrial work, came through San Antonio with $45,000 in their possession, all being carried back to Mexico.

The dollars which return to Mexico, whether in the pockets of wetbacks or in money orders sent by *braceros*, are gone from the channels of trade in the United States It is impossible to believe that the retail businessmen of the border country actually favor continuance of the wetback system which operates so much to their disadvantage. The fate of their businesses lies in the development of a sound employment system which will ring their cash registers.

25-CENT LABOR: On farm operated by Texan Care Co. near Mission, wetback broom corn balers earn 25 cents an hour.

WETBACK RECOMMENDATIONS

This survey does not qualify us as experts on immigration laws, but we believe there are certain corrections for which the need is obvious.

An augmented Border Patrol force with more vehicular, detention, and other facilities could go a long way toward controlling the wetback traffic, but even more important are modifications in the immigration laws to make them more effective. The records disclose that apprehension and deportation are not sufficient deterrents. For example, in one 11-day period, from July 20 to July 31, 1953, the Border Patrol made a detailed survey of 10,831 aliens who were being processed for voluntary departure in the bus-lift through Laredo and Zapata, voluntary departure meaning just that—the return to Mexico without the expensive and lengthy process of the trial in federal court required for formal deportation. Of the 10,831 surveyed, 2,970 (27 per cent) admitted having been returned to Mexico by bus-lift (which had been operating only a few months) from one to six times before! It is obvious that apprehensions are not the final answer.

The law must be amended to provide an enforceable penalty for harboring or aiding an alien, to permit the confiscation of vehicles used to transport aliens, and to provide an enforceable penalty for the employment of illegal aliens.

No further penalties, other than those now provided by law, need to be levied against the wetback or illegal alien himself. Illegal crossing is already a felony with adequate statutory penalties which will be found sufficient when immigration authorities have the facilities and personnel to prosecute rather than to allow voluntary departure.

Present statutes making it a felony to harbor, transport, and otherwise aid an alien do not make the harboring, transportation or aid felonious when it is "incidental to employment." Thus the very one who enjoys the subsidy of illegal alien labor is the one not covered by the statute. Furthermore, even the present provision has the loophole which requires that the person harboring, transporting or otherwise aiding an alien do so "knowingly." Under this loophole the courts have held that "reasonable inquiry" consists of asking the alien the simple question of "Are you a wetback?" and that no further inquiry need be made.

Furthermore, the penalty, under the statute is not effective, first, because it is too strict, and second, because it requires a jury trial for its enforcement. The statute needs revision to provide for inclusion of the alien's employer within its provisions and to make the illegal acts a misdemeanor rather than a felony.

Confiscation of vehicles of persons illegally transporting aliens would also go a long way in the solution of the problem. The Customs Service can confiscate a vehicle on which one ounce of marijuana is found; yet the same penalty cannot be levied by the Immigration Service on the same vehicle if it is found carrying fifty human beings as contraband labor.

Two persons can walk into the county judge's office in some counties and swear that they have knowledge that Jose Wetback was born in Harlingen on a certain date in a certain year and get a delayed birth certificate for Jose. One reporter to this survey was issued a delayed birth certificate in a Texas county without anyone appearing before the judge. Two letters were sufficient. They stated that the writers were present at the time of his birth and had personal knowledge that he was born at the place stated. A wetback can do the same thing, and many do.

This traffic in false papers is one of the most serious problems facing the Immigration Service in its enforcement of the laws along the border. Not until the State adopts adequate legislation to curtail the easy manner in which delayed birth certificates are issued can this traffic be stopped. And if the State will not do it, then the national Congress must decide that this is one field in which the national government must step in.

It has become common practice for Mexican women living near the border to come across into Texas to bear their children because the child born in the United States is an American citizen with all citizenship rights. Should the family ever decide to move to the United States, the Immigration authorities would be practically powerless to deport them. They cannot deport a citizen, and it is against policy to divide a family; so usually the whole family is allowed to stay. Only by strengthening the Border Patrol can this practice be stopped. In addition the Patrol must be provided with more detention facilities.

Another vital need is for an international agreement that will close the border effectively and will provide for returning illegal aliens to their homes in the interior of Mexico instead of dumping them just across the river to have them return the same night. Statistical information compiled by the Saunders-Leonard report on wetbacks shows that the vast majority of wetbacks come from states in the interior of Mexico, removed 800 or more miles from the border.

The same problem arises in connection with proposed schemes for recruiting of *braceros* along the U.S.-Mexican border (as well as with adoption of a crossing-card system). Records for one 10-day period of apprehensions in the San Antonio Immigration Service District show, for example, that of 6,711 wetbacks apprehended, most came from states in the interior of Mexico. San Luis Potosi, in Central Mexico, provided 1301 of those apprehended; Guanajuato, also in Central Mexico, 870; Michoacan, Central Mexico, 500; Zacatecas, north central, 344; Jalisco, west central, 325; Durango, central, 205. Nuevo Leon, Coahuila and Tamaulipas, the three states adjacent to the border, provided less than half (2754) of the 6711 wetbacks apprehended.

This same pattern could be expected to hold if border recruiting of *braceros* or a crossing-card system were used. Mass emigration of thousands of residents of interior states to the border, where they could get legalized jobs in the United States, would naturally follow. And those unable to obtain legalized entry would, by and large, take the wetback route, thus further complicating matters.

After the sacrifices these people have made to reach the border, it is most unlikely that they will return that long distance to their homes in the interior when the farmers on the American side are continually luring them to try it one more time. Curtailment and final abandonment of the air-lift, the most successful means the Immigration Service ever devised for returning illegal Mexican citizens, was the sheerest of false economy and a complete abdication of responsibility at the behest of interests bent on exploiting human beings in a form worse than the slavery practiced prior to the Civil War.

THE CROSSING CARD — SEMI-LEGAL WETBACKISM

While we have concentrated in this report on the wetbacks and the *braceros*, there is a large group of Mexican aliens working in the U. S. who fall into a third category. Primarily, this group consists of Mexican border residents who are extended the privilege of visiting in the United States to shop, to transact personal business, to consult professional men, etc.—but not to work. They hold a Border Resident's Crossing Card which permits the holder to cross freely into the United States simply by displaying the card at the Immigration Service checking points.

Despite the fact that these cards do not give the holder the right to work in the U. S., a tremendous number of these card-holders do work—every day—on the U. S. side of the Rio Grande. This is true in every border town or city which is joined to Mexico by a bridge or a ferry—Brownsville, Eagle Pass, Laredo, El Paso and points in between. Thousands of Mexicans cross daily, perform their work, then return south of the border after work—all with a semblance of legality. Their crossing is legal, their work is not. Yet they are to be found in the United States as retail clerks, auto mechanics, janitors, housemaids, nurses, skilled and semi-skilled craftsmen, and in many other capacities.

Local Immigration Service officials are perfectly aware of the practice. They see the same faces crossing daily or at regular intervals. They see the same faces behind the counters of retail stores, typing briefs in law offices, behind reception desks in medical offices, repairing flats in garages, and perhaps in their own backyards mowing the lawn or in their own dining rooms serving dinner.

The violators of the privileges afforded by the Border Resident's Crossing Card are not completely ignored. The Border Patrol apprehends violators regularly, but the pressure of the wetback invasion on the limited Patrol force is too heavy in other fields to permit strict enforcement of the laws governing the crossing-card holders. The card holder cannot be arrested at the time of his crossing, because his crossing is legal. He must be arrested while he is at work and violating the privileges afforded him by the card. But most card holders who plan to violate the law take the precaution of hiding the valuable card, so that it will not be taken away. By giving fictitious names, they win voluntary deportation without their true identity becoming known. They then arrange to recover their cards and resume their daily trek to work on the U. S. side of the river.

Many users of illegal alien labor—whether crossing-card holder or just plain wetback—for the past several years have demanded legalization of a crossing card which would permit aliens to work in the United States. Known as tne "white card system," such a scheme would be nothing more than legalized wetbackism. Aliens would be permitted to cross the river at will and to work in the United States at wetback wages, while still living in Mexico and spending their earnings in Mexico. Protections now afforded legally contracted workers under the Bracero Program (minimum wages, housing, insurance, etc.) would be discarded. Likewise, protections afforded U. S. citizens (physical examinations to screen out the diseased, labor shortage certifications, etc.) would be discontinued. The wetback would become a legalized card holder working for the same wetback wages. All of the evils of the wetback system would be perpetuated and expanded.

The answer to the problem lies not in adoption of the white card system and its attendant evils; it lies in stricter enforcement of the law governing the Border Resident's Crossing Card holders and the other immigration laws.

OUT OF THE FIELDS come the wetbacks rounded up by Border Patrol.

AT PATROL HEADQUARTERS they await voluntary deportation back to Mexico.

WETBACKS HEAD FOR MEXICO across bridge at Zapata.

THE BORDER PATROL

San Antonio Express

2ᵛ MONDAY, JULY 27, 1953

ALL VALLEY EDITION

Border Patrol's Percentage

A Valley man, according to some press reports, claimed recently that he was detained near Laredo by the border patrol under suspicion of being an alien. The report indicated that he thought an injustice had been done him.

His side of the case is the only one that has been publicized, so it's pretty early to judge the merits of his complaint. He has a right to complain if he thinks the circumstances warrant complaining, but sometimes complaints are warranted and sometimes they are not.

This is the first time in several months that the border patrol has had this kind of publicity. During that time the patrol, in its Valley sector alone, has been apprehending up to 1,000 aliens a day. Since the use of forged citizenship credentials is known to be fairly common, it is a proper part of the patrol's activity to question such credentials, including some which may be genuine.

When only one public complaint about the border patrol originates among tens of thousands of apprehensions, and the patrol itself makes a practice of promptly and thoroughly investigating such complaints, it is hard to believe that its intentions are less honorable, its treatment of individuals less courteous or its record in general less commendable than those of other law enforcement groups, or those of the general public.

The Border Patrol is the law enforcement body of the United States Immigration and Naturalization Service which, in turn, is a part of the U. S. Department of Justice. The functions of the Border Patrol are almost self-explanatory: it is charged with guarding our borders against illegal entrants, enforcing our immigration laws, apprehending and deporting illegal aliens. Those functions appear rather simple. The law is the law—and the border patrolmen are hired to enforce it.

Nevertheless, along the U. S.-Mexico border, particularly in Texas, the Border Patrol is a maligned, misunderstood and unappreciated agency. Its members, at least in the smaller communities, are social outcasts. The wives and children of patrolmen, who are enforcing United States law, are subjected by the community to many indignities, the result of the prevailing attitude that anyone interfering with the free movement of wetbacks is practically un-American and ought to be run out of town. In South Texas, the wife of the border patrolman needs as much fortitude as her husband.

Indicative of the physical and mental strain facing patrolmen in the Lower Valley, as a result of the attitude of Valley farmers on enforcement of the immigration laws, is an incident related to the survey investigators by a senior patrolman who has spent a number of years in the area. On one occasion this officer led a raid on the farm operated by two German-born immigrants whose Valley residence is of only a few years' standing and whose naturalization as American citizens is even shorter. One of the farmers, highly indignant, asked the inspector why the Patrol did not leave them alone and accused them of "Gestapo" tactics. In faulty, German-accented English, he then asked the officer and his men: "Why aren't you all in Korea?" The officer had already done his stint in World War II, seeing extensive service overseas, and frankly admitted it took utmost restraint on his part to refrain from causing an undesirable incident.

Despite these handicaps, the Border Patrol, with its limited personnel and facilities must be credited with an exceptionally high standard of performance in the execution of its duties.

Most of the individual officers in the Patrol are conscientious and interested in doing as good a job as possible. They ignore the 40-or-48 hour week customary for government employes, putting in as much as 75 or 80 hours in a week, particularly during the harvest seasons when the wetback tide is at its peak. Many stated

PICKED UP IN FIELDS and houses, these wetbacks on Kenmueller Farm in Lower Rio Grande Valley head for voluntary deportation.

COTTON-FIELD HIDING PLACE wasn't enough for this wetback on Schuster Farm near McAllen in Lower Rio Grande Valley.

WETBACKS WAIT on Kenmueller Farm in Hidalgo County while one busload of apprehendees is hauled away.

to these reporters, in all sincerity, that hours aren't important, that what is important is the enforcement of the law.

Naturally, there are misfits in the Patrol, men not so much interested in doing a good job as in completing the pay cycle. These officers are apt to succumb to the community attitude, to react to the adverse publicity by lying down on the job, to play ball with the wetback-users, or on occasion to lose their heads and abuse someone. Effects of the community pressure are seen in the turnover in patrolmen in the McAllen sector of almost 30 percent a year.

The patrolman who, in order to obtain social acceptance, adopts the wetback-user's viewpoint on wetbacks can become a demoralizing influence on his fellow-workers or subordinates. These reporters found at least one instance where the senior patrolman sees to it that only certain farms and ranches are raided, in effect providing protection for those farms and ranches whose owners he wishes to cultivate. Patrolmen working under him stated that they "dared not" enter certain properties for fear of having unfavorable efficiency reports filed on them.

We found this aggravated situation in only this one spot, but the entire community was aware of what was going on. Similar situations may well exist in other areas.

Most South Texas newspapers delight in emphasizing a minor incident on unproved charges of mistreatment by patrolmen. It may not be just by accident that these attacks usually come at the season when the crops are ripening and the farmers want to insure wetback availability. (Witness, for example, the vicious attacks by The Laredo Times on the so-called "hot-foot lift" at Zapata at the start of the Lower Valley cotton-picking season in 1953 and the more recent attacks of the same nature by other spokesmen over the deportations by "buslift" from the El Paso area through Presidio at the start of the harvest season in that area.)

The occasional abuses by Border Patrolmen are not condoned by the GI Forum, by the Texas State Federation of Labor, by the writers of this report or by officials of the Border Patrol and Immigration Service. District Director John W. Holland of San Antonio has been very strict in disciplinary measures involving Patrolmen who exceeded their authority. However, the occasional and isolated incidents which the area's papers play up out of all proportion should be taken in the light of the thousands upon thousands of persons handled daily, weekly and monthly by the harrassed Patrol officers. It is a remarkable record indeed that in a fiscal year as that of July 1, 1952, to June 30, 1953, when a grand total of 362,403 illegal aliens were apprehended in the San Antonio District by Patrol officers there was only a handful of cases in which these officers were charged with abuses of one type or another and some of these charges were subsequently proved false.

Effectiveness of the Border Patrol could be immensely increased by more cooperation between the Patrol and the U. S. Employment Service, which administers the Bracero Program. The same holds true, in some instances, with regard to Mexican Consulates.

Under the International Agreement, Article 7 sets out provisions under which an employer can be declared ineligible to contract *braceros* (i.e., be "blacklisted"). An employer can be declared ineligible for *braceros* if he employs wetbacks after certification for *braceros* or after 30 days from the effective date of the agreement. The question in ineligibility seems to revolve around the question of whether an employer has "knowingly" employed illegal aliens after making "reasonable inquiry" as to the applicant's status.

Here cooperation among the agencies involved would really be a help.

For example, the San Antonio District Immigration Office receives monthly reports from all senior patrolmen in the various sectors listing the employers and farms where wetbacks were apprehended. These lists are transmitted to the Dallas office of the U. S. Employment Service. The USES has a complete file on all farmers, farm associations and harvesting associations using *bracero* labor. A comparison of the two lists should provide a list of employers to be declared ineligible for *bracero* labor, but it apparently doesn't work that way.

The Border Patrol itself has no authority to blacklist an employer, a fact which many farmers seemingly do not realize, inasmuch as some refuse to cooperate with the Border Patrol on the grounds that the Patrol has had them blacklisted. The "blacklist" is drawn up periodically through joint action of agencies of the two governments, but the Immigration Service apparently is not consulted. The two principal agencies involved are the USES and the Mexican Consular Service.

It was found in the course of this investigation that the Border Patrol has made repeated raids on the farms of the most flagrant violators of Article 7, dutifully reporting the results in the reports sent to Dallas. Yet, months after such raids, they find that *braceros* still are working on the farms where the wetbacks were apprehended. Sanctions had not been applied against the

ROAD-BLOCK APPREHENDERS: Wetbacks caught in early-morning Border Patrol road-block.

WETBACK PAY-OFF: Apprehended wetbacks are paid off at Border Patrol headquarters by farm foreman.

SMALL CHANGE: Truck driver pays off apprehended wetbacks.

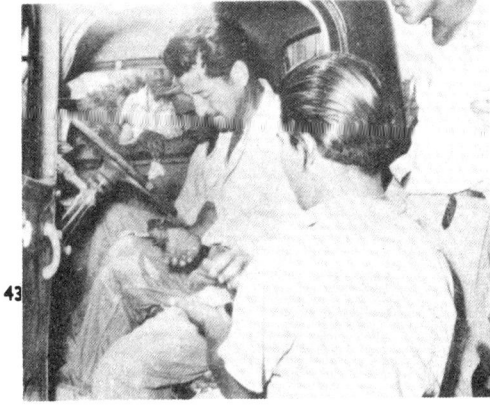

TBACK HAUL: Border Patrolman stops truck loaded wetbacks, signals road-block to pick them up.

EARLY CATCH: Border Patrol truck soon will be loaded with wetbacks.

wetback-users. The responsibility for initiating such sanctions lies with the USES.

In discussing this problem with the various compliance officers of the USES along the border, there seemed to be considerable question as to what constituted "reasonable inquiry" in an effort to establish the citizenship status of a job applicant. One compliance officer contended that merely asking the applicant whether he was a wetback was "reasonable inquiry" and that if the reply was negative, then there was no need to pursue the matter. Most farmers interviewed held to the same opinion, claiming that even though a later determination (after such "reasonable inquiry") showed the employe to be a wetback, the employer had not "knowingly" employed an alien.

Yet, time after time, the same names of employers hiring wetbacks appear in the weekly and monthly periodic reports on apprehensions filed with the San Antonio Immigration District Office and forwarded to the USES Regional Office at Dallas. The same wetbacks are time after time apprehended on the same farms—and the employers persist in asserting they make "reasonable inquiry" as to the citizenship status of these workers. In the Eagle Pass area, at the time the survey investigators were there, a spot check on apprehension files was made to select the most frequent violators, many on whose farms hardly a day passes without the apprehension of wetbacks. These same farmers were then checked against the official "blacklist" published by the USES and not one of them was found therein. All of them, however, had *braceros* certified to them — a flagrant violation of the International Agreement.

There is no procedure for providing the Border Patrol officers in the field with the periodic "blacklists," information which would be of great value in enforcing the immigration laws. Except in those areas where there is close cooperation between the USES compliance officers and the Border Patrol, the latter never learns what farmers or associations have been declared ineligible.

Another example of the lack of cooperation hampering law enforcement occurred in April, 1953, when a shipment of *braceros* arrived at the Eagle Pass Contracting Center. In the group were some *braceros* who were suspected of being agitators or subversives. The FBI was called in, and, after a lengthy examination, some were screened out and returned to Mexico.

AWAITING DEPORTATION: Wetbacks at McAllen Deportation Center of Border Patrol.

CHOW TIME: Wetbacks are fed at government expense while awaiting deportation in McAllen Detention Center.

TRUCK-LIFT: Trucks on Mexican side of Rio Grande at Zapata load up with wetbacks for haul to Enpalme.

WETBACK AND CHILD: Apprehended by Border Patrol on Kenmueller Farm, Hidalgo County.

One of the oldest and most astute Immigration Service Investigators on the entire border at that time was John Chamberlain, who was stationed at the Eagle Pass Border Patrol headquarters but who has recently retired and has been named Chief of Police of Eagle Pass. Chamberlain was born and raised in Laredo and speaks fluent Spanish. His duties, as an investigator, included the detection and apprehension of smugglers and subversives. His record is an enviable one. Yet, John Chamberlain was not called into the investigation either as an observer or as a participant.

The FBI investigation of this group was confidential, and the only information made available to the reporters of this survey was that the men had been screened out and returned to Mexico. But if they were subversives—and the presence of the FBI at the investigation lends credence to such speculation—just being returned across the border at Eagle Pass would not be enough to deter them from re-entering the United States as wetbacks.

As an Immigration Service investigator, Chamberlain might well have been called upon to investigate members of this same group at some future date, providing they entered as wetbacks—and also provided they were apprehended. As an observer during the Contracting Station investigation, Chamberlain would have materially benefited: first, by seeing and identifying the members of the group; second, by following closely the line of interrogation used in the examination, and third, knowing the futility of voluntary deportation which deposits the aliens just across the border, by seeing to it that the Border Patrol unit in the sector was extra vigilant in case the deported group tried to re-enter the country.

The writers of this report are not attempting to lay the blame for the lack of cooperation among the various agencies on any single agency. Certainly, both the U. S. Employment Service and the Border Patrol are understaffed for the jobs assigned them. Mexican consulates have neither the facilities nor the personnel to check adequately on the compliance with the International Agreement. But it does seem that a little more effort at cooperation would result in better enforcement of the terms of the *bracero* contracts and would enable everybody concerned to enforce the immigration laws better.

OFF TO MEXICO: Wetbacks board deportation buses at McAllen Detention Center.

TRAVELING LIGHT: Few wetbacks have many personal belongings.

Patrolman Shortage Aids Wetbacks, Brownell Says

DENVER, Aug. 17 (AP)—President Eisenhower was told by Attorney General U. S. B...

Influx of Wetbacks Poses Growing Problems for U.S.

BY GLADWIN HILL
New York Times Service

LOS ANGELES, May 9—Illegal immigration from Mexico into the southwestern United States, on the increase since World War II, has reached such overwhelming proportions that officers of the United States Immigration Service admit candidly, if unofficially, that there is nothing to stop the whole nation of Mexico moving into the United States if it wants to.

The numerical equivalent of more than 10 per cent of the population of Mexico has come in already.

A record total of 87,416 border-jumpers was caught last month by Immigration Service patrol officers along the 1,600-mile boundary between Brownsville and San Diego, Cal. That is equal to more than two a minute, day and night, the whole month.

The month's roundup brought the total number of wetbacks caught since 1945 to somewhere around 3,000,000. Many of the cases represent "repeaters," the bulk of the traffic being...

Why The Mexicans?

President Eisenhower has seen fit to take official notice of Attorney General Brownell's alarm over the Mexican "wetback" situation and has instructed the Department of Justice to throw all resources of the federal government to stem the "ever increasing" tide of wetbacks entering this country from Mexico.

The Times is in sympathy with any move the federal government to cope with aliens illegally in our country but this newspaper fails to see why Attorney General Brownell and President Eisenhower should confine themselves to Mexican "wetbacks."

Without a doubt, hundreds of thousands of Europeans are in this country illegally and centered in the big cities of the East and...

All anyone has to do is visit any big city to observe the seemingly endless stream of foreigners. We wonder how they got here...

Mexican laborers are needed on the 85,8... near the border. For many, many years 1952, prior can laborers crossed the Rio Grande son p border elsewhere to work on farms on in the That was an accepted custom and nobody vincing said or thought about it. Those workers ordinary returned to their homes in Mexico when hension. no longer was a need for their services of this new level.

The A... If the federal government is going above the all its resources at the disposal of Attorney more than eral Brownell to stem the flow of "wetbacks" 13,465 m from Mexico, why does it not also open previous. A fledged warfare against aliens illegally in parts of our country?

The Times would dislike very much to see this country turned into a police state where the authorities—and all citizens—had to keep the average person posted as to their whereabouts.

The Times also resents the singling out of Mexican aliens and turning all the resources of the federal government into stopping and rounding them up. In many cases these aliens are much more acceptable than the aliens here from some other parts of the world.

Cotton Men Blast Pact On Braceros

(Continued from Page 1)

...of cotton pickers that was the governing factor in the decision of association members to vote Monday in favor of accepting the terms of international agreement now in...

Find A Solution

Resentment of Valley farmers toward U. S. Immigration officials and the Mexican government over the bracero problem is something to think about.

George Spence, president of the El Paso Valley Cotton Association, was quoted as saying at a meeting of that association Monday:

"We've had a blitz here these past few days. The purpose was to bring us to our knees. The tactics of rounding up and transporting helpless Mexicans are similar to who...

The Times Ti... Mexican "wetbacks" transported all... ported. It is ass... more difficult for... back to their home munities from whe...

Wetback Problem Put Before Ike

DENVER—(AP) President Eisenhower was told by Atty Gen Brownell Monday that the U. S. Border Patrol, hampered by a existing manpower shortage, is powerless to halt the illegal entry of thousands of Mexican wetbacks into California.

Brownell called it "a very serious" and said he plans...

Brownell Sees Big Problem In Wetbacks

SAN FRANCISCO, Calif. (P)—Atty. Gen. Herbert Brownell Jr. said Sunday the "wetback" invasion from Mexico...

Ike Orders Sessions on 'Wetbacks'

DENVER, Colo. (UP)—President Eisenhower Monday authorized Atty. Gen. Herbert Brownell Jr. to use all resources of the Federal Government to stem the ever increasing tide of "wetbacks" entering this country illegally from Mexico.

Brownell, following a conference with the President at the summer White House here Monday morning...

Captured Wetbacks' Crowd Buses

...do, Texas (UP)—The U. S. Immigration Service said Monday it will have to charter additional buses the downstream heavy influx of "wetbacks" continues.

Service has been using all its automotive equipment in addition to several weeks to carry the Mexicans estimated to be back across the Rio Grande. In addition, it has used buses several times. 389,000 wetbacks first four months of fiscal year. John W. Holland district said 124... aliens had been apprehended compared with 76,187 for the same period of 1952.

During April alone, the figure was 31,423. The district comprises roughly two-thirds of Texas, including the cities of Laredo... heaviest influx of "wetbacks"...

Cotton Men Blast Pact On Braceros

A scorching blast against the U. S. Immigration Service and Department of Labor followed the decision of members of El Paso Valley Cotton Association Monday to contract bracero farm labor under terms of the current international agreement, which was negotiated two years ago and expires this...

"We learned last week we would not get a new agreement," Spence said. "So, it was decided to hold a meeting Monday and have the membership vote on accepting the present one, which expires Dec. 31. By that time we hope to have a new agreement."

The meeting was held in Hotel Paso del Norte. The unanimous vote of some 200 farmers in the hotel ballroom in favor of abiding by the current agreement, broke a six weeks deadlock during which the cotton association had refused to contract for Mexican farm laborers.

This refusal is believed to have caused the recent crackdown by the U. S. Immigration Service which has been apprehending wetbacks along the El Paso border and taking them to Presidio, Texas...

...not pleased" by progress of his small administration program setting up state and local private capital for the establishment and expansion of businesses.

William Mitchell, Small Business Administrator, gave the President a first-hand report on the program Monday.

Mitchell said the SBA has the authority to approve loans to small firms up to $150,000 from a revolving fund of $55,000,000, but pointed out it was his conception of the program that this federal money should be used for backstop, rather than primary lending purposes.

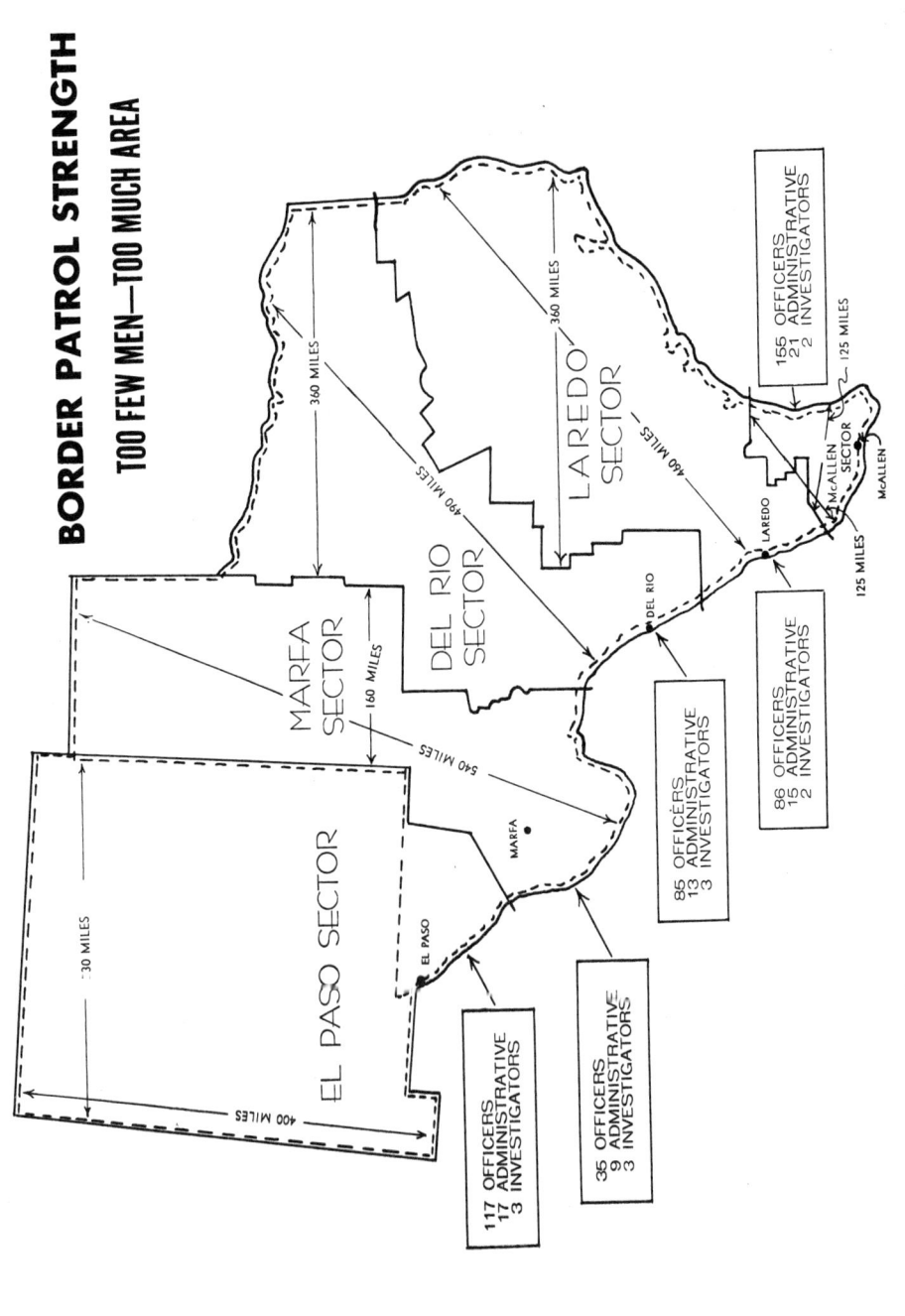

THE BRACERO

Mexico's Third Largest Industry

The miracle of America's production during World War II was accomplished only by drawing millions of workers into industrial employment. But in accomplishing this industrial miracle we created another problem almost as grave: farm labor practically disappeared and an intensive nationwide drive to persuade urban families to assist the local farmers in their harvest failed to solve the problem.

The products of agriculture were as important as the products of industry; so, as a last resort, our government drew upon the supply of Mexican farm laborers, contracting them and bringing them into this country temporarily to help harvest our food and fiber. This was an emergency measure and was not intended originally as permanent policy. But here was a farm laborer who was docile to the extreme, easy to handle (or mishandle), willing to work for 25 cents an hour or less and to suffer many privations for a short period in order to return to Mexico with a pocketful of yankee dollars. He could live by his standards in the interior of Mexico for many months on these savings. The farmer had no obligation to him beyond the short-term contract period and for the most part found this a very desirable and profitable arrangement. No domestic worker, living at even the bottom of the scale of American standards, could work for so little. Naturally, when the emergency ended, the farmer sought some reason for extending this international agreement which provided him with cheap, docile labor.

While this was happening, another change was taking place. The war had ended, defense production was sharply reduced, and the farm laborers who had gone away to win a war were returning home to find their work being done by these contracted *braceros* and by wetbacks at wages of from 15 to 25 cents per hour. Ten hours a day, six and seven days a week for $75 a month or less was a rather dismal prospect for an American who had to support himself and family at post-war prices. The returned farm worker couldn't afford to work at those wages—and he couldn't afford not to work. Up north, where this south-of-the border competition didn't exist, the wages were much higher; so, in the early spring he took his children out of schoool, packed his essentials and began the long haul north. He would return in late fall but not in time for the beginning of school.

One South Texas politician has called this trip a product of "a gypsy spirit that makes them want to travel"* and accused them of not being willing to do hard farm labor. But at the end of the long haul north was the very same kind of "hard farm labor" that the worker couldn't af-

* Saunders-Leonard Report on Wetbacks.

BRACERO LIVING: Top and middle, bracero housing in El Paso area; bottom, Idar checks cistern from which braceros get water on Ritchie Bros. Farm near Eagle Pass, bracero housing in background.

BRACERO SLEEPING: Cot in bracero house in El Paso area.

BRACEROS SIGN UP: At El Paso contracting center.

BRACERO EATING: Idar and John Apodaca check facilities in El Paso area.

BRACEROS AT WORK: In cotton field near El Paso.

TRACTOR REPAIR: By braceros on A. D. Candelaria Farm, El Paso County.

BRACERO MESS HALL: On El Paso area farm.

ford to do in the Valley at 25 cents an hour and that the farmer claimed he **wouldn't do.** Valley farm work at these low wages was left to the wetback and the *bracero.* The farmers took up the cry of people like this politician and were able to convince enough people in far removed places that the *bracero* was needed. So, another international labor agreement was signed and has been continued, except for a short lapse until the present.

(The Lower Rio Grande Valley farmers were the chief proponents of the *bracero* agreements. There seemed to be no limit to their efforts to extend the International Agreement. Their spokesmen drew heart-rending pictures of the harvest rotting in the fields. The reader or the listener could visualize the ragged Valley farmer selling his few baskets of oranges on the street corner, all for the lack of a few *braceros.*

(Yet, the survey investigators found that, in the summer of 1953, little effort was made by the Valley farmers to abandon the use of wetback labor and to comply with the *bracero* program. Even in areas where a more determined effort was being made to employ *braceros,* as in Eagle Pass, farmers were violating provisions of the international agreement in regard to wages, housing, sanitary drinking water and other facilities. In the Lower Valley, the use of *braceros* was practically nil. The wetback still provided the bulk of the farm labor.

(It is interesting to note an editorial in the Valley edition of the **San Antonio Express** under dateline of Thursday, August 20, 1953, which stated:

"A U. S. Farm Placement Service officer, explaining why the Harlingen bracero contracting center was closed recently, rather plainly stated that it didn't appear to be worthwhile to maintain the center when not a single cotton picker has been contracted there this year for work in Texas."

(The Eagle Pass and El Paso centers in Texas are still doing a big business.)

The argument was extended, but it contained a few "safeguards" intended to protect U. S. workers. For example, it provided that *braceros* could be contracted only if "sufficient domestic workers who are able, willing and qualified are not available at the time and place needed to perform the work."

In 1950, the Rio Grande Valley had 38,385 such domestic farm laborers who were very "able" and completely "qualified," (*Labor Requirements and Labor Resources in the Lower Rio Grande Valley of Texas* by Nelson & Meyers) but who could not possibly afford to be "willing"

to work for the 25 cents an hour offered them. The farmer cleared that hurdle easily by offering the wetback wage.

The law provides also that the *bracero* can be contracted only if "the employment of such workers will not adversely affect the wages and working conditions of domestic agricultural workers similarly employed." How does this work out?

The President's Commission on Migratory Labor, after conducting extensive hearings throughout the Southwest, found that under the international agreements during wartime, California got 63 percent of all the *bracero* workers who entered the United States in 1945 and raised its cottonpicking wages 136 percent. During the same year Texas got no contract workers from Mexico and raised its cotton wages 236 percent.

Under the postwar Bracero Program, the Commission found that in 1949 California got only 8 percent of the *braceros* and raised its wage rate 15 percent. Texas, on the other hand, got 46 percent of the *braceros* and lowered its wage rate 11 percent.

The law of supply and demand at work!

The effect of these contracts upon the farm labor wage is also apparent in the recent demand of farm organizations that the minimum wage provision of fifty cents an hour be removed because the wage is too high. They demand that the local prevailing wage be the minimum. But how is this local prevailing wage determined? Let us say that in Lubbock County, Texas, the cotton-picking season is near, and the farmers are preparing their requests for *bracero* labor. It would be the height of foolishness for the farmer to wait until the picking season started before ordering his *braceros,* for by the time he received them, it would be too late. So he submits his orders in time to have his labor on hand for the first picking. This means that he must place his order before the picking season actually begins, and, in submitting his request, the minimum wage must be specified. The law provides that this minimum wage shall be not less than the prevailing wage in that area as determined by the Secretary of Labor. So— a meeting is called to determine the prevailing rate for cotton picking—which, of course, hasn't started yet. Since there is no cotton being picked, naturally no wages are being paid—still, a prevailing cotton-picking wage is determined. The farmers admit that this "prevailing wage" is agreed upon in their pre-season meetings as the rate they plan to pay.

The "prevailing wage," thus, generally becomes the wage which the farmers have previously agreed they are going to pay. Through their organizational, financial and other resources they are able to get the Department of Labor and other agencies to implement their agreed-to wage rate.

It is interesting to note that in hearings before the Senate Sub-Committee on Labor and Labor Management

Relations during the Spring of 1951, time after time Senator Hubert Humphrey asked the Department of Labor representatives before the committee why the Department had taken no steps to set up representation for organized labor and the public in its Farm Labor Advisory Committee or why a separate committee with labor and the public represented was not set up on the same subject.

It is also interesting to note that several years ago the Texas Employment Commission came under severe, public criticism from farmers and farm organizations in the Lubbock area because a printed farm labor news bulletin distributed by the Commission specified wage rates being offered in the various localities. At that particular time farmers to the South of Lubbock were offering a 60-cent hourly wage for chopping cotton, while those in the Lubbock area offered only 50 cents. As a result, many migratory labor crews were by-passing the Lubbock area and going to the areas with the higher wage rate. The Lubbock growers criticized the TEC as being responsible for raising the wage rate when the agency was merely distributing wage information given it by the farmers in the various areas.

The manner of setting the "prevailing wage" rate is particularly obnoxious in the Lower Rio Grande Valley. Because the domestic agricultural worker has been pushed out of that labor market by the wetback since the end of World War II, the wetback wages of from 25 to 30 cents an hour have become, in effect, the prevailing wage.

In the latest international agreement on *bracero* contracting, there is a provision that, in all instances, *braceros* are to be paid the "prevailing wage" of the area wherein they are to be employed or fifty cents an hour, whichever is highest. It is obvious, therefore, that, because of the wetback wages in the Lower Valley—which have become the "prevailing wage"—the fifty-cent provision in the international agreement has become a minimum wage provision even though such was not the intent of negotiators of both countries when the agreement was drawn up. Even this low minimum wage, however, is unacceptable to farmers used to paying an average of twenty-five cents—as evidenced by the fact that nearly all farmers in the area have refused to make use of *bracero* labor, preferring the easily obtainable and exploitable wetback.

The constant hue and cry in the Lower Valley as the harvest approaches is on the shortage of domestic labor. But never once do the area's newspapers, except in isolated cases such as the Valley edition of the *San Antonio Express,* urge the farmers editorially to offer decent American wages—or even the fifty-cent wage required by the International Agreement—as a means of obtaining plentiful labor. This wage factor, in effect, brings about not a real but a purely artificial labor shortage for the area, since American citizens migrate because they cannot, and should not be required, to work for wetback wages—the only offer that Lower Valley farmers make.

Of the hundreds of wetback farm laborers interviewed in the Lower Valley during this investigation, very few were receiving more than 25 cents an hour. Is this the "local prevailing wage" referred to in the farmer's demands? Certifying to the existence of a severe labor shortage, on the one hand, and at the same time insisting there is a declining wage rate is an economic phenomenon that is difficult to understand. It doesn't take an economist to know that a *real* labor shortage is certain to result in higher wages being offered to workers who thus would be attracted to the work.

The law further provides that no Mexican labor may be contracted unless "reasonable efforts have been made to attract domestic workers for such employment at wages and standard hours of work comparable to those offered to foreign workers." In a few areas an honest effort is being made to attract domestic workers by offering a reasonably "comparable wage." An offer of the *bracero* wage rate is not comparable, for it does not include the value of the other guarantees in the *bracero* contract. In these few areas, the domestic worker is being offered an additional 15 cents per hour over the *bracero* wage, and an increasing number are returning to farm labor.

For the purposes of this survey, we have divided the Texas border into five districts: El Paso Valley, Del Rio, Eagle Pass, Laredo, and the Lower Rio Grande Valley.

This survey began in the El Paso area, in which, for the purposes of this report, we include Hudspeth and Culbertson Counties. Practically all of the farmers in this area are members of the El Paso Valley Cotton Growers Association. The Association is the prime contractor for *braceros* and assigns them to its members as they are needed. At the time of this survey, Samuel Sosa, USES Compliance officer, declared that the Association policed its membership and could penalize its members for contract violations. Sosa reported that, generally speaking, good housing was provided and the farmers were sincerely striving to make the program workable. He had investigated only six complaints since September, 1952, and there were no farmers on the blacklist (and so ineligible for *braceros*) at that time. District Director Joseph Minton of the Immigration Service in El Paso reported that the cooperation from the Association was excellent and that the farmers were making a genuine effort to stay clear of wetbacks.

Braceros were interviewed on various farms in the El Paso area, and all reported that they were receiving the guaranteed wage rate—fifty cents an hour.

There was excellent cooperation between the Mexican Consul, USES Compliance Officer and the Immigration Service in the area.

This "fairly adequate" situation found to exist in the El

Paso area at the time of the field survey had deteriorated by the time this report went to press late in October, but it showed signs of improving once again. For a time, the El Paso Valley Cotton Growers Association discontinued using the International Bracero Program as a means of meeting labor requirements in the area. Farmers reverted to the use of wetbacks and apprehensions went up to 500 a day. Intensive efforts by the Border Patrol in apprehending the wetbacks who flowed into the area brought on the usual flood of charges of mistreatment of wetbacks, but the Patrol stuck to its job of enforcing the law.

Meantime, some El Paso farmers joined the clamor for a "white card crossing system" which would do away with the protective provisions of the Bracero Program. After a short period of widespread wetback use, subject to disruption by the steady apprehension work and the effectiveness of the Ojinaja bus lift, the growers once again started using *braceros*.

This retrogression in the El Paso Valley may be attributed in part to the fact that El Paso agricultural interests, seeing their brethren in the Lower Rio Grande Valley enjoying a rich subsidy of cheap, illegal labor, would like to share in it as well. It is further proof of how one cancerous spot in a body politic will spread to other areas if not controlled.

Del Rio has long been the "hot spot" for smuggling that it is today. Del Rio and Eagle Pass are the focal points of all the highways serving the Central border, and, naturally, the smuggling traffic is funneled through these cities. Smuggling has developed into a multi-million dollar business.

The wetback traffic in Del Rio is heavy, and it can be reasonably assumed that many European aliens are smuggled in or come across with the wetbacks that commute regularly. This area is devoted largely to ranching with the West Texas Sheep and Goat Raisers Association as the predominant organization. But each individual farmer contracts his own labor. A few ranchers use only *bracero* labor and keep clear of wetbacks. But, most users of *braceros* make little effort to live up to the contract.

Chris Aldrete, Del Rio attorney and city commissioner, who has been elected State Chairman of the GI Forum since this field survey was made, stated that before the war native resident labor used to do most of the ranch work, but since the war *braceros* and many wets have taken over.

The ranch hand receives $50 to $60 per month (20 cents an hour). Some domestic labor is still found on the ranches, but annual migration out of the area is heavy. School enrollments increase 33 percent from September to March as the domestic migrant returns home during the winter.

There is not even the slightest trend toward resuming use of domestic labor in this area. In fact, the very

BRACERO HOUSING: On Ritchie Bros. Farm, Eagle Pass area.

BRACERO IN HOME: Santiago Alonzo Torres, Coahuila, on Ritchie Bros. Farm.

BRACEROS: Antonio Sanchez Juarez and Oscar Ramos Salas, Coahuila, on Ritchie Bros. Farm.
BRACERO INTERVIEW: Idar asks braceros on Springfield Farm near Quemado about their work.

opposite is true. The alien can afford to work much cheaper than the citizen and few, if any, of the employers show any concern over the attendant ills of wetback labor.

Eagle Pass has the same smuggling problems as Del Rio. At the time of this investigation, there were over forty smuggled aliens being held in jail, ready to serve as witnesses against the smuggling operators.

Most of the Eagle Pass area is ranchland, but farms have increased greatly in number and acreage in recent years. The predominant organization is the El Indio Growers Association, and most *bracero* users contract through this Association. Little effort is made to comply with the contract, including the fifty-cent wage rate set forth in it. It is quite common to find *braceros* and wetbacks living in the same crude, miserable huts and working in the same field, but with the wetbacks earning from 5 to 15 cents less per hour. A *bracero* generally receives 35 cents per hour while the wetback alongside him gets 30 cents per hour or less. No effort is made to attract domestic labor, and Border Patrol officials estimate that 5,000 citizens migrate annually from Eagle Pass to other areas and other states for seasonal farm work. One group of ten *braceros* was interviewed on the Springfield farm one mile southeast of Quemado in Maverick County. Their leader was Jesus Gaona of Guerrero. They said they were receiving $4.00 per day for 10-11-12 hours work with $4.00 deducted weekly for subsistence. The workers said they had no blankets and no bathing or washing facilities.

John James, USES compliance officer, was interviewed May 20, 1953. He stated that he had received 29 informal and 18 formal complaints since January, 1953. There appeared to be no liaison among the Mexican Consul, USES Compliance Officer and the Border Patrol. Compliance Officer James stated that he had had little to do with the Border Patrol in two years. The situation in this area can be explained partially by the fact that James has almost 40 counties to cover.

In the Eagle Pass area we begin to see the attitude that becomes so prevalent in the Lower Valley. The farmers, and to some degree the public generally, seem to feel that they have an inherent right to use wetbacks. Anyone who challenges that "right" is practically un-American.

In the Laredo area the situation improves slightly, inasmuch as there is some trend toward the use of domestic labor, according to Cesar Ochoa, USES Compliance Officer for the Laredo district. He said that while about 8,000 domestic workers have been migrating from the district each year, there has been a decrease in migration recently.

During the peak harvest season the district uses 1,650 *braceros*. Local domestic labor earns less than the *bracero*, drawing about 40 cents per hour, according to Ochoa. One might ask then: Why does the farmer prefer the *bracero* to the domestic laborer? The *bracero* is afraid of being sent home if he complains about violations of his contract by the farmer. With the constant threat of being sent home hanging over his head, the *bracero* becomes little more than a slave or bondsman. Should the farmers succeed in removing the minimum wage and working conditions guarantee provisions from the international agreement, the alien *braceros* would be even more at the farmer's mercy, and the threat of sending them home would be even more effective.

Even with the thousands of citizen laborers being forced to migrate annually and even with their willingness to work for the fifty-cent *bracero* wage rate, still the Secretary of Labor through the Texas Employment Commission, continues to certify the need for alien labor in the Laredo and other areas. According to Ochoa, some farmers fear being blacklisted for employing wetbacks and, as a result, are cooperating by not using them. This has helped keep down somewhat the wetback influx as indicated by the Border Patrol report that only about 5,000 wetbacks were apprehended in the area in 1952. Nevertheless, the trend toward higher apprehensions, evidenced in the Lower Valley up to midsummer of 1953, was also present in the Laredo area, although to a lesser degree.

There does appear to be good cooperation between the Mexican Consul, USES Compliance Officer and the Border Patrol in the Laredo area. While the situation in the district is not as good as it is in the El Paso and Trans-Pecos areas, it is much better than the rest of the Valley.

The Lower Valley (Hidalgo, Cameron, Willacy and Starr Counties) is the worst wetback area on the border. Very few farmers bother to use *braceros*, preferring to employ the more convenient and cheaper wetback. It is difficult to find a farm in this area not using wetbacks. The general wetback wage is about 25 cents per hour, with the worker, except in camps like Tampiquito, living in the brush. Most provide their own food, shelter and clothing, such as they are. Little effort is made to maintain a workable bracero program. Most farmers show little interest in any labor other than wetbacks, and are highly resentful and indignant over any move to deprive them of this labor.

There is an extremely heavy migration out of the area by citizen labor which cannot begin to compete with the wetbacks for jobs at the wages being paid.

There is very little liaison between the Mexican Consul and the USES Compliance Officer, and practically none between either of these and the Border Patrol.

The El Paso area at the time of this survey had made the bracero program fairly workable, while the Laredo area was making some progress toward a workable program. These two areas have certain things in common. In each area there is good cooperation between the Mexican Consul, USES Compliance Officer and the Border Patrol. The program works best where the prime contractor is a dependable and conscientious farm organization. In every case where the farm labor problem is approached with reason, the trend is toward the use of domestic labor, instead of bracero or wetback labor.

In the other areas along the border, there is a distinct absence of the conditions mentioned above. There is little or no cooperation between agencies concerned, no effort by a farm organization to make the program work; refusal to pay domestic labor a living wage, or even the same wage paid the *bracero*.

In international negotiations of labor contracts, the farmer is represented by strong farm organizations, the chambers of commerce, and the United States government. The *bracero* is represented only by his government which also is highly interested in continuing the program. When the negotiations are concluded, the worker is no longer in a position to improve the terms of the contract.

On August 13, 1952, a Texas editor said this, "If the Mexican Government persists in becoming a Petrillo or a John L. Lewis in saying what the rate of pay shall be for its citizens in New Mexico and Texas — it may be heading into difficulties closer home."

In the **San Antonio Express,** November 11, 1952, C. B. Ray, manager of the Rio Grande Valley Farm Bureau, proposed that Mexicans be permitted to work in labor short areas as free agents with their wages and conditions of employment to be decided between them and their employer. With the threat of deportation hanging over the worker's head, the farmer could make him a virtual slave. Add to this the confessed apprehension felt by the farmers over the provision in the International Agreement that permits the bracero to select a representative or spokesman to deal with the employer, and one is caused to wonder to what lengths some farmers would go to completely dominate their employes. At present, when the contract is violated by the farmer, the *bracero's* only recourse is the Mexican Consul. The Compliance Officer is charged with the enforcement of the contract, but when there is no liaison between the Consul and the Compliance Officer, contract violations become common. When the conditions of his employment become intolerable, he has only one choice—to "jump contract." In 1951 there were 107,851 *braceros* unaccounted for. They were neither re-contracted, nor were they returned to Mexico. In 1952 there were 42,313 *braceros* unaccounted for. As to why they left, where they went, their effect upon our economy, our society and our security—all are questions that deserve serious thought.

This survey does not have the accurate figures but it can be reasonably assumed that during the past eleven years, those unaccounted for *braceros* have made a sizeable contribution to the 5,000,000 illegal aliens Sen. Pat McCarran estimates reside within our borders.

How much longer can the American people afford to provide this luxury to the farmer?

RECOMMENDATIONS ON THE BRACERO PROGRAM

First of all, we want to emphasize that we are opposed to the Bracero Program whenever the *braceros* brought into the United States displace American citizen workers. We believe that U. S. citizens, if offered comparable wages to those paid *braceros*, together with the other contract guarantees, will supply a much greater proportion of the agricultural labor needed than at present. But we agree, that where a genuine labor shortage does exist, *braceros* may be used rather than lose the crop.

But we, the public, must learn not to become infected with the panic that grips the farmer the moment his product is ready to harvest. When his cotton is open, it is almost impossible for him to have too many pickers available. He would like to have it picked immediately, and, since he pays for picking by hundredweight, it costs no more to pick it with one thousand workers than it does with twenty. Until his harvest is out of the field, he is apt to consider that he has a labor shortage, regardless of the number of hands already in his fields. The same holds true in crops other than cotton. Whatever the product, to the farmer it represents a season's labor and investment. Naturally he wants it harvested before it is damaged by weather, pests or time, but seldom does he stop to consider the problems his haste creates. We must remember that his "critical labor shortage" does not necessarily mean that there are not enough laborers to harvest his crop but may only mean that there are not enough to harvest it as cheaply or as quickly as he would like. Even Mexico is concerned with the inaccuracy of our labor requirement estimates. Too many *braceros* are contracted, then left idle after their arrival because the farmer shoved his requirement date up so as to be doubly sure he would have plenty of labor when he wanted it.

We must devise a more accurate method of determining labor requirements, taking into consideration the wages and conditions of employment offered citizen workers. Any employer who offers American citizens only 25 cents an hour is going to be faced with a labor shortage. Farmers should not be permitted to evade the clear intent of the International Agreement with this subterfuge. The *bracero* contract specifies a minimum wage below which the farmer cannot go, but it never was intended that this "minimum wage" should become the "prevailing wage." Unfortunately, that is the way it has worked. And now even this "minimum wage" is under attack by farm groups as being too high. The method of determining the prevailing wage must be strengthened with a firm guarantee that employes will be represented at the hearings where they are determined.

The letter of the law should be enforced. Labor shortages must not be certified unless domestic labor has been given a genuine offer of employment under terms, wages and conditions of employment at least equal to those offered foreign workers. If the offer concerns wages only, then the wage should be increased a reasonable amount to compensate for the additional guarantees in the *bracero* contract.

A primary factor in a successful Bracero Program is the personnel and facilities available to enforce compliance with contract provisions. The field survey determined that at the time of the survey the United States Employment Service was sadly understaffed with regard to the number of compliance officers it had in the field. In the Eagle Pass area, for example, John James had 40 counties to cover the year round with the help only of an office secretary and another fieldman who was available to him only during the peak harvest period. Since that time, the limited staff of compliance men has been further reduced — for reasons of economy in government — and the offices at San Benito and Laredo have been closed.

In concluding this section, it is recognized that, in certain areas, a genuine labor shortage may exist and that it may be necessary to continue to contract alien labor in limited numbers to fill these shortages. If as much effort and money were expended to attract domestic labor as has been devoted to obtaining alien labor, we feel sure that our farm labor requirements would be filled — or nearly so, at any rate — by American citizens. The American people, with a great stake in both the economic and physical health of the nation, should demand that the national policy work toward that end.

THE MIGRANT WORKER

Thousands of words have been written and spoken and thousands of dollars have been spent in spreading the myth that the American citizens who migrate in search of work do so because they are by nature nomads, gypsies with itching feet who travel for the sheer love of traveling. With a patronizing air, many a self-styled expert on American citizens of Mexican extraction (and many who may have just finished paying off a wetback crew at the rate of 25 cents an hour) has explained that "these Mexicans (meaning American citizens of Mexican extraction) are too lazy to do field work" or that "all they want to do is travel" or that "you can't trust them to do a job right."

What he really means is that American citizens—living in the U. S., paying taxes in the U. S., raising their families in the U. S.—can't work for 25 cents an hour and manage to survive. The wetbacks can—and do. So the wetbacks move in, and the American citizens are forced to look elsewhere for a living. They take to the road, following the cotton crop through Texas or going to the better paying jobs in farm or industrial work in northern and western states.

Does it stand to reason that Juan Garcia, a property-owning, tax-paying citizen of Hidalgo County, Texas, prefers to pack his family into a truck each year and travel from 1000 to 1500 miles in order to work for 70 or 80 cents an hour if work at comparable wages were available in Hidalgo County?

Is it wanderlust that sends the same worker back to the same area and the same farm in California or Colorado or Wyoming or Illinois each year? Is it a desire to see the country which results in workers following the same route up and back year after year?

Is it laziness that forces these workers to do the same type of work picking or chopping cotton in the Gulf Coast Area, Central Texas, Lubbock, the Panhandle or the same exhausting work in the beet fields of the Midwest — the same work at the same long hours which the Lower Valley farmer says the same workers will not do in the Valley because they are "lazy"? This myth which has been fabricated in the Valley and which the press of that section promulgates and promotes in its editorials is an unmitigated lie and a shameful defamation of a large group of American citizens of Mexican descent who built the railroads, laid the basis for our agricultural development, and have done every other type of backbreaking toil in the history of Texas and the Southwest.

The answer to all these questions is a flat "no." The records show that most of the 100,000 or more Texas citizens who migrate each year for agricultural work return year after year to the same jobs for the same employers. They are searching for a form of temporary seasonal security, and the relatively higher wages to be found in the other areas justify their departure from the 25-cent wage area along the border.

The Texan of Mexican descent no more enjoys the numerous difficulties and domestic problems entailed in the annual migration than would any other American citizen. The children must be withdrawn from school weeks before the school year ends. The house must be boarded up with the windows and doors nailed tight to keep out intruders. Domestic animals must be sold or pastured out with some neighbor. Chickens and pigs must be sold or eaten. Clothing, personal items and equipment to be carried must be carefully rationed—just enough clothes to get by with, enough kitchen utensils to handle the cooking, as little of everything as is possible. After all, the two-ton-stake-body truck has to carry 25 passengers as well as the equipment.

Utilities have to be disconnected. The post office must be notified either to hold mail or to forward it to the temporary address in the north. Milk deliveries must be discontinued. The health of the women and children must be watched carefully for fear that illness in the family at the time scheduled for departure might upset plans.

Then, at the end of the season, the same petty details must be attended to for the return trip to Texas where the children will enter school several weeks or months late.

Nobody knows how many Texas citizens migrate each year, following the seasonal crops. Official records of the Texas Bureau of Labor Statistics and the Texas Employment Commission show that at least 59,033 farm workers were recruited for out-of-state work in 1950, while 65,666 followed the out-of-state crop trails in 1951 and 51,329 in 1952. But those reports cover only workers legally recruited for out-of-state work and do not include the thousands of workers traveling only within Texas or who go out of the state on their own. Conservative estimates place the number of farm workers moving within the state at not less than 100,000 and probably considerably higher.

It is not the intention of this report to cover in detail the lives, the problems, the difficulties, the plight of the migrant American citizen. It is our intention to point up the simple fact that these migrant citizens of Mexican descent are in the fullest sense of the word "displaced persons"—displaced by the hordes of illegal aliens pouring in from across the Rio Grande to work at starvation wages.

The plight and the problem of the migrant citizen have been fully covered—by the Report of the President's Commission on Migratory Labor in 1951, by innumerable magazine articles and other reports, by surveys such as those sponsored by the University of Texas, and by such organizations as the Bishop's Committee for the Spanish-Speaking. In the light of the great volume of information, statistics and opinion contained in these numerous reports, there is no disputing the fact that the migrants are a national problem or the fact that they are a problem almost solely as a result of the wetback invasion.

Over 80 per cent of the present-day national migratory farm labor force is made up of American citizens of Mexican descent (variously referred to as Latin-Americans, Mexicans, or Texas-Mexicans). Many are third and fourth generation Americans, and most are at least second generation citizens of Texas. Generally they are residents of agricultural communities and are skilled agricultural workers. Most are property-owners, either owning their homes or small acreages. A recent survey by a public utilities company shows that 80 percent own mechanical refrigerators. Most own cars or trucks. In their home communities, they are considered solvent citizens, devout, interested in community projects—first class citizens in every respect.

Is it logical to adopt the reasoning of the wetback employers that these first class citizens, of their own choice and desire, lower themselves to the second-class rank they are given as migrant workers?

Scattered among the workers in almost every truckload of migrants are a number of wetbacks, some with false identification papers, some with just a baptismal certificate, some without papers at all. They hope to get beyond the border area where the Border Patrol is most likely to apprehend them. Once they cross a line running almost due west from Corpus Christi, they are pretty well in the clear and have an excellent chance of serving out their tour of work in the northern states without being picked up. Government agencies concerned with the migrant workers make no attempt to determine whether a crew member is a citizen or a wetback. The Texas Employment Commission which clears many farm workers for migration each year reports that the only requirement made is that the applicant for work give the local TEC office a Texas address where he can be reached.

These migrant workers are the immediate victims of the wetback invasion. They felt the effects first when they were displaced from their jobs and their homes. But the effects in the long run, will go far beyond this group, hitting all levels of the population in the border country first, then spreading the virus to other sections—unless the wetback tide is halted.

The displaced persons of South Texas are the first victims—but not the last.

NO FAMILY BREAK-UP: Border Patrol keeps husband and wife together.

TRAVELING FAMILIES: Awaiting their turn to cross bridge to Mexico.

MEXICO BOUND: Deportees cross bridge into Mexico at Reynosa.

WAITING AT BRIDGE: Family groups ready to cross back to Mexico are interviewed by Idar.

BIBLIOGRAPHY

Castillo, Ed. Four articles in San Antonio Light, July 12-15, 1953.

Garner, Claud. *Wetback*. New York: Coward-McCann, Inc., 1947.

Hearings before the Subcommittee on Labor and Labor-Management Relations of the Committee on Labor and Public Welfare, United States Senate, 82nd Congress, Second Session, on Migratory Labor. U.S. Government Printing Office, 1952.

Kibbe, Pauline. *Latin Americans in Texas*. Albuquerque: The University of New Mexico Press, 1946.

Leibson, Art. "The Wetback Invasion." Common Ground, Autumn, 1949, pp. 11-19.

Meador, Bruce, *"Wetback Labor in the Lower Rio Grande Valley."* Unpublished Master's Thesis. The University of Texas, Austin, Texas, 1951.

McWilliams, Carey. *North from Mexico*, Philadelphia: J. B. Lippincott Co., 1949.

Nelson, Eastin, and Frederic Meyers. *Labor Requirements and Labor Resources in the Lower Rio Grande Valley of Texas*. Austin: The University of Texas Press, December, 1950.

President's Commission on Migratory Labor. *Migratory Labor in American Agriculture*. Washington: United States Government Printing Office, 1951.

Radtke, Theodore J. *The Wetback Situation in the Rio Grande Valley*. Mimeographed report of the Bishop's Committee for the Spanish Speaking. Corpus Christi, August 31, 1950.

Ramirez, Emilia S. *'Wetback' Children in South Texas*. Unpublished Master's Thesis. The University of Texas, Austin, Texas, 1951.

Sanchez, George I. and Lyle Saunders. *Wetbacks — A Preliminary Report*. Mimeographed Report of the Advisory Committee, Study of Spanish-Speaking People, the University of Texas, Austin, 1949.

Saunders, Lyle, and Leonard, Olen E. *The Wetback in the Lower Rio Grande Valley of Texas*. Occasional Papers VII. Austin: The University of Texas Press, July 1951. 92 pp.

WHAT PRICE WETBACKS?

Truly, the American people are entitled to ask: "What price wetbacks?"

What is the price in terms of depressed wages for citizens of the United States who have a right to a wage on which they can live according to American standards of living?

The 25-cent hourly wage of the wetback cannot support American citizens.

What is the price in disease and death?

Disease and death rates in the areas of heaviest wetback concentration are an indication of the stupendous price we pay in that regard.

What is the price in criminal activities?

Crime is a natural result of the presence of thousands of people who already are living beyond the law.

What is the price in danger to our national security?

An open border is a constant invitation to subversives and spies.

What is the price in lost business?

Dollars **not** paid in wages don't go into trade channels; dollars sent to Mexico don't ring cash registers in the United States.

What is the price in human misery?

You have seen part of the answer in this report on the lives and living conditions of the wetback and the people he displaces, the American citizens who are forced from their homes and their jobs by these illegal workers.

The answer must be found. It doesn't lie in opening the border still wider through the use of a crossing-card system which would be nothing but legalized wetbackism. Nor does it lie in maintaining a semblance of immigration law enforcement which results in only partial control of the wetback tide.

The answer lies in strengthening the immigration laws — and then enforcing them. Only then can the American people relax, secure in the knowledge that the threat of the wetback invasion has been halted.

THE CHICANO HERITAGE

An Arno Press Collection

Adams, Emma H. **To and Fro in Southern California.** 1887

Anderson, Henry P. **The Bracero Program in California.** 1961

Aviña, Rose Hollenbaugh. **Spanish and Mexican Land Grants in California.** 1976

Barker, Ruth Laughlin. **Caballeros.** 1932

Bell, Horace. **On the Old West Coast.** 1930

Biberman, Herbert. **Salt of the Earth.** 1965

Casteñeda, Carlos E., trans. **The Mexican Side of the Texas Revolution (1836).** 1928

Casteñeda, Carlos E. **Our Catholic Heritage in Texas, 1519-1936.** Seven volumes. 1936-1958

Colton, Walter. **Three Years in California.** 1850

Cooke, Philip St. George. **The Conquest of New Mexico and California.** 1878

Cue Canovas, Agustin. **Los Estados Unidos Y El Mexico Olvidado.** 1970

Curtin, L. S. M. **Healing Herbs of the Upper Rio Grande.** 1947

Fergusson, Harvey. **The Blood of the Conquerors.** 1921

Fernandez, Jose. **Cuarenta Años de Legislador:** Biografia del Senador Casimiro Barela. 1911

Francis, Jessie Davies. **An Economic and Social History of Mexican California** (1822-1846). Volume I: Chiefly Economic. Two vols. in one. 1976

Getty, Harry T. **Interethnic Relationships in the Community of Tucson.** 1976

Guzman, Ralph C. **The Political Socialization of the Mexican American People.** 1976

Harding, George L. **Don Agustin V. Zamorano.** 1934

Hayes, Benjamin. **Pioneer Notes from the Diaries of Judge Benjamin Hayes, 1849-1875.** 1929

Herrick, Robert. **Waste.** 1924

Jamieson, Stuart. **Labor Unionism in American Agriculture.** 1945

Landolt, Robert Garland. **The Mexican-American Workers of San Antonio, Texas.** 1976

Lane, Jr., John Hart. **Voluntary Associations Among Mexican Americans in San Antonio, Texas.** 1976

Livermore, Abiel Abbot. **The War with Mexico Reviewed.** 1850

Loyola, Mary. **The American Occupation of New Mexico, 1821-1852.** 1939

Macklin, Barbara June. **Structural Stability and Culture Change in a Mexican-American Community.** 1976

McWilliams, Carey. **Ill Fares the Land:** Migrants and Migratory Labor in the United States. 1942

Murray, Winifred. **A Socio-Cultural Study of 118 Mexican Families Living in a Low-Rent Public Housing Project in San Antonio, Texas.** 1954

Niggli, Josephina. **Mexican Folk Plays.** 1938

Parigi, Sam Frank. **A Case Study of Latin American Unionization in Austin, Texas.** 1976

Poldervaart, Arie W. **Black-Robed Justice.** 1948

Rayburn, John C. and Virginia Kemp Rayburn, eds. **Century of Conflict, 1821-1913.** Incidents in the Lives of William Neale and William A. Neale, Early Settlers in South Texas. 1966

Read, Benjamin. **Illustrated History of New Mexico.** 1912

Rodriguez, Jr., Eugene. **Henry B. Gonzalez.** 1976

Sanchez, Nellie Van de Grift. **Spanish and Indian Place Names of California.** 1930

Sanchez, Nellie Van de Grift. **Spanish Arcadia.** 1929

Shulman, Irving. **The Square Trap.** 1953

Tireman, L. S. **Teaching Spanish-Speaking Children.** 1948

Tireman, L. S. and Mary Watson. **A Community School in a Spanish-Speaking Village.** 1948

Twitchell, Ralph Emerson. **The History of the Military Occupation of the Territory of New Mexico.** 1909

Twitchell, Ralph Emerson. **The Spanish Archives of New Mexico.** Two vols. 1914

U. S. House of Representatives. **California and New Mexico:** Message from the President of the United States, January 21, 1850. 1850

Valdes y Tapia, Daniel. **Hispanos and American Politics.** 1976

West, Stanley A. **The Mexican Aztec Society.** 1976

Woods, Frances Jerome. **Mexican Ethnic Leadership in San Antonio, Texas.** 1949

Aspects of the Mexican American Experience. 1976
Mexicans in California After the U. S. Conquest. 1976
Hispanic Folklore Studies of Arthur L. Campa. 1976
Hispano Culture of New Mexico. 1976
Mexican California. 1976
The Mexican Experience in Arizona. 1976
The Mexican Experience in Texas. 1976
Mexican Migration to the United States. 1976
The United States Conquest of California. 1976
Northern Mexico On the Eve of the United States Invasion:
    Rare Imprints Concerning California, Arizona, New Mexico, and Texas, 1821-1846. Edited by David J. Weber. 1976